ECONOMIC ISSUES, PROBLEMS AND PERSPECTIVES

THE U.S. NATIONAL DEBT: BACKGROUND, ISSUES, SIGNIFICANCE

Economic Issues, Problems and Perspectives

Additional books in this series can be found on Nova's website under the Series tab.

Additional E-books in this series can be found on Nova's website under the E-books tab.

ECONOMIC ISSUES, PROBLEMS AND PERSPECTIVES

THE U.S. NATIONAL DEBT: BACKGROUND, ISSUES, SIGNIFICANCE

CHARLOTTE G. WILSON
AND
EMILY O. BROWN
EDITOR

Nova Science Publishers, Inc.
New York

For permission to use material from this book please contact us:
Telephone 631-231-7269; Fax 631-231-8175
Web Site: http://www.novapublishers.com

LIBRARY OF CONGRESSCATALOGING-IN-PUBLICATION DATA

The U.S. national debt : background, issues, significance / editors,
Charlotte G. Wilson and Emily O. Brown.
p. cm.
Includes index.
ISBN 978-1-61761-767-6 (hbk.)
1. Debts, Public--United States. 2. Budget deficits--United States. 3.
Government spending policy--United States. I. Wilson, Charlotte G. II.
Brown, Emily O. III. Title: US national debt. IV. Title: United States
national debt.
HJ8101.U135 2010
336.3'43373--dc22
2010033091

Published by Nova Science Publishers, Inc. † New York

CONTENTS

PREFACE

This book explains the different measures of the U.S. government debt, discusses the historical growth in the debt, identifies the current owners of the debt, presents comparisons with government debt in other countries, and examines the potential economic risks associated with a growing federal debt.

Chapter 1- After several years of surpluses in the late 1990s, the federal budget has been in deficit since FY2001. Deficits represent the additional borrowing required in each year to bridge the gap between tax revenues and spending outlays. Each deficit adds to the already existing stock of outstanding federal debt.

Some of those deficits may have seemed large at the time, but the budget deficit for FY2009 was unprecedented, in dollar terms, and the FY2010 deficit is also expected to be much larger than those of past years. The prospect of such rapid growth in the federal debt may seem alarming, and some might wonder how much the debt can grow before it poses significant economic risks.

Chapter 2- Total debt of the federal government can increase in two ways. First, debt increases when the government sells debt to the public to finance budget deficits and acquire the financial resources needed to meet its obligations. This increases *debt held by the public*. Second, debt increases when the federal government issues debt to certain government accounts, such as the Social Security, Medicare, and Transportation trust funds, in exchange for their reported surpluses. This increases *debt held by government accounts*. The sum of *debt held by the public* and *debt held by government accounts* is the total federal debt. Surpluses generally reduce debt held by the public, while deficits raise it.

A statutory limit has restricted total federal debt since 1917 when Congress passed the Second Liberty Bond Act. Congress has voted to raise the debt limit ten times since 2001. Deficits each year since 2001 and the persistent increases in debt held by government accounts repeatedly raised the debt to or near the limit in place at the time. Congress raised the limit in June 2002, and by December 2002 the U.S. Department of the Treasury asked Congress for another increase, which was passed in May 2003. In June 2004, the Treasury asked for another debt limit increase. After Congress recessed in mid-October 2004 without acting, the Secretary of the Treasury told Congress that the actions he was taking to avoid exceeding the debt limit would suffice only through mid-November. Congress approved a debt limit increase in a post-election session, which the President signed on November 19, 2004.

Chapter 3- Almost all borrowing by the federal government is conducted by the Treasury Department, within the restrictions established by a single, statutory limit on the total amount of debt that may be outstanding at any time. Most adjustments to the debt limit have been increases, but sometimes the change has been a reduction.

The annual budget resolution includes recommended levels of the public debt limit for each fiscal year covered by the resolution. Because a budget resolution does not become law, Congress and the President must enact legislation in order to implement budget resolution policies. The House and Senate may develop and consider legislation adjusting the debt limit in any one of three ways: (1) under regular legislative procedures in both chambers, either as freestanding legislation or as a part of a measure dealing with other topics; (2) pursuant to House Rule XXVIII (the so- called Gephardt rule); or (3) as part of the budget reconciliation process provided for under the Congressional Budget Act of 1974. During the period from 1940 to the present, Congress and the President have enacted a total of 91 measures adjusting the public debt limit—72 under regular legislative procedures in both chambers, 15 under the Gephardt rule, and 4 under reconciliation procedures. The current debt limit is $1 4.294 trillion.

Chapter 4- The amount of money the federal government is allowed to borrow generally is subject to a statutory limit. From time to time, Congress and the President enact legislation to adjust this limit.

The House may develop debt-limit legislation under House Rule XXVIII, commonly referred to as the Gephardt rule, named after its author, former Representative Richard Gephardt. The rule, which was established by P.L. 96-78 and first applied in calendar year 1980, provides for the automatic engrossment and transmittal to the Senate of a joint resolution changing the public debt limit, upon the adoption by Congress of the budget resolution, thereby avoiding a separate vote in the House on the public debt-limit legislation. The Senate has no comparable procedure; if it chooses to consider a House-passed joint resolution, it does so under the regular legislative process.

Chapter 5- Of the three broad categories of federal spending, the only category that cannot be reduced by legislative action is net interest payments. Net interest payments accounted for about 7% of federal spending between 1962 and the late 1970s. With the high interest rates in the late 1970s and the large budget deficits in the 1980s, net interest payments eventually rose to 15% of federal spending. The low interest rates combined with budget discipline in the 1990s reduced net interest payments back down to 7% of federal outlays by 2003. Low interest rates kept net interest payments low to 2009. However, net interest payments are projected to increase dramatically over the next 10 years.

Chapter6- This chapter presents current data on estimated ownership of U.S. Treasury securities and major holders of federal debt by country. Federal debt represents the accumulated balance of borrowing by the federal government. To finance federal borrowing, U.S. Treasury securities are sold to investors. Treasury securities may be purchased directly from the Treasury or on the secondary market by individual private investors, financial institutions in the United States or overseas, and foreign, state, or local governments. Foreign investment in federal debt has grown in recent years, prompting questions on the location of the foreign holders and how much debt they hold.

Chapter 7- This chapter is part of GAO's requirement, under the Emergency Economic Stabilization Act of 2008, to monitor the Department of the Treasury's (Treasury) implementation of the Troubled Asset Relief Program and submit special reports as warranted from oversight findings. It evaluates Treasury's borrowing actions since the start of the crisis, and how Treasury communicates with market participants in the context of the growing debt portfolio and the medium- and long-term fiscal outlook. GAO analyzed market data; interviewed Treasury, the Federal Reserve Bank of New York, and market experts; and surveyed major domestic holders of Treasury securities.

Chapter8- The United States has been free of a national debt for only two years, 1834 and 1835. In its first year, 1790, the country faced a debt of $75 million. From FY1998 to FY2001, the federal government ran budget surpluses. Since then, the budget has returned to deficit, and the debt had risen to $7.5 trillion by 2009. It rose to a high of 108.6% of gross domestic product (GDP) at the end of World War II; declined to a post-World War II low of 23.8% of GDP in 1974; and, then, rose to another high of 49.5% of GDP in 1993.

The national debt results from borrowing to finance budget deficits. Historically, the major cause of debt accumulation has been war. The United States has financed the extraordinary expenditures associated with war by borrowing rather than by raising taxes or printing money. This pattern was broken by the large budget deficits of the 1980s, the first half of the 1990s, and the period subsequent to 2001, which caused the national debt to rise substantially as a fraction of GDP.

Chapter 9- The U.S. Department of the Treasury (Treasury), among other roles, manages the country's debt. The primary objective of Treasury's debt management strategy is to finance the government's borrowing needs at the lowest cost over time. To accomplish this Treasury adheres to three principles: (1) to issue debt in a regular and predictable pattern, (2) to provide transparency in the decision-making process, and (3) to seek continuous improvements in the auction process.

Specifically, the Office of Debt Management (ODM) makes all decisions related to debt issuance and the management of the United States debt portfolio. When federal spending exceeds revenues, the ODM directs the Bureau of Public Debt (BPD) to borrow the funds needed to finance government operations by selling securities to the public and government agencies via an auction process. BPD manages the operational aspects of the issuance of Treasury securities, including the systems related to and the monitoring of the auction process.

Chapter 10- Financing the obligations of the United States has always been a central concern of Congress and the President. Levels of government spending and revenue collection are a focus of congressional debate in every fiscal year. Policy decisions and economic growth also play a large role in influencing federal debt levels over time. Historical trends can help illustrate the reasons behind large movements in debt levels. Understanding ebbs and flows of federal debt levels can be useful in synthesizing how budget policy affects the debt outlook.

Federal debt can be defined and reported in a number of ways. In the President's budget submission to Congress, information is presented on the federal surplus or deficit, gross (total) federal debt, debt held by federal government accounts (intragovernmental), and debt held by the public. In most years, debt held by the public has increased on a nominal basis. However, in order to compare the size of debt to the size of the economy over time, debt held by the public will be measured in this chapter as a percentage of gross domestic product (GDP) to control for effects such as inflation and economic growth.

In: The U.S. National Debt: Background, Issues, Significance ISBN: 978-1-61761-767-6
Editor: Charlotte G. Wilson and Emily O. Brown

Chapter 1

THE FEDERAL GOVERNMENT DEBT: ITS SIZE AND ECONOMIC SIGNIFICANCE

Brian W. Cashell

SUMMARY

After several years of surpluses in the late 1990s, the federal budget has been in deficit since FY2001. Deficits represent the additional borrowing required in each year to bridge the gap between tax revenues and spending outlays. Each deficit adds to the already existing stock of outstanding federal debt.

Some of those deficits may have seemed large at the time, but the budget deficit for FY2009 was unprecedented, in dollar terms, and the FY2010 deficit is also expected to be much larger than those of past years. The prospect of such rapid growth in the federal debt may seem alarming, and some might wonder how much the debt can grow before it poses significant economic risks.

In a slack economy, federal borrowing and spending can stimulate growth in output in the short run. As the economy approaches full employment, federal government borrowing adds to total credit demand and tends to push up interest rates. Higher interest rates increase the cost of financing new investment in plant and equipment and thus may tend to reduce the stock of productive capital below what it might otherwise have been. That would tend to reduce the long- run rate of growth.

In the long run, the relationship between the growth rate of the federal debt and the overall rate of economic growth is critical to economic stability. As long as the debt grows more rapidly than output, the ratio of debt to gross domestic product (GDP) will rise. Debt growth in excess of economic growth is ultimately unsustainable. Whether the debt-to-GDP ratio is on such a path depends on the size of the budget deficit, the rate of interest, and the rate of growth in GDP.

What matters most, as far as economic stability is concerned, is what investors believe to be the long-run outlook for the debt-to-GDP ratio. If large deficits are expected to persist, or if the interest rate on the debt is expected to exceed the growth rate indefinitely, then at some point the federal government may begin to find it more difficult to sell new securities.

Should the federal government be unable to find private sector buyers, the Federal Reserve might buy Treasury securities in order to sustain their marketability. Should it decide to do so, then the threat is no longer one of government insolvency, but rather of inflation.

INTRODUCTION

After several years of surpluses in the late 1990s, the federal budget has been in deficit since FY2001. Deficits represent new borrowing required in each year to bridge the gap between tax revenues and spending outlays. Each deficit adds to the already existing stock of outstanding federal debt.

Some of the deficits in recent years may have seemed large at the time, but the budget deficit for FY2009 was unprecedented, in dollar terms, and the deficit in FY2010 is expected to be considerably larger than in past years as well. The prospect of such rapid growth in the federal debt may seem alarming, and some might wonder how large, or how rapidly, the debt might grow before it poses significant economic risks.

One way in which policymakers have expressed their concerns over the level of federal government debt is in the form of a statutory debt limit.[1] Although the debt limit tends to rise as necessary, those increases serve as occasions to consider the debt itself separately from the policies that account for it.

There is more than one measure of federal debt, and that may be a source of confusion. This chapter explains the different measures of the U.S. government debt, discusses the historical growth in the debt, identifies the current owners of the debt, presents comparisons with government debt in other countries, and examines the potential economic risks associated with a growing federal debt.

MEASURING THE FEDERAL DEBT

The statutory debt limit is a ceiling set by Congress restricting the total amount of federal debt outstanding. Gross federal debt, with some minor adjustments, is the measure that is subject to the limit.

Although gross federal debt is the broadest measure of the debt, it may not be the most important one. Not all of the gross debt actually represents past borrowing in credit markets. Some of the debt is held by the so-called trust funds, primarily the one for Social Security, but also others such as unemployment insurance, the highway trust fund, and one for federal employee pensions. Relatively small amounts of debt are also held by selected federal agencies.

The assets held by the trust funds consist entirely of non-marketable federal debt. That debt exists only as a bookkeeping entry, and does not reflect past borrowing in credit markets. The trust fund balances represent the cumulative amount that the government has not had to borrow in credit markets since they were simply credited to the trust fund accounts.[2]

The debt measure that is relevant in an economic sense is debt held by the public. This is the measure of debt that has actually been sold in credit markets, and which has influenced interestrates and private investment decisions. At the beginning of calendar 2010, the debt held by the public was $7.8 trillion, whereas total gross federal debt was $12.3 trillion.

The dollar amount of the debt, however large it may seem to be, is not the best measure of its burden on the economy. Just as an individual with a larger income can afford to take on more debt, the importance of the debt can only be measured relative to the overall size of the economy.[3] For a given amount of debt, the larger the potential tax base is, the less of a burden on the economy the interest payments on that debt will be. The most common way of putting the size of the debt in perspective is to express it as a percentage of total gross domestic product (GDP).

RECENTHISTORY OF THE FEDERALDEBT

Prior to World War II, the federal budget was in surplus about as often as it was in deficit. Some of the largest increases in the debt resulted from wartime spending. There were large increases in the debt held by the public related to the Civil War and also to World War I. Since World War II, the federal budget has been in deficit most of the time and the debt has steadily grown. Since 1940, revenues exceeded outlays in only 12 years.[4]

Figure 1 shows gross federal debt held by the public since 1940. The red line plots the dollar value of the debt held by the public since 1940. These are nominal amounts (i.e., they have not been adjusted for inflation). The black line shows the debt held by the public as a percentage of GDP.

The dollar value of the debt rose gradually until the late 1 970s and early 1 980s, at which time its growth accelerated. It peaked in 1997, fell through 2001, but since then has reached a new high each year. Measuring the debt relative to GDP tells a different story. The surge in debt to finance the costs of World War II is much more pronounced and indicates that recent debt levels are far from unprecedented, in terms of the burden to the economy. Following that surge and until the late 1 970s, however, debt grew much less rapidly than did the overall economy and so the ratio fell steadily. Between 1980 and 1995, the debt grew more rapidly than the economy so the ratio rose. Between 1995 and 2001, with the decline in debt levels, the ratio fell. Between 2002 and 2005, it rose again, but then fell in 2006 and 2007 even with significant deficits. It is above the recent peak reached in 1993 but, for now, it is below what it was in 1955. Given current projections the debt-to-GDP ratio seems likely to continue to rise over the next few years.

THE SHORT- AND LONG-RUNEFFECTS OF FEDERALBORROWING

In the short run, growth in the public debt (i.e., budget deficits) affects the composition of economic output. When there is considerable slack in the economy, the main effect of an increase in the deficit may be to stimulate demand and raise output. That's the reasoning behind the fiscal stimulus in the American Recovery and Reinvestment Act of 2009 (P.L. 111-5).

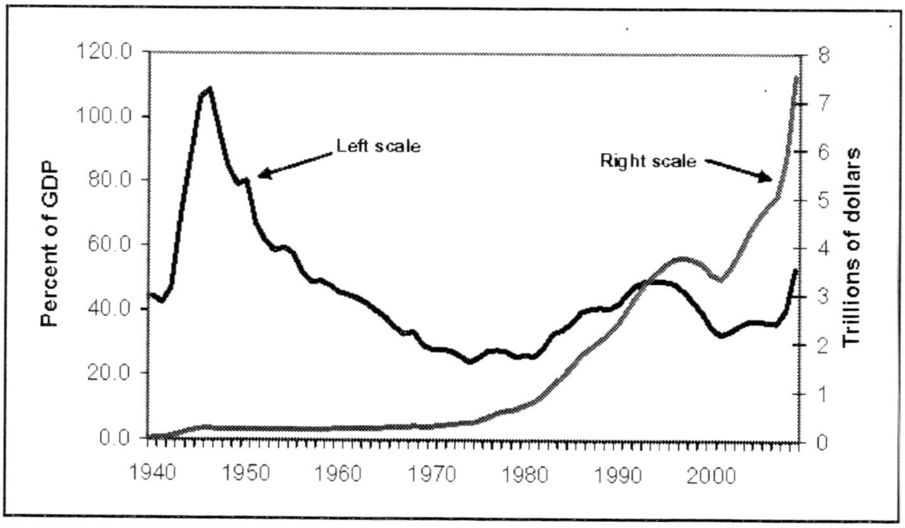

Source: Congressional Budget Office.

Figure 1. Federal Debt Held by the Public

Eventually, however, as the economy approaches full employment, and credit markets tighten, federal government borrowing tends to push up interest rates. Higher interest rates increase the cost of financing new investment in plant and equipment and thus may tend to reduce the stock of productive capital below what it might otherwise have been. Thus, there may be a shift in the composition of output towards consumption and away from investment. Consumption that might otherwise have been deferred (i.e., saving) is reduced and current consumption rises.

The higher interest rates may also have an effect on international capital flows, and thus on the trade balance. Other things being equal, they make dollar-denominated assets more attractive to foreign investors because of the relatively higher yield. Foreign investors, in order to buy U.S. securities, must first buy dollars with which to pay for them. The increased demand for dollars in exchange markets tends to push up the price of the dollar in terms of other currencies.[5]

The increase in the exchange value of the dollar has two mutually reinforcing effects. First, the price of imported goods falls because it takes fewer dollars to buy the same quantity of goods and services abroad. Lower prices for imported goods means, other things being equal, that U.S. consumers spend more on goods and services produced abroad. Second, the price of U.S.- produced goods and services rises for foreigners because the amount of foreign currency required to buy a given quantity of U.S. exports rises. Because U.S. exports are more expensive, they tend to decline.

Both the rise in imports and the drop in exports contribute to a larger trade deficit. Because of the increased domestic borrowing associated with the rising federal debt, firms that sell a significant share of their production abroad, and those that compete directly with foreign firms selling in the United States, experience a drop in the demand for their goods and services. The increased capital inflow, however, may offset to some extent the reduction in investment that might otherwise result from the increase in domestic credit demand.[6]

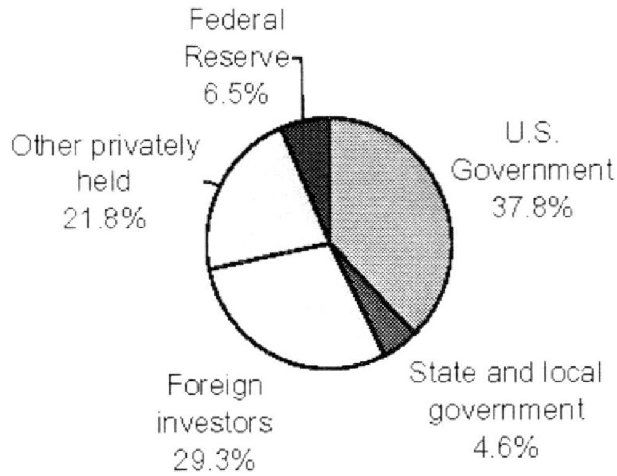

Source: Department of the Treasury.

Figure 2. Ownership of the Gross Federal Debt, June 2009

Table 1. Major Foreign Holders of Treasury Securities as of November 2009

Country	Holdings (billions of dollars)	Percentage of Foreign Held Debt
Total Foreign Held	3,597.5	100.0
Mainland China	789.6	21.9
Japan	757.3	21.1
United Kingdom	277.5	7.7
Oil Exporters	187.7	5.2
Caribbean Banking Centers	179.8	5.0
Brazil	157.1	4.4
Hong Kong	146.2	4.1
Russia	128.1	3.6
Luxembourg	91.7	2.5
Taiwan	78.4	2.2
Switzerland	63.0	1.8
Germany	53.6	1.5

Source: Department of the Treasury; Federal Reserve Board.

Notes: Oil Exporters include Ecuador; Venezuela; Indonesia; Bahrain; Iran; Iraq; Kuwait; Oman; Qatar; Saudi Arabia; the United Arab Emirates; Algeria; Gabon; Libya; and Nigeria.

WHO OWNS THE FEDERAL DEBT?

Because Treasury securities are seen as relatively safe, they are held by a wide range of investors. Next to cash they are the most liquid asset, meaning they can easily be converted to cash when necessary, on short notice. Because of that, investors hold them as a way of managing the overall risk associated with their portfolios.

Figure 2 shows a breakdown of the holders of the outstanding gross federal debt. The U.S. government is itself the largest holder of the debt, mainly in the trust funds. Included in the "other" category are financial institutions, including banks, insurance companies, and mutual funds, as well as private pension funds. The Federal Reserve holds a significant share of the debt. The Federal Reserve buys and sells Treasury securities in its open market operations in order to manage short-term interest rates.[7] State and local governments hold Treasury securities as well, mainly in pension funds for their employees. Foreign investorshold 29.3% of the debt.

The Treasury Department publishes estimates of major foreign holdings of Treasury securities. Mainland China, Japan, and the United Kingdom are the three largest holders. Table 1 presents recent data for countries with the largest holdings of Treasury securities.

THE RELATIONSHIP BETWEENFEDERALDEBT AND GDP

In the long run, the relationship between the growth rate of the federal debt and the overall rate of economic growth is critical to economic stability. As long as the debt grows more rapidly than output, the ratio of debt to GDP will rise. Perpetual debt growth in excess of economic growth is inherently unsustainable.

Whether the debt-to-GDP ratio is on such a path depends on the budget deficit, of course, but also on the rate of interest and the rate of growth in GDP.[8] To illustrate, consider the case where the budget is balanced except for the interest payment on the debt. In other words, the budget deficit is equal to the interest payment. In this case, the debt would grow each year by an amount equal to the interest cost of financing the debt. Thus, the growth rate of the debt would equal the interest rate. If the interest rate were higher than the growth rate of GDP, then the debt would grow faster than GDP and the ratio of debt to GDP would rise. If, instead, the interest rate stays below the economic growth rate, then the ratio of debt to GDP would fall.

Figure 3 compares the average interest rate on the federal debt with the growth rate of nominal GDP. This measure of economic growth reflects changes in both real output and inflation. The green line shows the annual growth rate of nominal GDP, and the red line shows the average interest rate on the outstanding federal debt held by the public.

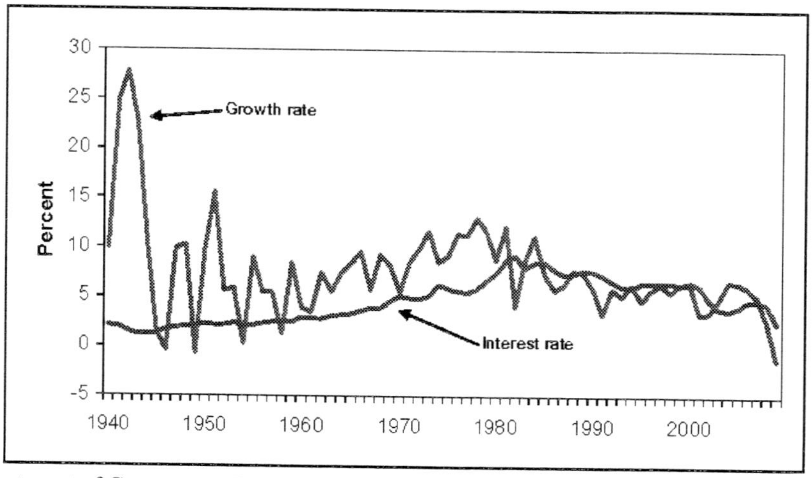

Source: Department of Commerce, Bureau of Economic Analysis; Congressional Budget Office.

Figure 3. Economic Growth and Interest on the Federal Debt

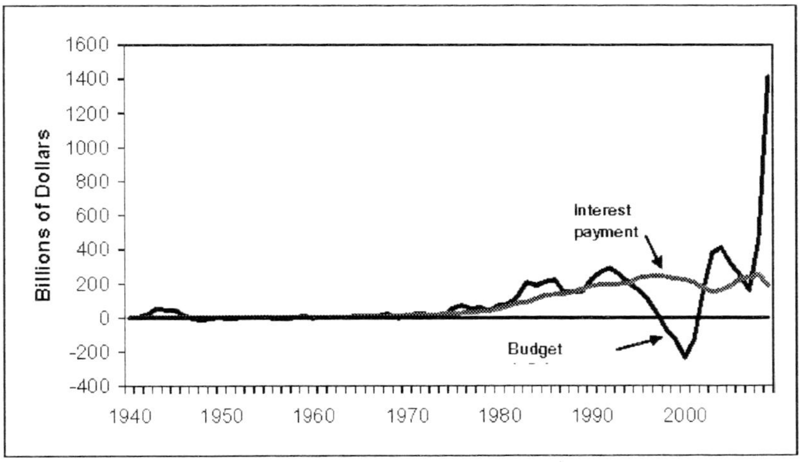

Source: Congressional Budget Office.

Figure 4. The Budget Deficit and Net Interest Outlays

For most of the period between 1940 and 1980, the interest rate remained well below the growth rate of the economy. For much of the past 25 years, however, the interest rate has been above the growth rate, which through the mid-1990s contributed to the rising debt-to-GDP ratio. If the interest rate is less than the growth rate, it is possible for the debt ratio to fall even with a modest budget deficit. When the interest rate is above the growth rate, a surplus is required to keep the debt-to-GDP ratio from rising.

Consider the case where the budget deficit is larger than the interest payment on the debt. When the budget deficit is larger than the interest payment, the difference between the two is sometimes referred to as the "primary" deficit. In that case, the growth rate of the debt would be larger than the interest rate, and so, even with an interest rate below the GDP growth rate, the debt-to-GDP ratio could still rise. Figure 4 shows the relationship between the budget deficit and the interest payment on the debt from 1940 through 2009. The black line shows the deficit (which in some cases is negative, i.e., a surplus), and the red line shows the interest payment.

Although there were clearly exceptions, the overall pattern until recently was for the budget deficit and the interest payment to rise in tandem, which is not surprising since the deficits represents additional debt which requires a larger interest payment. In the late 1 990s, when the budget was in surplus (i.e., a negative deficit), the budget deficit was clearly substantially less than the interest payment which contributed to the decline in the debt-GDP ratio. Since FY2003 that situation has reversed, and except for FY2007 the deficit has been larger than the interest payment.

WHAT ARE THE RISKS OF RISINGFEDERALDEBT?

The federal government usually has little difficulty in marketing securities when revenues fall short of outlays. As long as there is a ready market for federal debt, the risks are small.

What matters most, as far as economic stability is concerned, is what investors believe the long- run trend in the debt-GDP ratio to be. If large primary deficits (deficits in excess of the net interest payment) are expected to persist, or if the interest rate on the debt is expected to exceed the growth rate indefinitely, then at some point the federal government may find it more and more difficult to sell new securities. In other words, it may become harder for the federal government to find willing lenders to finance its deficits. At worst, private investors might come to doubt the federal government's ability even to meet its interest payments, and would be reluctant, if not completely unwilling, to hold government bonds.

Inability to borrow money in credit markets can be fatal to private businesses. Firms that are losing money and cannot find willing lenders are on the road to bankruptcy. The federal government, however, has a source of credit not available to individual businesses, the Federal Reserve Bank.

There are two possible outcomes should the federal government be unable to find private sector buyers, either domestic or foreign, for its securities. First, the federal government could simply find itself unable to meet all of its obligations. In that case outlays would have to fall unless taxes were increased enough to eliminate the shortfall. Second, rather than allow the government to default, the Federal Reserve might buy sufficient Treasury securities in order to sustain their marketability.[9]

Although subject to congressional oversight, the Federal Reserve is independent and under no legal obligation to ensure the sale of government securities. But should it decide to do so, then the threat is no longer one of government insolvency, but rather of inflation.

When the Federal Reserve buys Treasury securities, it increases the stock of reserves to commercial banks. Those increased reserves, in turn, increase the banks' capacity to lend money and create demand deposits, increasing the stock of money in circulation. The historical record demonstrates that continued financing of large government budget deficits by "printing money" runs a substantial risk of rapidly accelerating inflation.

Current and projected federal debt, however, are both short of the levels thought to be associated with this risk. For the moment, federal debt remains well below the level it reached following World War II.

History provides a number of examples where large public sector debt led to serious economic consequences. In the aftermath of World War I, four countries experienced episodes of rapid inflation directly attributable to the central bank financing of very large budget deficits through money creation: Germany, Poland, Austria, and Hungary. In each of these cases, more than one- half of the total central government expenditures was deficit financed. As a result, the public lost confidence in the governments' ability to bring growth in public sector debt under control by either raising taxes or cutting expenditures. [10]

Immediately following World War II, Hungary experienced the most extreme episode of inflation on record. Between July 1945 and August 1946, the price level in Hungary rose by a factor of 3×10^{25}. As is characteristic of instances of very rapid inflation, tax revenues fell far short of public expenditures during this time. For much of the period, revenues covered less than 10% of total expenditures.[11]

During the mid-1980s, Bolivia experienced an episode of very rapid inflation. In 1984, general government revenues represented less than 20% of total government expenditures, and the budget deficit surpassed 20% of GDP. Annual inflation in 1984 was over 1,000%, and in 1985 the inflation rate topped 11 ,000%.[12]

These are all examples of extreme cases, but they serve to put the U.S. experience in perspective. Even in instances of much more modest federal government credit demand, there remains the possibility that the Federal Reserve might seek to mitigate any upward pressure on interest rates due to the Treasury's borrowing needs at the risk of pushing up the inflation rate. But as long as the Treasury can find buyers for its securities in private credit markets, the Federal Reserve will likely find it easier to pursue an anti-inflationary policy.

In any country with a large government debt there may be temptation to reduce the real value of that debt with inflation. In cases where that is perceived to be a real possibility, nominal interest rates may be higher than they otherwise would be because investors demand a higher rate of return to protect themselves from the possible decline in the value of their assets. The independence of the Federal Reserve is generally believed to reduce the possibility that will happen.[13]

GOVERNMENT DEBT IN OTHER INDUSTRIALIZED COUNTRIES

Short of the extreme examples cited in the previous section, it is useful to compare the federal government debt in the United States with that of other developed countries. The United States is not the only country whose central government has issued a significant amount of debt.

Table 2. Gross General Government Debt as a Percentage of GDP

Country	2000	2009
Austria[a]	71.1	72.9
Belgium[a]	113.8	101.2
Canada	82.1	82.8
Finland[a]	52.3	43.7
France[a]	65.6	84.5
Germany[a]	60.4	77.4
Greece[a]	114.9	114.9
Ireland[a]	40.2	65.8
Italy[a]	121.0	123.6
Japan	135.4	189.3
Luxembourg[a]	9.2	18.2
Netherlands[a]	63.9	71.4
Portugal[a]	62.0	83.8
Spain[a]	66.5	59.3
Switzerland	52.5	44.4
United Kingdom	45.1	71.0
United States	54.4	83.9

Source: Organization for Economic Co-operation and Development.
a. Member of the European Economic and Monetary Union (Euro country).

Among the countries shown in Table 2 are all those participating in the European Economic and Monetary Union (EMU). These are the countries who now use the Euro as their currency. The Maastricht Treaty established conditions for European Union countries' participation in the EMU. Among them was the condition that a member country's public sector financial condition must be "sustainable." In particular, the standards for assessing the sustainability of public sector finances were that the public sector deficit not exceed 3% of GDP, and that the public sector debt not exceed 60% of GDP. More than half of the Euro countries now have debt-to-GDP ratios above 60%.

As the figures in Table 2 indicate, the United States is far from having the largest government debt. Of the 17 countries shown, five had a higher debt-to-GDP ratio in 2009 than did the United States. Twelve countries increased their debt ratio between 2000 and 2009. Four of the countries had public debt larger than their GDP in 2009.

CONCLUSION

It appears that the federal debt is likely to rise significantly in the near future. The Congressional Budget Office now projects the budget to be in deficit through 2020. In the current economy, however, there is significant slack and debt growth is likely to affect aggregate demand much more than prices or interest rates.

At current and even at projected levels, most economists would agree the debt poses little immediate risk to economic stability. But continued deficits on the order of 10% of GDP eventually might, and are likely unsustainable. Ultimately the risk of a very large, and rapidly growing, government debt is extremely high rates of inflation, as pressure would mount on the Federal Reserve to monetize the debt.

End Notes

[1] CRS Report RL3 1967, *The Debt Limit: History and Recent Increases*, by D. Andrew Austin and Mindy R. Levit.

[2] Interest paid on the trust fund accounts is also strictly a bookkeeping entry and does not constitute an actual outlay of the federal government.

[3] Prospects for economic growth may also affect perceptions about the advisability of taking on more debt.

[4] See also CRS Report RL34712, *Ebbs and Flows of Federal Debt*, by Mindy R. Levit.

[5] In the current international economic environment a desire for quality investments may also affect capital flows. See CRS Report R40007, *Financial Market Turmoil and U.S. Macroeconomic Performance*, by Craig K. Elwell.

[6] In the longer run, as the amount of foreign holdings of U.S. assets increases, an increasing share of U.S. income will flow abroad in the form of interest, dividend, and rent payments. While this outflow does not necessarily mean a decline in U.S. living standards, it may mean that future living standards will not be as high as they would have been if a greater share of domestic investment had been financed by borrowing at home instead of abroad.

[7] Recently the share of Treasury securities held by the Federal Reserve has fallen. In an effort to add liquidity to credit markets, the Federal Reserve has swapped substantial amounts of Treasury securities for relatively riskier assets that were held by other financial institutions. See CRS Report RL34427, *Financial Turmoil: Federal Reserve Policy Responses*, by Marc Labonte.

[8] In the current discussion, both the growth rate and the interest rate are nominal (i.e., not adjusted for inflation).

[9] By law (section 14(b) of the Federal Reserve Act), the Federal Reserve can only buy Treasury securities in the open market. It cannot buy them directly from the Treasury.

[10]Thomas J. Sargent, "The Ends of Four Big Inflations," in Robert Hall, ed., *Inflation: Causes and Effects* (National Bureau of Economic Research, 1982), pp. 41-97.

[11] William A. Bomberger and Gail E. Makinen, "The Hungarian Hyperinflation and Stabilization of 1945-1946," *Journal of Political Economy*, vol. 91, no. 5 (1983), pp. 801-824.

[12] Juan-Antonio Morales, "Inflation Stabilization in Bolivia," in Michael Bruno et. al., eds., *Inflation Stabilization* (MIT Press, 1988), pp. 307-346.

[13] See CRS Report RL3 1056, Economics of Federal Reserve Independence, by Marc Labonte.

In: The U.S. National Debt: Background, Issues, Significance ISBN: 978-1-61761-767-6
Editor: Charlotte G. Wilson and Emily O. Brown

Chapter 2

The Debt Limit: History and Recent Increases

D. Andrew Austin and Mindy R. Levitt

Summary

Total debt of the federal government can increase in two ways. First, debt increases when the government sells debt to the public to finance budget deficits and acquire the financial resources needed to meet its obligations. This increases *debt held by the public*. Second, debt increases when the federal government issues debt to certain government accounts, such as the Social Security, Medicare, and Transportation trust funds, in exchange for their reported surpluses. This increases *debt held by government accounts*. The sum of *debt held by the public* and *debt held by government accounts* is the total federal debt. Surpluses generally reduce debt held by the public, while deficits raise it.

A statutory limit has restricted total federal debt since 1917 when Congress passed the Second Liberty Bond Act. Congress has voted to raise the debt limit ten times since 2001. Deficits each year since 2001 and the persistent increases in debt held by government accounts repeatedly raised the debt to or near the limit in place at the time. Congress raised the limit in June 2002, and by December 2002 the U.S. Department of the Treasury asked Congress for another increase, which was passed in May 2003. In June 2004, the Treasury asked for another debt limit increase. After Congress recessed in mid-October 2004 without acting, the Secretary of the Treasury told Congress that the actions he was taking to avoid exceeding the debt limit would suffice only through mid-November. Congress approved a debt limit increase in a post-election session, which the President signed on November 19, 2004.

In 2005, reconciliation instructions in the FY2006 budget resolution (H.Con.Res. 95) included a debt limit increase. With no action having been taken by December 2005, the Secretary of the Treasury sent several letters warning Congress that the Treasury would exhaust its options to avoid default by mid-March 2006. Congress passed an increase in mid-March, which the President signed on March 20. The House's adoption of the conference report on the FY2008 budget resolution in the spring of 2007 automatically created and deemed passed legislation (H.J.Res. 43) raising the debt limit by $850 billion to $9,815 billion. The Senate approved the resolution on September 27, 2007, and it was signed by the President two days later.

The current economic slowdown led to sharply higher estimates of the FY2008 and FY2009 deficits, which led to a series of debt limit increases. A debt limit increase was included in the Housing and Economic Recovery Act of 2008 (H.R. 3221) and signed into law (P.L. 110-289) on July 30. The Emergency Economic Stabilization Act of 2008 (H.R. 1424), signed into law on October 3 (P.L. 110-343), raised the debt limit again. The debt limit was increased for the third time in less than a year with the passage of American Recovery and Reinvestment Act of 2009 on February 13, 2009 (ARRA; H.R. 1), which was signed into law on February 17, 2009 (P.L. 111-5), which raised the debt limit to $12,104 billion.

The House's adoption of the conference report on the FY2010 budget resolution (S.Con.Res. 13) on April 29, 2009, triggered the automatic passage of H.J.Res. 45 to raise the debt limit to $13.029 trillion. In August 2009, Treasury reportedly said that the debt limit would be reached in mid-October, although the Treasury later stated that the limit would not be reached until mid or late December 2009. H.R. 4314, passed by the House on December 16, 2009, and by the Senate on December 24, raised the debt limit to $12.394 trillion when the President signed the measure (P.L. 111-123) on December 28. On January 28, the Senate passed an amended version of H.J.Res. 45, which the House passed on February 4 and the President signed on February 12.

INTRODUCTION

The statutory debt limit applies to almost all federal debt.[1] The limit applies to federal debt held by the public (that is, debt held outside the federal government itself) and to federal debt held by the government's own accounts. Federal trust funds, such as Social Security, Medicare, Transportation, and Civil Service Retirement accounts, hold most of this internally held debt.[2] The government's surpluses or deficits determine essentially all of the change in debt held by the public.[3] The government's on-budget fiscal balance, which excludes a small U.S. Postal Service net surplus or deficit and a large Social Security surplus of payroll taxes net of paid benefits, does not directly affect debt held in government accounts.[4] Increases or decreases in debt held by government accounts result from net financial flows into accounts holding the debt, such as the Social Security Trust Fund. Legal requirements and government accounting practices also affect levels of debt held by government accounts.[5]

The Debt Limit and the Treasury

Standard methods of financing federal activities or meeting government obligations used by the U.S. Department of Treasury (Treasury) can be hobbled when federal debt nears its legal limit. If the limit prevents the Treasury from issuing new debt to manage short-term cash flows or to finance an annual deficit, the government may be unable to obtain the cash needed to pay its bills or it may be unable to invest the surpluses of designated government accounts (federal trust funds) in federal debt as generally required by law. In either case, the

Treasury is left in a bind; the law requires that the government's legal obligations be paid, but the debt limit may prevent it from issuing the debt that would allow it to do so.

The government's income and outlays vary over the course of the year, producing monthly surpluses and deficits that affect the level of debt, whether or not the government has a surplus or deficit for the entire year. The government accounts holding federal debt also can experience monthly deficits and surpluses, even if most of them currently show annual surpluses.

Why Have a Debt Limit?

The debt limit can hinder the Treasury's ability to manage the federal government's finances, as noted above. In extreme cases, when the federal debt is very near its statutory limit, the Treasury must take unusual and extraordinary measures to meet federal obligations.[6] While the debt limit has never caused the federal government to default on its obligations, it has at times caused great inconvenience and has added uncertainty to Treasury operations.

The debt limit also provides Congress with the strings to control the federal purse, allowing Congress to assert its constitutional prerogatives to control spending.[7] The debt limit also imposes a form of fiscal accountability that compels Congress and the President to take visible action to allow further federal borrowing when the federal government spends more than it collects in revenues. In the words of one author, the debt limit "expresses a national devotion to the idea of thrift and to economical management of the fiscal affairs of the government."[8] On the other hand, some budget experts have advocated elimination of the debt limit, arguing that other controls provided by the modern congressional budget process established in 1974 have superseded the debt limit, and that the limit does little to alter spending and revenue policies that determine the size of the federal deficit.[9]

A Brief History of the Federal Debt Limit

Origins of the Federal Debt Limit

The statutory limit on federal debt began with the Second Liberty Bond Act of 1917,[10] which helped finance the United States' entry into World War I.[11] By allowing the Treasury to issue long-term Liberty Bonds, which were marketed to the public at large, the federal government held down its interest costs.[12]

Before World War I, Congress authorized specific loans, such as the Panama Canal loan, or allowed the Treasury to issue specific types of debt instruments, such as certificates of indebtedness, bills, notes and bonds.[13] In other cases, Congress provided the Treasury with limited discretion to choose debt instruments.[14] With the passage of the Second Liberty Bond Act, Congress enacted aggregate constraints on certificates of indebtedness and on bonds that allowed the Treasury greater ability to respond to changing conditions and more flexibility in financial management. Debt limit legislation in the following two decades also set separate limits for different categories of debt, such as bills, certificates, and bonds.

In 1939, Congress eliminated separate limits on bonds and on other types of debt, which created the first aggregate limit that covered nearly all public debt.[15] This measure gave the Treasury freer rein to manage the federal debt as it saw fit. Thus, the Treasury could issue debt instruments with maturities that would reduce interest costs and minimize financial risks stemming from future interest rate changes.[16] On the other hand, although the Treasury was delegated greater independence of action, the debt limit on the eve of World War II was much closer to total federal debt than it had been at the end of World War I. For example, the 1919 Victory Liberty Bond Act (P.L. 65-328) raised the maximum allowable federal debt to $43 billion, far above the $25.5 billion in total federal debt at the end of FY1919.[17] By contrast, the debt limit in 1939 was $45 billion, only about 10% above the $40.4 billion total federal debt of that time.

World War II and After

The debt ceiling was raised to accommodate accumulating costs for World War II in each year from 1941 through 1945, when it was set at $300 billion.[18] After World War II ended, the debt limit was reduced to $275 billion. Because the Korean War was mostly financed by higher taxes rather than by increased debt, the limit remained at $275 billion until 1954. After 1954, the debt limit was reduced twice and increased seven times, until March 1962 when it again reached $300 billion, its level at the end of World War II. Since March 1962, Congress has enacted 74 separate measures that have altered the limit on federal debt.[19] Most of these changes in the debt limit were, measured in percentage terms, small in comparison to changes adopted in wartime or during the Great Depression. Some recent increases in the debt limit, however, were large in dollar terms. For instance, in May 2003, the debt limit increased by $984 billion.

Table 1. Components of Debt Subject to Limit, FY1996-FY2009 (in billions of current dollars and as percentage of GDP)

End of Fiscal Year	Debt Limit	Debt Subject to Limit					
		Total		Held by Government Accounts		Held by the Public	
		$ Billion	% of GDP	$ Billion	% of GDP	$ Billion	% of GDP
1996	$5,500	$5,137.2	65.7%	1,432.4	18.3%	3,704.8	47.4%
1997	5,950	5,327.6	64.2	1,581.9	19.0	3,745.8	45.1
1998	5,950	5,439.4	62.2	1,742.1	19.9	3,697.4	42.3
1999	5,950	5,567.7	60.1	1,958.2	21.1	3,609.5	38.9
2000	5,950	5,591.6	57.0	2,203.9	22.4	3,387.7	34.5
2001	5,950	5,732.8	56.6	2,436.5	24.1	3,296.3	32.5
2002	6,400	6,161.4	58.9	2,644.2	25.3	3,517.2	33.6
2003	7,384	6,737.6	61.4	2,846.7	25.9	3,890.8	35.5
2004	7,384	7,333.4	62.5	3,056.6	26.0	4,276.8	36.4
2005	8,184	7,871.0	64.0	3,301.0	26.9	4,570.1	37.2

Table 1. (Continued)

End of Fiscal Year	Debt Limit	Debt Subject to Limit					
		Total		Held by Government Accounts		Held by the Public	
		$ Billion	% of GDP	$ Billion	% of GDP	$ Billion	% of GDP
2006	8,965	8,420.3	64.2	3,610.4	27.5	4,809.8	36.7
2007	9,815[a]	8,921.3	65.4	3,903.7	28.6	5,017.6	36.8
2008	10,615[b]	9,960.0	70.0	4,180.0	29.4	5,780.3	40.6
2009	12,104[c]	11,909.8	84.1	4,358.0	30.8	7,551.9	53.3
Change during FY1998 - FY2001		$405.2		$854.6		$-449.5	
Change during FY2002 - FY2009		$5,748.4		$1,713.8		$4,034.7	

Source: U.S. Department of the Treasury, Financial Management Service, *Treasury Bulletin*, June 2001 and December 2006. Bureau of the Public Debt, *Monthly Statement of Public Debt*, various issues. CRS calculations.

Notes: For the fiscal years 1996 through 2000, the amounts held by government accounts and held by the public are approximations. In 2001, the Treasury publications began distinguishing holders of debt subject to limit. The numbers in the table showing this breakdown for FY1996 through FY2000 were calculated by subtracting debts of the Federal Financing Bank, an arm of the Treasury whose debt is not subject to limit, from total debt held by government accounts. This calculation approximates the amount of that debt subject to limit. This approximation overestimates debt by billions of dollars because estimates of unamortized discount are unavailable. This adjusted amount was then subtracted from total debt subject to limit to produce an approximate measure of debt held by the public subject to limit. Because the amount held by government accounts is overestimated, the resulting measure of debt held by the public subject to limit is underestimated. Totals may not sum due to rounding.

a. Debt limit increased September 29, 2007, to $9,815 billion.

b. The debt limit was increased twice in 2008—to $10,615 billion on July 30 and then to $11,315 billion on October 3, at the start of FY2009.

c. Debt limit was increased February 17, 2009, to $12,104 billion.

THE DEBTCEILING IN THE LAST DECADE

During the four years (FY1998-FY2001) the government ran surpluses, federal debt held by intergovernmental accounts grew by $855 billion and debt held by the public fell by almost $450 billion. Since FY2001, however, debt held by the public has grown due to persistent and substantial budget deficits. Debt held in government accounts also has grown, in large part because Social Security payroll taxes have exceeded payments of beneficiaries. Table 1 shows components of debt in current dollars and as percentages of gross domestic product (GDP).[20]

Figure 1 shows the components of federal debt as shares of gross domestic product (GDP) from FY1940 through FY2009.[21] Federal debt held by government accounts has grown steadily since 1980. Debt held by the public, which changes in response to total surpluses or deficits, grew as a share of GDP through the mid-1990s. After FY1992, deficits shrank, and from FY1998 through FY2001 the federal government ran surpluses.[22] Those surpluses, along with rapid GDP growth, reduced debt held by the public as a percentage of GDP. When large deficits returned and GDP growth slowed in the early 2000s, debt held by the public as a share of GDP again increased. Smaller deficits in FY2006 and FY2007 led to smaller increases in publicly held debt. The total FY2007 deficit fell to 1.2% of GDP according to the Congressional Budget Office (CBO).[23] As a result of the recession, which began in December 2007, and federal action taken to stabilize the housing and financial markets, deficits rose in FY2008 to 3.2% of GDP. Federal debt, according to CBO and Treasury projections, is on track to exceed the debt limit before the end of December 2009.

The Debt Limit Issue in 2002

Accumulating debt in government accounts produced most of the pressure on the debt limit that occurred early in 2002. As deficits reemerged in FY2002, increases in debt held by the public added to the pressure on the debt limit in the spring of 2002. During the four fiscal years with surpluses (FY1998-FY2001), the increases in federally held debt and decreases in debt held by the public produced a net increase of $405 billion in total debt subject to limit. At the beginning of FY2002 (October 1, 2001), debt subject to limit was within $217 billion of the existing $5,950 billion debt limit.[24] Between then and the end of May 2002, debt subject to limit increased by another $217 billion, divided between a $117 billion increase in debt held by government accounts and a $100 billion increase in debt held by the public, putting the debt close to the $5,950 billion limit. Table A-1, presented in the Appendix, shows month-by-month debt totals and accumulations from September 2001 through November 2009.

In the fall of 2001, the Administration recognized that a deteriorating budget outlook and continued growth in debt held by government accounts were likely to lead to the debt limit soon being reached. In early December 2001, it asked Congress to raise the debt limit by $750 billion to $6.7 trillion. As the debt moved closer to and reached the debt limit over the first six months of FY2002, the Administration asked Congress repeatedly to increase the debt limit, warning of adverse financial consequences were the limit not raised.

On April 4, 2002, the Treasury held debt below the limit by invoking its legislatively mandated authority to suspend reinvestment of government securities in the G-Fund of the federal employees' Thrift Savings Plan (TSP). This allowed the Treasury to issue new debt and meet the government's obligations. On April 15, debt subject to limit stood at $5,949,975 million, just $25 million below the limit. Once April 15 tax revenues flowed in, the Treasury "made whole" the G-Fund by restoring all of the debt that had not been issued to the TSP over this period and crediting the fund with interest it would have earned on that debt.[25] By the end of April, debt subject to limit had fallen back $35 billion below the limit.

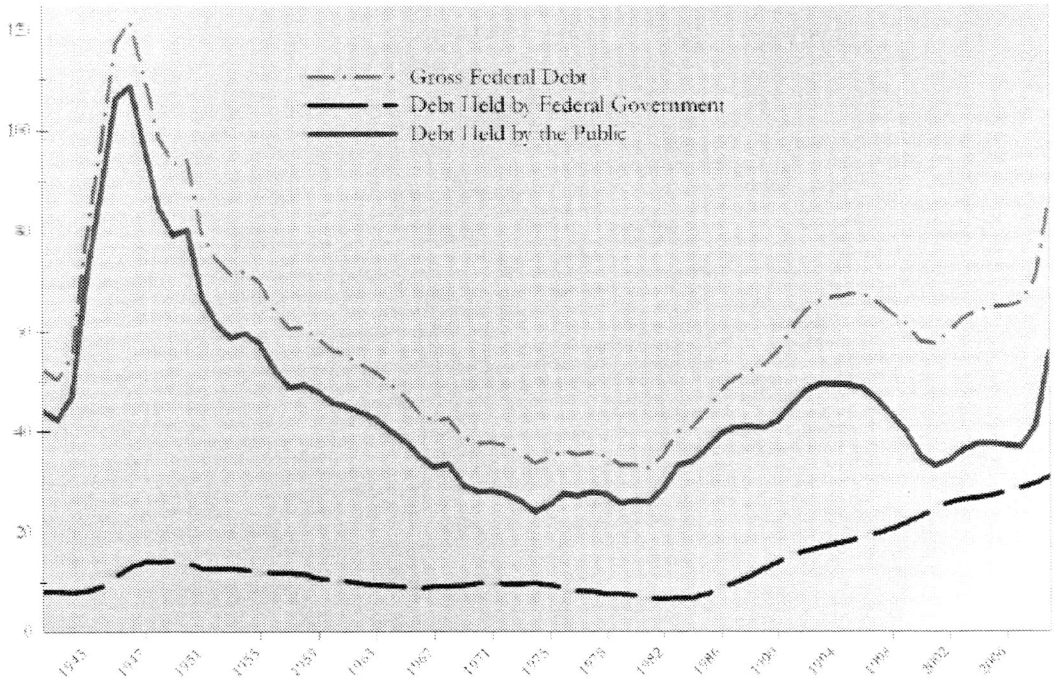

Source: OMB, Budget of the United States for FY2010, Historical Tables, February 2009; Mid-Session Review, August 2009.

Figure 1. Components of Federal Debt As a Percentage of GDP, FY1940-FY2009

Resolving the DebtLimit Issue in 2002

By the middle of May 2002, debt subject to limit had again risen to within $15 million of the statutory limit. At the FY2002 average spending rate, $15 million equaled about five minutes of federal outlays. The Treasury, for the second time in 2002, used its statutory authority to avoid a default. The Treasury's financing problems, however, would persist without an increase in the debt limit. On May 14, the Treasury asked Congress to raise the debt limit or enact other statutory changes allowing the Treasury to issue new debt. A Treasury news release stated "absent extraordinary actions, the government will exceed the statutory debt ceiling no later than May 16," and that

> a "debt issuance suspension period" will begin no later than May 16 [2002].... [This] allows the Treasury to suspend or redeem investments in two trust funds, which will provide flexibility to fund the operations of the government during this period.[26]

The Treasury reduced federal debt held by these government accounts by replacing it with non-interest-bearing, non-debt instruments, which enabled it to issue new debt to meet the government's obligations. The Treasury claimed these extraordinary actions would suffice, at the latest, through June 28, 2002. Without a debt limit increase by that date, the Treasury indicated it would need to take other actions to avoid breaching the ceiling. By June 21, the Treasury had postponed a regular securities auction, but took no other actions. With large payments and other obligations due at the end of June and at the beginning of July, the

Treasury stated it would soon exhaust all options to issue debt and fulfill government obligations, putting the government on the verge of a default.

During May and June 2002, Congress took steps to increase the debt limit. The FY2002 supplemental appropriations bill (H.R. 4775) passed by the House on May 24 included, after extended debate, language allowing any eventual House-Senate conference on the legislation to increase the debt limit. However, the Senate's supplemental appropriations bill (S. 2551; incorporated as an amendment to H.R. 4775, June 3, 2002) omitted debt-limit-increasing language. The Senate leadership expressed strong reluctance to include a debt limit increase in the supplemental appropriation bill. Instead, on June 11, the Senate adopted a bill (S. 2578), without debate, to raise the debt limit by $450 billion to $6,400 billion. At that time, a $450 billion debt limit increase was thought to provide enough borrowing authority for government operations through the rest of calendar year 2002, if not through the summer of 2003. With the possibility of default looming over it, the House passed the $450 billion debt limit increase by a single vote on June 27. The President signed the bill into law on June 28 (P.L. 107-199, 116 Stat. 734), ending the 2002 debt limit crisis.[27]

The Debt Limit Issue in 2003

On Christmas Eve, 2002, Kenneth Dam, Deputy Secretary of the Treasury sent a letter to Congress requesting an unspecified increase in the debt limit by late February 2003, signaling that the $6,400 billion debt limit would then be reached.[28] The 108th Congress, still in the process of organizing itself, did not immediately respond. Through the winter and into the spring, the Treasury repeatedly requested that the debt limit be raised to avoid serious financial problems. By February 20, 2003, the Treasury, as in 2002, used legislatively mandated measures to manage debt holdings of certain government accounts to avoid reaching the debt limit. These actions included the replacement of internally held government debt with non-debt instruments in certain government accounts and not issuing new debt to these accounts. These actions allowed the Treasury to issue additional debt to the public to acquire the cash needed to pay for the government's commitments or to issue new debt to other federal accounts.

Through the rest of February and into May, the Treasury held debt subject to limit $15 million below the debt ceiling.[29] The adoption of the conference report on the FY2004 budget resolution (H.Con.Res. 95; H.Rept. 108-71) on April 11, 2003, in the House triggered the "Gephardt rule" (House Rule XXVII) that deems to have passed legislation (in this case, H.J.Res. 51) raising the debt limit to accommodate the spending and revenue levels approved in the adopted budget resolution.[30]

The Senate received the debt-limit legislation on April 11, but did not act until May 23, after receiving further Treasury warnings of imminent default. On that day, debt subject to limit was $25 million (or 0.0004%) below the existing $6,400 billion limit. The Senate adopted the legislation, after rejecting eight amendments and sent it to the President, who signed it on May 27. This legislation raised the debt limit to $7,384 billion (P.L. 108-24, 117 Stat. 710).

The Debt Limit Issue in 2004

In January 2004, CBO estimated that the debt limit, then set at $7,384 billion, would be reached the following summer.[31] In June 2004, the Treasury asked Congress to raise the debt limit in order to avoid the disruptions to government finances experienced in the previous two years.[32] In August, and again in September, the Treasury declared that the debt limit would be reached in the first half of October. On October 14, debt subject to limit reached $7,383,975 million, just $25 million below the existing limit. The Treasury employed methods used in the previous two years to keep debt under the legal limit. On October 14, Secretary of the Treasury John Snow informed Congress, just before the election recess, that available measures to avoid breaching the debt limit would be exhausted by mid-November.[33] Without an increase in the debt limit, the Treasury would be unable to meet all of the government's existing obligations, and the government could default.[34]

Although the House passed a budget resolution for FY2005 in the spring of 2004, it did not reach final agreement with the Senate on the measure. Without a budget resolution passed by Congress, no resolution to raise the debt limit could be deemed passed by the House automatically under the Gephardt rule. Consequently, no measure was available to send to the Senate. As the debt approached the limit through the summer and into the fall, no legislation was moved to raise the debt limit.

Earlier, in September 2004, the House had added an amendment to the FY2005 Transportation-Treasury appropriations (H.R. 5025) in an effort to remove the Treasury's flexibility in financing the government as federal debt approached and reached the existing limit. Without that flexibility, the government would be unable to meet its financial obligations as the amount of debt neared the limit. The legislation cleared the House, but the Senate did not act on it.

After the elections, Senator Frist, on November 16, 2004, introduced legislation (S. 2986) to raise the debt limit by $800 billion, from $7,384 billion to $8,184 billion. The Senate approved the increase on November 17, 2004. The House considered and approved the increase on November 18. The President signed the legislation into law (P.L. 108-415, 118 Stat. 2337) on November 19, 2004. Estimates made at that time anticipated the new limit would be reached between August and December 2005.

Shortly before the increase in the debt limit, the Treasury delayed a debt auction and informed Congress that it would invoke a "debt limit suspension period" as it had in previous years. The increase in the debt limit in mid-November allowed the Treasury to reschedule the debt auction and cancel, before it began, the "debt limit suspension period."

The Debt Limit Issue in 2005, 2006, and 2007

Debt limit increases in 2005, 2006, and 2007 took a less dramatic path than those in President Bush's first term. In 2005, Congress included three reconciliation instructions in the FY2006 budget resolution (H.Con.Res. 95, 109th Congress; April 28, 2005), the third of which directed the House Committee on Ways and Means and the Senate Finance Committee to report bills raising the debt limit. The instructions specified a $781 billion debt limit increase, to $8,965 billion, with a reporting date of no later than September 30, 2005. Neither committee reported a bill to raise the debt limit.

The adoption of the conference report on the FY2006 budget resolution in late April 2005 also triggered the Gephardt rule (House Rule XXVII), producing a House Joint Resolution (H.J.Res. 47) that also would raise the debt limit by $781 billion to $8,965 billion. Under the rule, the resolution was automatically deemed passed by the House and sent to the Senate. Through the end of the first session of the 109th Congress, the Senate had not considered H.J.Res. 47, nor had Congress considered a reconciliation bill raising the debt limit as called for in the budget resolution.

At the end of December 2005, Secretary of the Treasury Snow wrote Congress that the debt limit would probably be reached in mid-February 2006, although the Treasury could take actions that maintain the debt below its limit until mid-March. He therefore requested an increase in the debt limit.[35] In two more letters, sent on February 19 and March 6, Secretary Snow advised Congress that the Treasury was taking measures within its legal discretion to avoid reaching the limit and that these measures would suffice only until the middle of March 2006. Secretary Snow authorized actions used previously by the Treasury, including declaring a debt issuance suspension period. As March began, the government was again close to becoming unable to meet its obligations. During the week of March 13 the Senate took up H.J.Res. 47. On March 16, the Senate passed a debt limit increase after rejecting several amendments. The President's signature on March 20, 2006, then raised the debt limit (P.L. 109-182) to $8,965 billion.

In mid-May 2007, Congress passed the conference report (H.Rept. 110-153) on the FY2008 budget resolution. The House's Gephardt rule, triggered by the adoption of the conference report on the budget resolution, resulted in the automatic engrossment of a joint resolution (in this case, H.J.Res. 43, 110th Congress) raising the debt limit by $850 billion to $9,815 billion, and sending it to the Senate. At the end of July 2007, the Treasury asked Congress to raise the debt limit, stating the limit would be reached in early October 2007. In August, the CBO Director said that projections suggested that the limit would be reached in late October or early November. Without an increase, the Treasury indicated that it would take steps within its legal authority to avoid exceeding the debt limit. The Senate Finance Committee approved the House resolution (H.J.Res. 43) without changes on September 12, 2007. The Senate then passed the measure on September 27, which the President signed on September 29, 2007 (P.L. 110-91).

The Economic Slowdown and Federal Debt

Fiscal Policy Considerations

The United States entered a severe economic recession in the last quarter of 2007. The economic slowdown began with a rapid deceleration of housing prices and a rise in interest rate spreads between private lending rates and benchmark Federal Reserve rates, indicating an increasing reluctance of major financial institutions to lend to each other as well as to firms and individuals. This led to sharply higher federal deficit spending in FY2008 spurred by several major actions taken by Congress to unfreeze credit markets, boost consumption, and increase spending. Deficit spending was even higher in FY2009, with higher than average deficits as a percentage of GDP persisting into the next decade, likely leading to further increases in the federal debt and debt limit.

An economic recession affects the federal deficit in several ways. First, falling prices of many assets and equities can sharply reduce federal revenues from capital gains taxes and from the corporate tax. Second, individual income taxes, the largest component of federal revenues, may also fall if jobs are cut and unemployment increases due to economic conditions. Third, "automatic stabilizers" such as unemployment insurance and income support programs pay out more money as unemployment rises and the number of households eligible for means-tested benefits rises, thus increasing federal spending.

Boosting the economy through deficit spending provides a fiscal stimulus if the output levels of goods and services produced in the nation are below their potential levels. Deficit spending, however, can help accelerate inflation if output levels are near or at potential levels, and in addition, exacerbates long-term fiscal challenges. Several economists have expressed concerns that inflation, which had been relatively low since the early 1980s, could accelerate due to rising prices of food, energy, and primary commodities. While inflation would reduce the market value of the federal deficit, it would require Treasury to pay higher nominal interest rates on federal debt.

Raising the DebtCeilingin 2008, 2009, and 2010

In a March 2008 report, CBO estimated the President's budget would lead to a $396 billion deficit in FY2008 and a $342 billion deficit in FY2009.[36] The actual deficit for FY2008 reached $455 billion. In August 2009, CBO estimated the deficit would total $1,587 billion in FY2009 and $1,381 billion in FY2010.[37] As a result of the current economic conditions and the actions of the federal government to bring the economy out of recession, the federal debt limit was raised twice in the second half of 2008 and twice in 2009.

The House Concurrent Resolution on the Budget (H.Con.Res. 312) recommended policies that would result in a $10.2 trillion debt in FY2009. The Senate Concurrent Resolution on the Budget S.Con.Res. 70) recommended policies that would result in a total debt of $10,278 billion in FY2009.[38] Implementing either set of policies would require an increase in the federal debt limit. The conference agreement (H.Rept. 110-659) also recommended spending levels that would lead to a debt subject to limit of $10,207 billion in FY2009, a level that would require an increase in the statutory debt limit. The budget conference report passed the Senate on a 48-45 vote on June 4, 2008. The House passed the measure on the next day by a 214-210 vote. Agreement on the FY2009 budget resolution automatically created and deemed passed in the House legislation (H.J.Res. 92) that would increase the debt limit from its current level of $9,815 billion to $10,615 billion. Because the Senate did not take up H.J.Res. 92, the debt limit remained at $9,815 billion.

Subsequently, the House passed an amended version of the Housing and Economic Recovery Act of 2008 (H.R. 3221) by a vote of 272-152 that included a debt limit increase to $10,615 billion on July 23, 2008. The Senate then passed the measure on July 26 on a 72-13 vote. The President signed the bill on July 30 (P.L. 110-289), increasing the debt limit. In addition to increasing the debt limit, the act also contained provisions that would temporarily authorize the Secretary of Treasury to extend a line of credit to mortgage guarantee agencies Freddie Mac and Fannie Mae. The act also created the a new independent agency called the Federal Housing Finance Agency (FHFA), which replaced the Department of Housing and

Urban Development Office of Federal Housing Enterprise Oversight (OFHEO) and the Federal Housing Finance Board (FHFB).

While CBO indicated that it was more likely than not that such intervention would not be needed, it also estimated a 5% chance of a cost to taxpayers of more than $100 billion.[39] Because debt subject to limit was just $339 billion less than the debt ceiling of $9,815 billion when the Senate passed H.R. 3221, some financial market participants may have worried that the debt limit, without an increase, might have hindered the Treasury Secretary's ability to intervene to support Freddie Mac and Fannie Mae. On September 7, 2008, the FHFA placed Fannie Mae and Freddie Mac in conservatorship, providing FHFA with the full powers to control the assets and operations of the firms.

Since the deprivatization of Fannie Mae and Freddie Mac, the federal government has acted to provide stability to financial markets.[40] On September 20, 2008, the U.S. Treasury submitted a proposal to Congress to authorize the Treasury Secretary to buy mortgage-related assets in order to stabilize financial markets. The Treasury proposal would allow Treasury holdings of mortgage-related securities up to $700 billion and would raise the debt limit to $11,315 billion.[41] The House introduced the Emergency Economic Stabilization Act of 2008 (H.R. 3997), which incorporated the main tenets of the Treasury proposal including raising the debt limit to $11,315 billion.[42] On September 29, 2008, however, the House rejected this measure. On October 1, 2008, the Senate voted on, and passed, a different version of the Emergency Economic Stabilization Act of 2008 (H.R. 1424) that included the same debt limit increase.[43] The House passed H.R. 1424 on October 3, 2008, and it was signed into law by the President (P.L. 110-343) on the same day, raising the debt limit to $11,315 billion.

Current economic conditions led Congress to consider another economic stimulus measure. This measure contains both tax cuts and spending increases, which will increase the deficit by reducing revenues and increasing outlays. The American Recovery and Reinvestment Act of 2009 (ARRA) as passed by the Senate on February 10, 2009 (Division B of the Senate Substitute amendment to H.R. 1 and S. 350), contained a provision which would raise the debt limit to $12,140 billion. The version of this legislation originally passed by the House omitted this provision. The final conference agreement on ARRA was passed by the House and Senate on February 13, 2009, and signed by the President on February 17, 2009 (P.L. 111-5). This measure contained a provision increasing the debt limit to $12,104 billion.

The conference report on the Concurrent Resolution on the Budget for FY2010 (S.Con.Res. 13) recommended policies that would lead to a debt subject to limit of $13,233 billion in FY2010, a level that would require an increase in the statutory debt limit. The budget resolution also contained a revised estimate of debt subject to limit of $12,016 billion for FY2009. The adoption of this conference report on April 29, 2009, triggered the Gephardt rule (House Rule XXVII), producing a House Joint Resolution (H.J.Res. 45) that would raise the debt limit by $925 billion to $13,029 billion. Under the rule, the resolution was automatically deemed passed by the House and sent to the Senate. The Senate, as of the date of this chapter, has not acted on H.J.Res. 45.

In August 2009, according to media reports, Secretary of Treasury Timothy Geithner notified Congress that the debt limit would be reached in mid-October.[44] On November 4, the U.S. Treasury announced that it could postpone the time when federal debt would reach its statutory limit until the middle or the end of December. [45] Treasury dropped nearly $185 billion from its balance sheet by reducing the amount of loans available through the Supplemental Financing Program, an emergency loan program created in the days following

Lehman Brothers' bankruptcy, from $200 billion to $15 billion, which extended the time until the debt limit would be reached.[46] According to media reports, the Obama Administration also contemplated scaling back the Troubled Asset Relief Program (TARP), which could also lower federal debt subject to statutory limit. Repayments of TARP funds by major financial institutions could also lower the amount of debt subject to limit.[47] Other measures, such as those taken in 2003 during a "debt issuance suspension period" (described above), could also have extended the U.S. Treasury's ability to operate within the debt limit. On the other hand, the U.S. Treasury was scheduled to issue $48 billion of nonmarketable securities to the FDIC on December 30 and to make interest payments to various federal trust funds on December 31 totaling about $100 billion, according to Wall Street analysts, which in the absence of a debt limit increase, could have challenged Treasury's debt management activities in the absence of special accounting measures.[48]

Table 2. Increases in the Debt Limit Since 1993

Date	Public Law (P.L.) Number	New Debt Limit ($ billion)	Change From Previous Limit ($ billion)
April 6, 1993	P.L. 103-12	$4,370[a]	$225
August 10, 1993	P.L. 103-33	4,900	530
February 8, 1996	P.L. 104-103	(b)	—
March 12, 1996	P.L. 104-115	(c)	—
March 29, 1996	P.L. 104-121	5,500	600[d]
August 5, 1997	P.L. 105-33	5,950	450
June 28, 2002	P.L. 107-199	6,400	450
May 27, 2003	P.L. 108-24	7,384	984
Nov. 19, 2004	P.L. 108-415	8,184	800
Mar. 20, 2006	P.L. 109-182	8,965	781
Sept. 29, 2007	P.L. 110-91	9,815	850
July 30, 2008	P.L. 110-289	10,615	800
Oct. 3, 2008	P.L. 110-343	11,315	700
Feb. 17, 2009	P.L. 111-5	12,104	789
Dec. 28, 2009	P.L. 111-123	12,394	290
February 12, 2010[e]	(H.J.Res. 45)	14.294	1,900

Source: CRS, compiled using the Legislative Information System, available at http://www.congress.gov; OMB.

a. Increased the debt limit temporarily through September 30, 1993.

b. Temporarily exempted from limit obligations in an amount equal to the monthly insurance benefits payable under Title II of the Social Security Act in March 1996, the exemption to expire on the earlier of an increase in the limit or March 15, 1996.

c. Temporarily exempted from limit (a) obligations in an amount equal to the monthly insurance benefits payable under Title II of the Social Security Act in March 1996 and (b) certain obligations issued to trust funds and other Federal Government accounts, both exemptions to expire on the earlier of an increase in the limit or March 30, 1996.

d. Difference from debt limit set on August 10, 1983.

e. Awaiting public law number.

In mid-December, according to media reports, senior Members of the House chose to forgo a larger increase in the debt limit in favor of a smaller increase in the debt limit that would allow the U.S. Treasury Department to continue normal debt management operations for two months or so.[49] H.R. 4314, a measure to raise the debt limit to $12.394 trillion, was introduced on December 15, 2009, and passed by the House the next day on a 218-214 vote. The Senate passed it on December 24 by a 60-39 vote, and the President signed the measure on December 28.

On January 28, the Senate passed an amended version of H.J.Res. 45 on a 60-39 vote. The measure would raise the debt ceiling by $1.9 trillion, to $14.294 trillion.[50] In addition, one amendment to impose certain pay-as-you-go (PAYGO) restrictions was approved on a 60-40 vote.[51]

Some Members of Congress have called for the creation of a national commission to address federal debt and the government's fiscal situation, which could be enabled through a measure linked to an increase in the debt limit.[52] An amendment (S.Amdt. 3302 to S.Amdt. 3299) to H.J.Res. 45 that would have established a "Bipartisan Task Force for Responsible Fiscal Action" was not approved on a 53-46 vote, having failed to reach 60 votes, on January 26, 2010.

The House approved H.J.Res. 45 on a 233-187 vote on February 4, forwarding the measure to the President. The Obama Administration had previously voiced its strong support for a debt limit increase.[53] The President signed the measure on February 12, 2010.

Table 2 summarizes the increases in the debt limit since 1993.[54]

DeficitEstimates

The size of the debt may remain a concern in the future due to the size of impending federal deficits necessitating further increases in the debt limit. CBO warns that the current trajectory of federal borrowing is unsustainable and could lead to slower economic growth in the long run as debt rises as a percentage of GDP. The total federal deficit reached $1.414 trillion in FY2009 CBO estimates the FY2010 deficit will be nearly as large at $1.349 trillion. In FY2008, the total federal deficit was $455 billion.[55] Much of the increase in deficits can be attributed to weak economic and financial market turmoil that started in late 2007, as well as to federal responses. Nonetheless, many budget experts are concerned that a slow economic recovery could keep federal revenues below previous trendline projections for several years, and that the federal government would continue to run large deficits.

CONCLUDINGCOMMENTS

Since the late 1950s, the federal government increased its borrowing from the public in all years, except in FY1969 following imposition of a war surcharge and in the period FY1997-FY2001. The persistence of federal budget deficits has required the government to issue more and more debt to the public.[56] The accumulation of Social Security and other trust funds, particularly after 1983 when recommendations of the Greenspan Commission were implemented, led to sustained growth in government-held debt subject to limit.[57] The growth in federal debt held by the public and in intergovernmental accounts, such as trust funds, has periodically obliged Congress to raise the debt limit.

Between August 1997, when the debt limit was raised to $5,950 billion, and the beginning of FY2002 in October 2001, federal budget surpluses reduced debt held by the public. From the end of FY2001, the last fiscal year with a surplus, until the end of FY2008, debt held by the public subject to limit grew by $2,484 billion. Federal debt held in intergovernmental accounts grew steadily throughout the period, rising by $1,743 billion since the beginning of FY2002.

In early 2001, the 10-year budget forecasts projected large and growing surpluses, indicating rapid reduction in debt held by the public. Some experts expressed concern about consequences of retiring all federal debt held by the public.[58] Most long-term forecasts computed at that time, however, showed large deficits emerging once the baby boomers began to retire. Short-term forecasts projected continuous growth in debt held by government accounts, largely due to the difference between Social Security tax revenues and benefit payments. The combination of falling levels of publicly held debt and rising levels of debt held by government accounts moderated the expected growth of total debt. The moderate growth in total debt those projections had forecast was expected to postpone the need to increase the debt limit until late into the decade, when accumulating debt in government accounts would overtake reductions in debt held by the public.

New budget projections released in early 2002 smashed expectations of large, persistent surpluses, and hopes for reductions in debt held by the public collapsed. The return to large federal deficits accelerated the growth of total debt. Increases in the debt limit would be necessary much sooner than previously expected.

Early in 2003, the FY2003 deficit and the persistent rise in debt held by government accounts drove the federal debt up to the $6,400 billion limit in effect at the time. The Treasury avoided breaching the limit into May. Congress adopted a debt limit increase of $934 billion on May 23, 2003, that provided enough room for the growing federal debt through the fall of 2004. The debt limit increase passed by Congress late in 2004 was expected, at the time, to accommodate the government's debt growth well into 2005, if not into early 2006. In late December 2005, and early in 2006, the Treasury informed Congress that the limit would be reached between mid-February and mid-March 2006. On March 16, 2006, the Senate passed the House-initiated debt limit increase, raising the debt limit to $8,965 billion. The debt limit crisis was resolved when the President signed the debt limit increase on March 20.

Smaller than expected deficits in FY2006 and FY2007 postponed, but did not end the need for a new, higher debt limit. The House passed legislation in May 2007 (H.J.Res. 43) to raise the debt limit. The Senate passed the measure (P.L. 110-91) on September 27, which the President signed on September 29. Turmoil in some financial markets in August 2007, according to some observers, appeared to constrain contention over the debt limit increase.

The 2008 economic slowdown, which reduced federal tax revenues and increased federal outlays, caused federal deficit spending to rise, thus bringing forward the projected date when the federal debt will reach its current limit. The House passed an amended version of the Housing and Economic Recovery Act of 2008 (H.R. 3221) that included a debt limit increase to $10,615 billion on July 23, 2008. The Senate passed the measure on July 26, and the President signed it on July 30, raising the debt limit for the first time in 2008. Subsequently, the Emergency Economic Stabilization Act of 2008 (H.R. 1424), signed into law on October 3 (P.L. 110-343), raised the debt limit for the second time in 2008 to $11,315 billion. The debt limit was raised for the third time in less than a year as a result of passage of the

American Recovery and Reinvestment Act of 2009. President Obama signed this measure on February 17, 2009 (P.L. 111-5), which raised the debt limit to $12,104 billion.

The debt limit was again raised in late 2009. H.R. 4314, passed by the House on December 16, 2009, and by the Senate on December 24, raised the debt limit to $12.394 trillion when the President signed the measure on December 28. In early 2010, Congress voted for a larger increase in the debt limit, which would put the limit at $14.294 trillion, raising the debt ceiling by $1.9 trillion. President Obama signed the measure on February 12, 2010. The new debt limit, according to projections, is high enough to allow the Treasury Department to issue new debt at projected levels for the coming year.

Amendments offered during consideration of the latest debt limit increase may signal a growing concern with the fiscal sustainability. One amendment, which was not approved, would have established a statutory commission to consider long-term fiscal issues. Another amendment, which was approved, would impose certain PAYGO restrictions.[59] Over the next decade, without major changes in federal policies, persistent and possibly growing deficits, along with the ongoing growth in the debt holdings of government accounts, would increase substantially the amount of federal debt subject to limit. Unless federal policies change, Congress would repeatedly face demands to raise the debt limit to accommodate the growing federal debt in order to provide the government with the means to meet its financial obligations.

Further Reading

Drishnakumar, Anita S, "In Defense of the Debt Limit Statute," *Harvard Journal on Legislation*, vol. *42*, 2005, pp. 135-185.

Gordon, John Steele, *Hamilton's Blessing: the Extraordinary Life and Times of Our National Debt*, New York: Penguin, 1998.

Hormats, Robert D, *The Price of Liberty: Paying for America's Wars from the Revolution to the War on Terror*, New York: Times Books, 2007.

Noll, Franklin, "The United States Public Debt, 1861 to 1975," EH.Net Encyclopedia, edited by Robert Whaples, May 26, 2004. Available at http://eh.net/encyclopedia/article /noll.publicdebt.

Wright, Robert E, *One Nation Under Debt: Hamilton, Jefferson, and the History of What We Owe*, New York: McGraw-Hill, 2008.

APPENDIX. DEBTSUBJECT TO LIMIT BY MONTHSINCESEPTEMBER 2001

Table A-1 provides data on the dollar amount, in current dollars, of federal debt and the changes in these amounts by month between the end of September 2001 (the end of FY2001) and the end of November 2009. The table shows outstanding monthly balances, subject to the debt limit, of total federal debt, debt held by government accounts, and debt held by the public. The final row shows the change for each category for the entire period, September 2001 to November 2009.

All three measures of debt subject to limit increased over this period. From the end of September 2001 (the end of FY2001) to the end of September 2009 (the most recently completed fiscal year), total federal debt increased by $6,121 billion, debt held in government accounts increased by $1,889 billion, and debt held by the public increased by $4,232 billion. All three measures experienced periodic reductions in some months. Because federal receipts and outlays are spread unevenly over the fiscal year, debt may rise or fall in a given month, even if debt measures follow an overall increasing trend.

Table A-1. Components of Debt Subject to Limit by Month, September 2001-November 2009 (in millions of current dollars)

End of Month	Total	Change from Previous Period	Held by Government Accounts	Change from Previous Period	Held by the Public	Change from Previous Period
Sept. 2001	$5,732,802	—	$2,436,521	—	$3,296,281	—
Oct. 2001	5,744,523	$11,721	2,451,815	$15,294	3,292,709	$-3,572
Nov. 2001	5,816,823	72,300	2,469,647	17,832	3,347,176	54,467
Dec. 2001	5,871,413	54,590	2,516,012	46,365	3,355,401	8,225
Jan. 2002	5,865,892	-5,521	2,525,755	9,743	3,340,138	-15,263
Feb. 2002	5,933,154	67,262	2,528,494	2,739	3,404,659	64,521
Mar. 2002	5,935,108	1,954	2,528,318	-176	3,406,789	2,130
Apr. 2002	5,914,816	-20,292	2,549,438	21,120	3,365,378	-41,411
May 2002	5,949,975	35,159	2,553,350	3,912	3,396,625	31,247
June 2002	6,058,313	108,338	2,630,646	77,296	3,427,667	31,042
July 2002	6,092,050	33,737	2,627,980	-2,666	3,464,070	36,403
Aug. 2002	6,142,835	50,785	2,620,946	-7,034	3,521,890	57,820
Sept. 2002	6,161,431	18,596	2,644,244	23,298	3,517,187	-4,703
Oct. 2002	6,231,284	69,853	2,680,812	36,568	3,550,472	33,285
Nov. 2002	6,294,480	63,196	2,680,788	-24	3,613,692	63,220
Dec. 2002	6,359,412	64,932	2,745,787	64,999	3,613,625	-67
Jan. 2003	6,355,812	-3,600	2,753,301	7,514	3,602,511	-11,114
Feb. 2003	6,399,975	44,163	2,750,471	-2,830	3,649,504	46,993
Mar. 2003	6,399,975	0	2,722,812	-27,659	3,677,163	27,659
Apr. 2003	6,399,975	0	2,731,042	8,230	3,668,933	-8,230
May 2003	6,498,658	98,683	2,755,895	24,853	3,742,763	73,830
June 2003	6,625,519	126,861	2,842,361	86,466	3,783,158	40,395
July 2003	6,704,814	79,295	2,835,566	-6,795	3,869,247	86,089
Aug. 2003	6,743,775	38,961	2,829,387	-6,179	3,914,388	45,141
Sept. 2003	6,737,553	-6,222	2,846,730	17,343	3,890,823	-23,565
Oct. 2003	6,826,668	89,115	2,869,493	22,763	3,957,175	66,352
Nov. 2003	6,879,626	52,958	2,879,117	9,624	4,000,509	43,334
Dec. 2003	6,952,893	73,267	2,940,736	61,619	4,012,157	11,648

Table A-1. (Continued)

End of Month	Total	Change from Previous Period	Held by Government Accounts	Change from Previous Period	Held by the Public	Change from Previous Period
Jan. 2004	6,966,851	13,958	2,951,219	10,483	4,015,633	3,476
Feb. 2004	7,049,163	82,312	2,953,123	1,904	4,096,040	80,407
Mar. 2004	7,088,648	39,485	2,941,195	-11,928	4,147,453	51,413
Apr. 2004	7,089,700	1,052	2,960,151	18,956	4,129,549	-17,904
May 2004	7,151,523	61,823	2,973,869	13,718	4,177,653	48,104
June 2004	7,229,320	77,797	3,039,987	66,118	4,189,334	11,681
July 2004	7,271,328	42,008	3,033,396	-6,591	4,237,933	48,599
Aug. 2004	7,305,531	34,203	3,037,149	3,753	4,268,382	30,449
Sept. 2004	7,333,350	27,819	3,056,590	19,441	4,276,760	8,378
Oct. 2004	7,383,975	50,625	3,096,207	39,617	4,287,768	11,008
Nov. 2004	7,464,740	80,765	3,087,834	-8,373	4,376,906	89,138
Dec. 2004	7,535,644	70,904	3,158,531	70,697	4,377,114	208
Jan. 2005	7,567,702	32,058	3,171,089	12,558	4,396,615	19,501
Feb. 2005	7,652,726	85,024	3,176,406	5,317	4,476,320	79,705
Mar. 2005	7,715,503	62,777	3,175,460	-946	4,540,042	63,722
Apr. 2005	7,704,041	-11,462	3,185,364	9,904	4,518,677	-21,365
May 2005	7,717,574	13,533	3,207,232	21,868	4,510,342	-8,335
June 2005	7,778,128	60,554	3,280,914	73,682	4,497,214	-13,128
July 2005	7,829,029	50,901	3,278,725	-2,189	4,550,304	53,090
Aug. 2005	7,868,395	39,366	3,284,696	5,971	4,583,699	33,395
Sept. 2005	7,871,040	2,645	3,300,969	16,273	4,570,071	-13,628
Oct. 2005	7,964,782	93,742	3,345,589	44,620	4,619,193	49,122
Nov. 2005	8,028,918	64,136	3,351,093	5,504	4,677,826	58,633
Dec. 2005	8,107,019	78,101	3,424,304	73,211	4,682,715	4,889
Jan. 2006	8,132,290	25,271	3,442,543	18,239	4,689,747	7,032
Feb. 2006	8,183,975	51,685	3,457,409	14,866	4,726,567	36,820
Mar. 2006	8,281,451	97,476	3,443,602	-13,807	4,837,849	111,282
Apr. 2006	8,262,718	-18,733	3,479,623	36,021	4,783,095	-54,754
May 2006	8,263,812	1,094	3,492,648	13,025	4,771,165	-11,930
June 2006	8,330,646	66,834	3,566,186	73,538	4,764,460	-6,705
July 2006	8,352,614	21,968	3,569,550	3,364	4,783,064	18,604
Aug. 2006	8,423,321	70,707	3,576,166	6,616	4,847,155	64,091
Sept. 2006	8,420,278	-3,043	3,622,378	46,212	4,828,972	-18,183
Oct. 2006	8,498,016	77,738	3,650,241	27,863	4,847,775	18,803
Nov. 2006	8,545,715	47,699	3,649,736	-505	4,895,979	48,204
Dec. 2006	8,592,513	46,798	3,724,450	74,714	4,868,063	-27,916
Jan. 2007	8,619,499	26,986	3,737,894	13,444	4,881,605	13,542
Feb. 2007	8,690,921	71,422	3,744,299	6,405	4,946,622	65,017

Table A-1. (Continued)

End of Month	Total	Change from Previous Period	Held by Government Accounts	Change from Previous Period	Held by the Public	Change from Previous Period
Mar. 2007	8,760,735	69,814	3,740,127	-4,172	5,020,608	73,986
Apr. 2007	8,753,070	-7,665	3,778,255	38,128	4,974,815	-45,793
May 2007	8,740,892	-12,178	3,792,201	13,946	4,948,691	-26,124
June 2007	8,779,168	38,276	3,867,819	75,618	4,911,348	-37,343
July 2007	8,845,417	66,249	3,873,239	5,420	4,972,178	60,830
Aug. 2007	8,918,493	73,076	3,854,115	-19,124	5,064,377	92,199
Sept. 2007	8,921,343	2,850	3,903,710	49,595	5,017,633	-46,744
Oct. 2007	8,994,639	73,296	3,958,357	54,647	5,036,281	18,648
Nov. 2007	9,065,827	71,188	3,950,468	-7,889	5,115,358	79,077
Dec. 2007	9,144,715	78,888	4,038,566	88,098	5,106,149	-9,209
Jan. 2008	9,155,842	11,127	4,053,199	14,633	5,102,644	-3,505
Feb. 2008	9,275,683	119,841	4,045,007	-8,192	5,230,676	128,032
Mar. 2008	9,358,135	82,452	4,051,685	6,678	5,306,450	75,774
Apr. 2008	9,298,567	-59,568	4,080,887	29,202	5,217,680	-88,770
May 2008	9,324,137	25,570	4,071,992	-8,895	5,252,144	34,464
June 2008	9,427,901	167,869	4,169,509	134,950	5,258,392	32,920
July 2008	9,520,220	92,319	4,144,377	-25,132	5,375,843	117,451
Aug. 2008	9,580,508	60,288	4,129,413	-14,964	5,451,095	75,252
Sept. 2008	9,959,850	379,342	4,179,574	50,161	5,780,276	329,181
Oct. 2008	10,504,702	544,852	4,231,878	52,304	6,272,824	492,548
Nov. 2008	10,595,725	91,023	4,228,270	-3,608	6,367,454	94,630
Dec. 2008	10,640,274	44,549	4,298,482	70,212	6,341,792	-25,662
Jan. 2009	10,569,310	-70,964	4,278,424	-20,058	6,290,886	-50,906
Feb. 2009	10,814,630	245,320	4,261,734	-16,690	6,552,896	262,010
Mar. 2009	11,066,217	251,587	4,258,272	-3,462	6,807,946	255,050
Apr. 2009	11,178,827	112,610	4,273,005	14,733	6,905,822	97,876
May 2009	11,260,445	81,618	4,265,719	-7,286	6,994,725	88,903
June 2009	11,487,470	227,025	4,336,673	70,954	7,150,797	156,072
July 2009	11,611,178	123,708	4,299,673	-37,000	7,311,505	160,708
Aug. 2009	11,755,205	144,027	4,294,923	-4,750	7,460,282	148,777
Sept. 2009	11,853,434	98,229	4,325,124	30,201	7,528,311	68,029
Oct. 2009	11,836,629	-16,805	4,372,308	47,184	7,464,321	-63,990
Nov. 2009	12,057,348	220,719	4,367,935	-4,373	7,689,413	225,092
Change, Sept. 2001-Sept. 2009	6,120,632		1,888,603		4,232,030	

Source: U.S. Treasury, Bureau of the Public Debt, Monthly Statement of the Public Debt, Sept. 2001-Nov. 2009, available at http://www.treasurydirect.gov/govt/reports/pd/mspd/mspd.htm; CRS calculations.

End Notes

[1] Approximately 0.5% of total debt is excluded from debt limit coverage. As of December 29, 2009, total public debt outstanding was $12,100 billion; debt subject to limit was $12,045 billion or 99.5% of total public debt outstanding. The Treasury defines "Total Public Debt Subject to Limit" as "the Total Public Debt Outstanding less Unamortized Discount on Treasury Bills and Zero-Coupon Treasury Bonds, old debt issued prior to 1917, and old currency called United States Notes, as well as Debt held by the Federal Financing Bank and Guaranteed Debt." For details, see http://www.treasurydirect.gov.

[2] Although there are hundreds of trust funds, the overwhelming majority are very small. The 12 largest trust funds hold 98.8% of the federal debt held in government accounts.

[3] Other means of financing—including cash balance changes, seigniorage, and capitalization of financing accounts used to fund federal credit programs—have relatively little effect on the changes in debt held by the public.

[4] In future years, when some trust funds are projected to pay out more than they take in, funds that the Treasury would use to redeem those intergovernmental debts must be obtained via higher taxes or lower government spending.

[5] Trust fund surpluses by law must be invested in special federal government securities.

[6] U.S. General Accounting Office (GAO), *Analysis of Actions Taken during the 2003 Debt Issuance Suspension Period,* GAO-04-526, May 2004, available at http://www.gao.gov/new.items/d04526.pdf.

[7] For a vigorous assertion of the utility of the debt ceiling, see Anita S. Drishnakumar, "In Defense of the Debt Limit Statute," *Harvard Journal on Legislation*, vol. 42, 2005, pp. 135-185.

[8] Marshall A. Robinson, *The National Debt Ceiling: An Experiment in Fiscal Policy*, Washington, DC: The Brookings Institution, 1959, p. 5.

[9] Bruce Bartlett, "Why Congress Must Now Abolish its Debt Limit," *Financial Times*, October 22, 2009, p. 11.

[10] P.L. 65-43, 40 Stat. 288, enacted September 24, 1917. Currently codified as amended as 31 U.S.C. § 3101.

[11] H. J. Cooke and M. Katzen, "The Public Debt Limit," *Journal of Finance*, vol. 9, no. 3 (September 1954), pp. 298-303.

[12] Robert D. Hormats, *The Price of Liberty,* (New York: Henry Holt, 2007), ch. 4.

[13] Treasury certificates of indebtedness were short-term, interest-bearing securities. Treasury bills are securities with a maturity of a year or less. Treasury notes are interest-bearing securities that generally have maturities of two to five years. Treasury bonds are interest-bearing securities that generally have maturities of 10 or more years.

[14] Marshall A. Robinson, *The National Debt Ceiling: An Experiment in Fiscal Policy*, (Washington, DC: The Brookings Institution, 1959), pp.1-6.

[15] P.L. 76-201. Some authors claimed the aggregate limit was first created in Public Debt Act of 1941 (P.L. 77-7). The 1939 Senate floor debate, however, makes clear that Congress intended to lift categorical debt restrictions. See Senate debate, *Congressional Record*, vol. 84, part 6 (June 1, 1939), pp. 6480, 6497-6501.

[16] This limit did not apply to certain previous public debt issues that constituted a minor portion of the federal debt.

[17] U.S. Bureau of the Census, *Historical Statistics of the United States: Colonial Times to 1970*, H. Doc. 93-78 (Washington: GPO, 1975), Series Y 493-504.

[18] Public Debt Acts of 1941 (P.L. 77-7), 1942 (P.L. 77-510), 1943 (78-34), 1944 (P.L. 78-333), and 1945 (P.L. 79-48).

[19] U.S. Office of Management and Budget, *FY2010 Budget of the U.S. Government: Historical Tables*, Table 7-3.

[20] Until 2001, Treasury publications did not divide debt subject to limit by that held by the public and that held by government accounts. **Table 1** uses CRS calculations that approximate levels of debt subject to limit held in these two categories for fiscal years prior to 2001.

[21] The data show components of debt compared to the size of the economy. This avoids possible distortions resulting from changing price levels over time and includes changes in per capita incomes. This percentage increases when debt grows faster than GDP and falls when it grows more slowly than GDP.

[22] Federal on-budget receipts and outlays nearly matched in FY1999, and the on-budget surplus in FY2000 was 0.9% of GDP. Prior to FY1999, the federal government last had an on-budget surplus in FY1960. Social Security receipts in excess of benefits make up most of the off-budget surplus, which has been positive since FY1985.

[23] U.S. Congress, Congressional Budget Office, An Analysis of the President's Budgetary Proposals for Fiscal Year 2009, March 2008, available at http://www.cbo.gov/ftpdocs/89xx/doc8990/03-19-AnalPresBudget.pdf.

[24] The debt limit was raised from $5,500 billion to $5,950 billion on August 5, 1997, as part of the Balanced Budget Act of 1997 (P.L. 105-33, 111 Stat. 251).

[25] For a comprehensive discussion of the Treasury's previous uses of its short-term ability to avoid breaching the debt limit, see U.S. General Accounting Office, *Debt Ceiling: Analysis of Actions During the 1995-1996 Crisis*, GAO/AIMD-96-130, August 1996.

[26] U.S. Department of the Treasury, Treasury News, *Treasury Statement on the Debt Ceiling*, May 14, 2002.

[27] For additional details, see U.S. General Accounting Office, *Debt Ceiling: Analysis of Actions During the 2002 Debt Issuance Suspension Period*, GAO-03-134, December 2002.

28 Kenneth Dam, Deputy Secretary of the Treasury, letter to Speaker of the House, Dennis Hastert, December 24, 2002, available at http://www.treas.gov/press/releases/po3718.htm.

29 The Treasury reduced the amount of debt held by selected federal accounts while it sold an equal (or smaller) amount of debt to the public. This raised cash needed to pay for ongoing obligations and kept the debt below the limit.

30 The House Budget Committee has some discretion in setting the debt limit level in the House Joint resolution generated by the Gephardt rule. See CRS Report 98-453, *Debt-Limit Legislation in the Congressional Budget Process*, by Bill Heniff Jr. and CRS Report RL31913, *Developing Debt-Limit Legislation: The House's "Gephardt Rule"*, by Bill Heniff Jr..

31 U.S. Congress, Congressional Budget Office, *The Budget and Economic Outlook: Fiscal Years 2005 to 2014*, January 2004.

32 Alan Fram, "Congress May Duck Debt Limit Raise," *Oakland Tribune*, June 5, 2004.

33 John W. Snow, Secretary of the U.S. Treasury, letter to Senate Majority Leader Bill Frist, October 14, 2004, available at http://www.treas.gov/press/releases/reports/frist.pdf.

34 Although not all the possible consequences of a government default are known, it would mean that the government could no longer meet all of its legal obligations. Not only the default, but the efforts to resolve it would arguably have negative repercussions on both domestic and international financial markets and economies.

35 John W. Snow, Secretary of the Treasury, letter to Senator Max Baucus, December 29, 2005, available at http://www.ombwatch.org/budget/pdf/snow_debtlimit_2006.pdf.

36 U.S. Congress, Congressional Budget Office, *An Analysis of the President's Budgetary Proposals for Fiscal Year 2009*, Table 1.1, March 2008, available at http://www.cbo.gov/ftpdocs/89xx/doc8990/03-19-AnalPresBudget.pdf.

36 U.S. Congress, Congressional Budget Office, *The Budget and Economic Outlook: An Update*, Table 1-1, August 2009, available at http://www.cbo.gov/doc.cfm?index=10521.

37 Goldman Sachs U.S. Research, "US Daily: The Fiscal 2008 Deficit—Likely to Top $500 Billion," March 25, 2008.

38 U.S. Congress, House Committee on the Budget, *Report to Accompany H. Con. Res. 312*, 110th Cong., 2nd sess., H.Rept. 110-543, March 2008, p. 99; U.S. Congress, Senate Committee on the Budget, *Report to Accompany S. Res. 70*, S.Prt. 110-039, March 2008.

39 U.S. Congress, Congressional Budget Office, *Cost Estimate for H.R. 3221 "Housing and Economic Recovery Act of 2008" As passed by the Senate on July 11, 2008, with an amendment transmitted to CBO on July 22, 2008*, July 24, 2008, available at http://www.cbo.gov/ftpdocs/95xx/doc9597/hr3221.pdf.

40 For additional information see CRS Report RS22956, *The Cost of Government Financial Interventions, Past and Present*, by Baird Webel, Marc Labonte, and N. Eric Weiss.

41 U.S. Department of Treasury, "Fact Sheet: Proposed Treasury Authority to Purchase Troubled Assets," Press release hp-1150, Sept. 20, 2008, available at http://www.treas.gov/press/releases/hp1150.htm.

42 U.S. Congress, House Financial Services Committee, Emergency Economic Stabilization Act of 2008 (Amendment to the Senate Amendment to H.R. 3997), available at http://www.house.gov/apps/list/press/financialsvcs_dem/ amend_001_xml.pdf.

43 U.S. Congress, Senate Banking, Housing, and Urban Affairs Committee, Emergency Economic Stabilization Act of 2008 (In the Nature of a Substitute to H.R. 1424), available at http://banking.senate.gov/public/_files/latestversionAYO08C32_xml.pdf.

44 *CQ Weekly*, "Fall 2009 Outlook: Debt Limit Increase," September 7, 2009, p. 1966.

45 U.S. Treasury, "November 2009 Quarterly Refunding Statement," press release tg346, November 4, 2009, http://www.ustreas.gov/press/releases/tg346.htm; David Clarke and CQ Staff, "Treasury Gives Congress More Breathing Room on Debt Limit," *CQ Today Online News*, November 4, 2009.

46 For details, see Joseph Haubrich and John Lindner, "The Supplemental Financing Program," *Economic Trends*, Federal Reserve of Chicago, September 28, 2009, available at http://www.clevelandfed.org/research/trends/2009/1009/ 03monpol.cfm.

47 *The Money Market Observer: Wrightson ICAP's Weekly Newsletter*, December 7, 2009.

48 *The Money Market Observer: Wrightson ICAP's Weekly Newsletter*, November 30, 2009.

49 Paul Kane, "House Democrats Discard Larger Debt Limit," *Washington Post*, December 15, 2009, p. A4.

50 *CQ Today Midday Update*, "Senate Sends Debt Ceiling Increase to House," January 28, 2010.

51 S.Amdt. 3305. A second amendment (S.Amdt. 3300), approved on a 97-0 vote, provides certain protections to the Social Security program. Other amendments were not approved.

52 Jonathan Weisman and John D. McKinnon, "White House Weighs New Panel to Tackle Deficit: Bipartisan Commission Considered As Administration Seeks to Show Resolve on a Problem that Dogs Its Broader Agenda," *Wall Street Journal*, November 26, 2009, p. A10.

53 U.S. Office of Management and Budget, "H.J.Res. 45—Increasing the Statutory Limit on the Public Debt," Statement Of Administration Policy, January 20, 2010, available at http://www.whitehouse.gov/omb/assets/sap_111/ saphjr45s_20100120.pdf.

[54] For a discussion of earlier debt limit increases, see CRS Report 98-805 E, *Public Debt Limit Legislation: A Brief History and Controversies In the 1980s and 1990s*, by Philip D. Winters, which is available from the authors upon request.

[55] U.S. Congress, Congressional Budget Office, *A Preliminary Analysis of the President's Budget and an Update of CBO's Budget and Economic Outlook*, March 2009; *The Budget and Economic Outlook: FY2010-FY2020*, January 2010.

[56] The ability to run fiscal deficits gives the federal government useful flexibility in managing its finances, although large deficits may harm economic performance. See CRS Report RL33657, *Running Deficits: Positives and Pitfalls*, by D. Andrew Austin.

[57] *Report of the National Commission on Social Security Reform*, January 1983, available at http://www.ssa.gov/history/reports/gspan.html.

[58] Testimony of Federal Reserve Chairman Alan Greenspan, in U.S. Congress, Senate Committee on the Budget, *Outlook for the Federal Budget and Implications for Fiscal Policy*, hearings, 107th Cong., 1st sess., January 25, 2001, available at http://www.federalreserve.gov/boarddocs/testimony/2001/20010125/default.htm.

[59] For a discussion of PAYGO in the past, see CRS Report R41005, *The Statutory PAYGO Process for Budget Enforcement: 1991-2002*, by Robert Keith.

In: The U.S. National Debt: Background, Issues, Significance ISBN: 978-1-61761-767-6
Editor: Charlotte G. Wilson and Emily O. Brown

Chapter 3

LEGISLATIVE PROCEDURES FOR ADJUSTING THE PUBLIC DEBT LIMIT: A BRIEF OVERVIEW

Bill Heniff Jr.

SUMMARY

Almost all borrowing by the federal government is conducted by the Treasury Department, within the restrictions established by a single, statutory limit on the total amount of debt that may be outstanding at any time. Most adjustments to the debt limit have been increases, but sometimes the change has been a reduction.

The annual budget resolution includes recommended levels of the public debt limit for each fiscal year covered by the resolution. Because a budget resolution does not become law, Congress and the President must enact legislation in order to implement budget resolution policies. The House and Senate may develop and consider legislation adjusting the debt limit in any one of three ways: (1) under regular legislative procedures in both chambers, either as freestanding legislation or as a part of a measure dealing with other topics; (2) pursuant to House Rule XXVIII (the so- called Gephardt rule); or (3) as part of the budget reconciliation process provided for under the Congressional Budget Act of 1974. During the period from 1940 to the present, Congress and the President have enacted a total of 91 measures adjusting the public debt limit—72 under regular legislative procedures in both chambers, 15 under the Gephardt rule, and 4 under reconciliation procedures. The current debt limit is $1 4.294 trillion.

INTRODUCTION

Almost all borrowing by the federal government is conducted by the Treasury Department, within the restrictions established by a single, statutory limit on the total amount of debt that may be outstanding at any time.[1] In a few instances, agencies such as the Tennessee Valley Authority operate within their own borrowing limits established separately in law. For years, the public debt limit has been codified in Section 3101(b) of Title 31, *United States Code*. Periodic adjustments in the debt limit take the form of amendments to 31 U.S.C. 3101(b), usually by striking the current dollar limitation and inserting a new one. Although most adjustments to the debt limit have been increases, in some instances the debt limit has been reduced or extended at its current level for a specified interval.[2]

The Congressional Budget Act of 1974 (P.L. 93-344, 2 U.S.C. 601-688) requires the House and Senate to adopt a concurrent resolution on the budget each year before considering revenue, spending, and debt-limit legislation. In addition to recommending the appropriate levels of total revenues, spending, and the deficit or surplus, the budget resolution also specifies the appropriate level of the debt limit for each fiscal year covered by the measure. Inasmuch as a budget resolution does not become law, Congress and the President must enact legislation implementing budget resolution policies, including any needed adjustment in the debt limit. Even if a budget resolution is not adopted by the House and Senate, as occurred in 1998, 2002, 2004, and 2006, legislation must be enacted to raise the debt limit whenever it becomes insufficient.

LEGISLATIVE PROCEDURES FOR ADJUSTING THE PUBLIC DEBT LIMIT

Under current legislative procedures, the House and Senate may develop and consider legislation adjusting the debt limit in any one of three ways: (1) under regular legislative procedures in both chambers, either as freestanding legislation or as a part of a measure dealing with other topics; (2) pursuant to House Rule XXVIII (the so-called Gephardt rule); or (3) as part of the budget reconciliation process provided for under the Congressional Budget Act of 1974. Although the Constitution requires that revenue measures originate in the House, this requirement is not considered to apply to debt-limit measures.[3] Over the years, however, most debt-limit legislation has originated in the House. In 2002 and 2004, a Senate-originated bill was the vehicle for the debt-limit increase. The House Ways and Means Committee and the Senate Finance Committee exercise jurisdiction over debt-limit legislation.

It is extremely difficult for Congress to effectively influence fiscal and budgetary policy through action on legislation adjusting the debt limit. The need to raise (or lower) the limit during a session is driven by many previous decisions regarding revenues and spending stemming from legislation enacted earlier in the session or in prior years. Nevertheless, the consideration of debt- limit legislation often is viewed as an opportunity to reexamine fiscal and budgetary policy and is marked by controversy. Consequently, House and Senate action on legislation adjusting the debt limit often is complicated, hindered by political difficulties, and subject to delay.

The three ways of developing and considering debt-limit legislation are discussed briefly below.

Regular Legislative Procedures in Both Chambers

The House Ways and Means Committee and the Senate Finance Committee may originate measures adjusting the debt limit at any time. The Senate usually acts on legislation originated by the House. In 2002 and 2004, however, the Senate originated debt-limit bills (S. 2578 and S. 2986, respectively), which became P.L. 107-199 and P.L. 108-415, respectively.

Consideration of debt-limit measures in the House usually is subject to special rules, reported by the House Rules Committee, that may include debate limitations, restrictions on the offering of amendments, and other expediting features. In the Senate, consideration of debt-limit measures generally is not subject to expedited procedures; nongermane amendments may be offered and the measures may be debated at length, unless cloture is invoked or other limitations are agreed to by unanimous consent.

In 2009, for instance, an adjustment to the public debt limit (Section 1604, Div. B, P.L. 111-5) was considered under the regular legislative process as part of the economic stimulus legislation considered in the early part of 2009. The House passed (on January 28) its version of the economic stimulus legislation (H.R. 1, the American Recovery and Reinvestment Act of 2009) without any provision increasing the public debt limit. The Senate, however, included an increase to the public debt limit in its version passed on February 10. The House and Senate subsequently agreed to the conference report to accompany H.R. 1, which included the Senate's provision to increase the public debt limit, on February 13. President Barack Obama signed the legislation on February 17, 2009 (P.L. 111-5).

Gephardt Rule Procedures

Debt-limit legislation may be initiated pursuant to House Rule XXVIII, commonly referred to as the Gephardt rule (named after its author, Representative Richard Gephardt).[4] The Gephardt rule was established by P.L. 96-78 (93 Stat. 589-591; September 29, 1979) and first applied in calendar year 1980. It provides for the automatic engrossment and transmittal to the Senate, upon the adoption of the budget resolution, of a joint resolution changing the public debt limit by the amount recommended in the budget resolution. The joint resolution is deemed to have passed the House by the same vote as the conference report on the budget resolution.

The Gephardt rule originally was designated as House Rule XLIX. The House recodified the rule as House Rule XXIII at the beginning of the 106th Congress, repealed it at the beginning of the 107th Congress, and reinstated it, as new Rule XXVII, at the beginning of the 108th Congress. Finally, the rule was redesignated (without change) as Rule XXVIII during the 110th Congress upon the enactment of the Honest Leadership and Open Government Act of 2007 (S. 1, P.L. 110- 81, September 14, 2007, see Section 301(a)).

The Senate has no comparable procedure. If the Senate chooses to consider a House joint resolution originated pursuant to the Gephardt rule, it does so under the regular legislative process. As noted above, under the regular legislative process, consideration of debt-limit measures, even those originated by the Gebhardt rule, generally is not subject to expedited procedures; nongermane amendments may be offered and the measures may be debated at length, unless cloture is invoked or other limitations are agreed to by unanimous consent.

The Senate sometimes has considered such debt-limit measures for days and amended them. In 1985, for example, the Senate added extensive budget enforcement procedures (the Balanced Budget and Emergency Deficit Control Act of 1985, also known as the "Gramm-Rudman- Hollings Act") to H.J.Res. 372, a measure that the House had originated under the Gephardt rule. More recently, in 2010, the Senate added statutory "pay-as-you-go" (PAYGO) enforcement procedures to H.J.Res. 45, a measure that the House had originated under the Gephardt rule pursuant to the adoption of the FY20 10 budget resolution (S.Con.Res 13, 111th Congress) on April 29, 2009. The Senate passed the measure, as amended, on January 28, 2010, and the House subsequently passed the measure without further amendment on February 4, 2010. President Obama signed it into law on February 12, 2010 (P.L. 111-139).

Overall, since the rule was established in 1980 (through March 18, 2010), the House has originated 20 joint resolutions under this procedure. The Senate has passed 16 of these joint resolutions, passing 10 without amendment and six with amendments.[5] Of the 20 joint resolutions originated by the House under the Gephardt rule, 15 have been enacted into law.

In 14 years during this period (calendar years 1988, 1990-1991, 1994-2002, 2004, and 2006), the rule did not apply or was not used due to its suspension or repeal, or a budget resolution was not finally agreed to. In most cases, the House suspended the rule because legislation changing the statutory limit was not necessary at the time.

The Budget Reconciliation Process

The reconciliation process is an optional procedure that operates as an adjunct to the budget resolution process.[6] The chief purpose of the reconciliation process is to enhance Congress's ability to change current law to bring revenue, mandatory spending, and debt-limit levels into conformity with the policies of the budget resolution. Reconciliation legislation is subject to expedited consideration in both chambers. In the Senate, in particular, debate on reconciliation legislation is limited, amendments must be germane, and extraneous matter is barred.

Although the predominant focus of reconciliation legislation has been to change revenue and spending levels, four such measures also were used to adjust the debt limit:

- the **Omnibus Budget Reconciliation Act of 1986** (P.L. 99-509; October 21, 1986), Section 8201 (100 Stat. 1968);
- the **Omnibus Budget Reconciliation Act of 1990** (P.L. 101-508; November 5, 1990), Section 11901 (104 Stat. 1388-560);
- the **Omnibus Budget Reconciliation Act of 1993** (P.L. 103-66; August 10, 1993), Section 13411 (107 Stat. 565); and
- the **Balanced Budget Act of 1997** (P.L. 105-33; August 5, 1997), Section 5701 (111 Stat. 648).

MEASURES ADJUSTING THE PUBLIC DEBT LIMIT

A total of 91 debt-limit measures were enacted into law during the period from 1940 to the present (see **Figure 1**). The number of laws rose steadily from the decade of the 1 950s through the decade of the 1980s, from 6 to 24, but dropped to 13 in the 1990s. Six of the 13 laws enacted in the 1990s were temporary extensions over a three-month period in 1990, enacted largely to accommodate lengthy negotiations during a budget summit between Congress and the President. Nine debt-limit laws were enacted in the 2000s, and one debt-limit law has been enacted so far in this decade.

As mentioned previously, debt-limit legislation may be considered under regular legislative procedures in both chambers, pursuant to the House's so-called Gephardt rule, or as part of the budget reconciliation process. Of the total 91 debt-limit measures enacted into law during the period from 1940 to the present, 72 were considered under regular legislative procedures, 15 were initiated pursuant to the Gephardt rule, and four were considered as part of omnibus budget reconciliation legislation. Compared with regular legislative procedures, the Gephardt rule accelerates action in the House (but not the Senate) and the budget reconciliation process expedites consideration in both chambers.

Table 1 provides information on the 16 measures adjusting the public debt limit enacted during the period from 1993 to the present. Of these 16 measures, 10 were considered under regular legislative procedures in both chambers, either as freestanding legislation (four measures) or as part of legislation involving other matters (six measures), four were initiated pursuant to the Gephardt rule, and two were considered as part of omnibus budget reconciliation legislation.

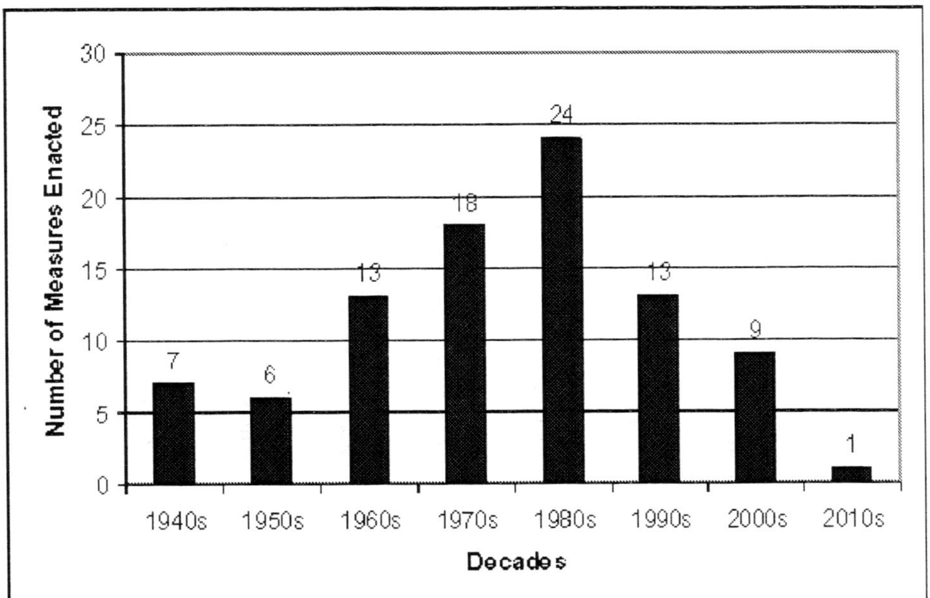

Source: Office of Management and Budget, Budget of the United States Government, Fiscal Year 2011, Historical Tables, Table 7.3, pp. 136-139.

Figure 1. Number of Measures Adjusting the Public Debt Limit Enacted by Decade: 1940s to the Present

Table 1. Legislation Adjusting the Public Debt Limit Enacted From 1993 to the Present

Bill Number	Procedure	Title of Act	Nature of Adjustment	Public Law (Date Enacted)
H.R. 1430	Regular legislative procedures	To provide for a temporary increase in the public debt limit	Temporary increase	P.L. 103-12 (04-06-1993)
H.R. 2264	Reconciliation process	Omnibus Budget Reco-nciliation Act of 1993	Permanent increase	P.L. 103-66 (08-10-1993)
H.R. 2924	Regular legislative procedures	To guarantee the timely payment of social security benefits in March 1996	Temporary exemption for certain borrowing	P.L. 104-103 (02-08-1996)
H.R. 3021	Regular legislative procedures	To guarantee the continuing full investment of Social Security and other Federal funds in obligetions of the United States	Temporary exemption for certain borrowing	P.L. 104-115 (03-12-1996)
H.R. 3136	Regular legislative procedures	Contract with America Advancement Act of 1996	Permanent increase	P.L. 104-121 (03-29-1996)
H.R. 2015	Reconciliation process	Balanced Budget Act of 1997	Permanent increase	P.L. 105-33 (08-05-1997)
S. 2578	Regular legislative procedures	A bill to amend title 31 of the United States Code to increase the public debt limit	Permanent increase	P.L. 107-199 (06-28-2002)
H.J.Res. 51	Gephardt rule procedures	Increasing the statutory limit on the public debt	Permanent increase	P.L. 108-24 (05-27-2003)
S. 2986	Regular legislative procedures	A bill to amend title 31 of the United States Code to increase the public debt limit	Permanent increase	P.L. 108-415 (11-19-2004)
H.J.Res. 47	Gephardt rule procedures	Increasing the statutory limit on the public debt	Permanent increase	P.L. 109-182 (03-20-2006)
H.J.Res. 43	Gephardt rule procedures	Increasing the statu-tory limit on the public debt	Permanent increase	P.L. 110-91 (09-29-2007)
H.R. 3221	Regular legislative procedures	Housing and Econo-mic Recovery Act of 2008	Permanent increase	P.L. 110-289 (07-30-2008)
H.R. 1424	Regular legislative procedures	Emergency Economic Stabilization Act of 2008	Permanent increase	P.L. 110-343 (10-03-2008)
H.R. 1	Regular legislative procedures	American Recovery and Reinvestment Act of 2009	Permanent increase	P.L. 111-5 (02-17-2009)

Table 1. (Continued)

Bill Number	Procedure	Title of Act	Nature of Adjustment	Public Law (Date Enacted)
H.R. 4314	Regular legislative procedures	To permit continued financing of Government operations	Permanent increase	P.L. 111-123 (12-28-2009
H.J.Res. 45	Gephardt rule procedures	Increasing the statutory limit on the public debt	Permanent increase	P.L. 111-139 (02-12-2010)

Sources: Office of Management and Budget, *Budget of the United States Government, Fiscal Year 2011, Historical Tables*, Table 7.3, pp. 136-139; and the Legislative Information System (LIS), http://www.congress.gov.

ACKNOWLEDGMENTS

This chapter was originally written with Robert Keith, Specialist in American National Government. The current author, however, assumes responsibility for its current content.

End Notes

[1] For a discussion of federal debt, the debt limit, and debt management practices, see the Office of Management and Budget, *Budget of the United States Government, Fiscal Year 2010, Analytical Perspectives*, Chapter 16—Federal Borrowing and Debt, pp. 223-23 7. For an additional discussion of issues related to increasing the debt limit, see CRS Report RL3 1967, *The Debt Limit: History and Recent Increases*, by D. Andrew Austin and Mindy R. Levit.

[2] For example, P.L. 455 of the 79th Congress (60 Stat. 316; June 26, 1946) reduced the debt limit from $300 billion to $275 billion as budget surpluses reemerged following World War II, and P.L. 101-461 (104 Stat. 1078; October 25, 1990) extended the current debt limit level of $3. 195 trillion for three days (as part of a series of short-term extensions) while a budget summit was underway.

[3] See the discussion under section "Other Legislation and the Origination Clause" of CRS Report RL3 1399, *The Origination Clause of the U.S. Constitution: Interpretation and Enforcement*, by James V. Saturno.

[4] For further information, see CRS Report RL31913, *Developing Debt-Limit Legislation: The House's "Gephardt Rule,"* by Bill Heniff Jr.

[5] Only one of these 16 joint resolutions was not signed into law. (Specifically, during the second session of the 99th Congress, the Senate passed, as amended, the joint resolution (H.J.Res. 668) automatically engrossed by the House and requested a conference with the House, but no further action was taken.) Of the remaining four joint resolutions, the Senate began consideration on one but came to no resolution on it, and took no action on three.

[6] For more information on the reconciliation process, see CRS Report RL33030, *The Budget Reconciliation Process: House and Senate Procedures*, by Robert Keith and Bill Heniff Jr.

In: The U.S. National Debt: Background, Issues, Significance ISBN: 978-1-61761-767-6
Editor: Charlotte G. Wilson and Emily O. Brown

Chapter 4

DEVELOPING DEBT-LIMIT LEGISLATION: THE HOUSE'S "GEPHARDT RULE"

Bill Heniff, Jr.

SUMMARY

The amount of money the federal government is allowed to borrow generally is subject to a statutory limit. From time to time, Congress and the President enact legislation to adjust this limit.

The House may develop debt-limit legislation under House Rule XXVIII, commonly referred to as the Gephardt rule, named after its author, former Representative Richard Gephardt. The rule, which was established by P.L. 96-78 and first applied in calendar year 1980, provides for the automatic engrossment and transmittal to the Senate of a joint resolution changing the public debt limit, upon the adoption by Congress of the budget resolution, thereby avoiding a separate vote in the House on the public debt-limit legislation. The Senate has no comparable procedure; if it chooses to consider a House-passed joint resolution, it does so under the regular legislative process.

The House also may develop and consider debt-limit legislation without resorting to the Gephardt rule, either as freestanding legislation, as part of another measure, or as part of a budget reconciliation bill. Of the 47 public-debt limit changes enacted into law during the period 1980 to the present (March 18, 2010), 32 were enacted without resorting to the Gephardt rule.

In 11 of the 30 years since the Gephardt rule was established, the rule did not apply, due to its suspension or repeal by the House (calendar years 1988, 1990-1991, 1994-1997, and 1999-2002). In most cases, the House suspended the rule because legislation changing the statutory limit was not necessary; at the time, the existing public debt limit was expected to be sufficient.

During the remaining 19 years, when the rule was in effect, the House originated 20 joint resolutions under this procedure; 15 were signed into law. The first seven of these 20 joint resolutions were generated under the Gephardt rule in its original form. The rule was modified in 1983; the current rule is substantively the same as the 1983 form of the rule. The subsequent 13 joint resolutions were generated under this modified language. In three years (calendar years 1998, 2004, and 2006), the House and Senate did not agree to a conference report on the budget resolution and therefore the automatic engrossment process under the Gephardt rule was not used.

The Senate passed 16 of the 20 joint resolutions automatically engrossed pursuant to the Gephardt rule, passing 10 without amendment and six with amendments. Only one of these 16 joint resolutions was not signed into law. Of the remaining four joint resolutions, the Senate began consideration on one but came to no resolution on it, and took no action on three.

INTRODUCTION

The amount of money the federal government is allowed to borrow generally is subject to a statutory limit, which is set forth as a dollar limitation in 31 U.S.C. 3101(b). From time to time, Congress and the President enact legislation adjusting the limit.[1] Legislation adjusting the debt limit takes the form of an amendment to 31 U.S.C. 3101(b), usually striking the current dollar limitation and inserting a new one.

The House may develop debt-limit legislation under House Rule XXVIII, commonly referred to as the Gephardt rule, named after its author, former Representative Richard Gephardt. The rule, which first applied in calendar year 1980, provides for the automatic engrossment and transmittal to the Senate of a joint resolution changing the public debt limit, upon the adoption by Congress of the budget resolution, thereby avoiding a separate vote in the House on the public debt-limit legislation. The Senate has no comparable procedure; if it chooses to consider a House-passed joint resolution, it does so under the regular legislative process.

The House also may develop and consider debt-limit legislation without resorting to the Gephardt rule, either as freestanding legislation, as part of another measure, or as part of a budget reconciliation bill.[2] Regardless of the process by which debt-limit legislation is developed, the House Ways and Means Committee maintains exclusive jurisdiction over debt-limit legislation. (In the Senate, the Finance Committee has exclusive jurisdiction over debt-limit legislation.)

This chapter describes the legislative history of the Gephardt rule, explains its current features, and reviews its implementation from its inception through the present.

LEGISLATIVE HISTORY OF THE GEPHARDT RULE

The Gephardt rule, initially codified as Rule XLIX of the Standing Rules of the House of Representatives, was established by P.L. 96-78 (93 Stat. 589-591), an act to provide for a temporary increase in the public debt limit. The House adopted the legislation (H.R. 5369) by a vote of 219-198 on September 26, 1979.[3]

During consideration of the measure, Representative Gephardt explained that the purpose of the new House rule was to place the consideration of the public debt limit within the context of the overall budget policies contained in the annual budget resolution. In addition, it was intended to reduce the amount of time spent and the number of votes in the House and in committees on the issue of raising the public debt limit.

One of the aggregate figures required to be included in the annual budget resolution is the appropriate level of the public debt. As the budget resolution has evolved over time from a single- year time frame to a multi-year time frame, the budget resolution has gone from including a debt- limit level for only one fiscal year to including debt-limit levels for each fiscal year over a multiyear period. Because a budget resolution does not become law, it is necessary to enact legislation in order to implement budget resolution policies regarding debt-limit adjustments. The Gephardt rule enables the House to combine the finalization of the budget resolution and the initiation of debt-limit legislation into a single step.

Representative Gephardt stated that the new automatic engrossment process:

> puts the consideration of the appropriate level for the debt ceiling where it legitimately and logically belongs. That is in the context of when we vote for the spending that creates the need to change the debt ceiling.[4]

In its original form, the rule required the engrossment of a joint resolution changing the temporary public debt limit. In 1983, the existing, separate temporary and permanent statutory limits on the public debt were combined into one permanent statutory limit (P.L. 98-34). Subsequently, the House amended the Gephardt rule to reflect this change by agreeing to H.Res. 241 (98th Congress) by voice vote on June 23, 1983.[5] Under the modified rule, the automatically engrossed joint resolution would contain a change to the permanent statutory limit. In addition to this modification,

> The rules change also provided that where a budget resolution contains more than one public debt limit figure (for the current and the next fiscal year), only one joint resolution be engrossed, containing the debt limit figure for the current fiscal year with a time limitation, and the debt limit figure for the following fiscal year as the permanent limit.[6]

During consideration of H.Res. 241, Representative Butler C. Derrick explained the limitation of a single joint resolution by stating that

> The Committee on Rules ... believes that it is unnecessary and confusing to have ... a single concurrent resolution on the budget trigger the engrossment and passage of two separate joint resolutions to increase or decrease the public debt [limit].[7]

At the beginning of the 106th Congress, the House recodified the rule as House Rule XXIII. Certain language was deleted and modified from the existing rule but the revisions were intended to continue the automatic engrossment process "without substantive change."[8]

The House repealed the rule at the beginning of the 107th Congress.[9] On the opening day of the 108th Congress, the House reinstated this automatic engrossing process as a new rule, Rule XXVII.[10] The current rule contains the exact language as Rule XXIII of the 106th Congress.

Finally, the rule was redesignated (without change) as Rule XXVIII during the 110th Congress upon the enactment of the Honest Leadership and Open Government Act of 2007 (S. 1, P.L. 110- 81, September 14, 2007, see Section 30 1(a)).

CURRENT FEATURES OF THE GEPHARDT RULE

House Rule XXVIII requires that the House clerk automatically engross and transmit to the Senate, upon the adoption of the budget resolution, a joint resolution changing the public debt limit to the level specified in the budget resolution. The rule stipulates that the joint resolution is deemed to have passed the House by the same vote as the conference report on the budget resolution.

Under clause 2 of the current rule:

> If an adopted concurrent resolution under clause 1 sets forth different appropriate levels of the public debt for separate periods, only one engrossed joint resolution shall be prepared under clause 1; and the blank referred to in the preceding sentence shall be filled with the limitation that is to apply for each period.

Further, clause 3(a) of Rule XXVIII requires the House Budget Committee and the conference committee on the budget resolution to issue a clear statement regarding the impact of the automatically engrossed joint resolution on the public debt.[11] Specifically, clause 3(a) states:

> The report of the Committee on the Budget on a concurrent resolution described in clause 1 and the joint explanatory statement of the managers on a conference report to accompany such a concurrent resolution each shall contain a clear statement of the effect the eventual enactment of a joint resolution engrossed under this rule would have on the statutory limit on the public debt.

The full text of the Gephardt rule in its current form is provided in the **Appendix**.

IMPLEMENTATION OF THE GEPHARDT RULE

Table 1 provides information on the joint resolutions changing the public debt limit that were engrossed and deemed passed by the House pursuant to the Gephardt rule during calendar years 1980-2010 (through March 18, 2010).

In 11 of the 30 years since the Gephardt rule was first established, the rule did not apply, due to its suspension or repeal by the House (calendar years 1988, 1990-1991, 1994-1997, and 1999- 2002).[12] In most cases, the House suspended the rule because legislation changing the statutory limit was not necessary; at the time, the existing public debt limit was expected to be sufficient. In three cases, the House passed, or was expected to pass, separate legislation to increase the statutory limit. As noted above, the rule was repealed at the beginning of the 107th Congress and therefore did not apply in 2001 and 2002.

During the remaining 19 years, when the rule was in effect, the House originated 20 joint resolutions under this procedure. The first seven of these 20 joint resolutions were generated under the Gephardt rule in its original form. As mentioned above, the rule was modified in 1983; the current rule is substantively the same as this 1983 form of the rule. The subsequent 13 joint resolutions were generated under this modified language. In three years (calendar years 1998, 2004, and 2006), while the rule was in effect, the House and Senate did not agree to a conference report on the budget resolution and therefore the automatic engrossment process under the Gephardt rule was not used. [13]

As **Table 1** shows, although budget resolutions adopted during this period contained debt limit amounts for between three and 11 different fiscal years (as the time frame of each budget resolution dictated), the joint resolutions automatically engrossed under the Gephardt rule contained debt limit amounts for only one or two fiscal years, depending on the requirements of the rule at the time. As noted above, the 1983 modification provided that the automatically engrossed joint resolution could include multiple debt-limit increases, one temporary and another permanent. The first three of the 11 joint resolutions automatically engrossed pursuant to this modified version of the rule contained two different public debt limits and the other eight contained a single public debt limit.

The Senate passed 16 of the 20 joint resolutions automatically engrossed pursuant to the Gephardt rule, passing 10 without amendment and six with amendments. Only one of these 16 joint resolutions was not signed into law. [14] Of the remaining five joint resolutions, the Senate began consideration on one but came to no resolution on it, and took no action on three.

Of the 20 joint resolutions originated by the House under the Gephardt rule, 15 were enacted into law. [15]

Table 1. House Joint Resolutions Increasing the Public Debt Limit Automatically Engrossed Pursuant to the Gephardt Rule, 1980-2010 (as of March 18, 2010)

	Budget Resolution		Debt-limit Resolution			
Congress/ Session	Fiscal Year and Resolution Number	Number of Public Debt Amounts Specified	Joint Resolution Number	Number of Public Debt Amounts Set Forth	Senate Initial Disposition (Date of Action)	Final Disposition (Date of Action)
96/2	FY1981 (first) H.Con.Res. 307	3	H.J.Res. 569	1	Passed without amendment (06-26-1980)	P.L. 96-286 (06-28-1980)
			H.J.Res. 570	1	Passed without amendment (12-12-1980)	P.L. 96-556 (12-19-1980)
	FY1981 (second) H.Con.Res. 448	3	H.J.Res. 636	1	Laid aside (12-12-1980)	—

Table 1. (Continued)

Congress/ Session	Budget Resolution		Debt-limit Resolution		Senate Initial Disposition (Date of Action)	Final Disposition (Date of Action)
	Fiscal Year and Resolution Number	Number of Public Debt Amounts Specified	Joint Resolution Number	Number of Public Debt Amounts Set Forth		
97/1	FY1982 H.Con.Res. 115	3	H.J.Res. 265	1	Passed without amendment (09-29-1981)	P.L. 97-49 (09-30-1981)
			H.J.Res. 266	1	Passed without amendment (09-29-1981)	P.L. 97-48 (09-30-1981)
97/2	FY1983 S.Con.Res. 92	3	H.J.Res. 519	1	Passed without amendment (06-23-1982)	P.L. 97-204 (06-28-1982)
			H.J.Res. 520	1	Passed without amendment (09-23-1982)	P.L. 97-270 (09-30-1982)
98/1	FY1984 H.Con.Res. 91	4	H.J.Res. 308	2	Passed, amended (11-17-1983)	P.L. 98-161 (11-21-1983)
98/2	FY1985 H.Con.Res. 280	4	H.J.Res. 654	2	Passed without amendment (10-12-1984)	P.L. 98-475 (10-13-1984)
99/1	FY1986 S.Con.Res. 32	4	H.J.Res. 372	2	Passed, amended (10-10-1985)	P.L. 99-177 (12-12-1985)
99/2	FY1987 S.Con.Res. 120	3	H.J.Res. 668	1	Passed, amended (08-09-1986)	Senate requested conference (08-09-1986) and no further action was taken
100/1	FY1988 H.Con.Res. 93	3	H.J.Res. 324	1	Passed, amended (07-31-1987)	P.L. 100-119 (09-29-1987)

Table 1. (Continued)

Congress/ Session	Budget Resolution		Debt-limit Resolution		Senate Initial Disposition (Date of Action)	Final Disposition (Date of Action)
	Fiscal Year and Resolution Number	Number of Public Debt Amounts Specified	Joint Resolution Number	Number of Public Debt Amounts Set Forth		
100/2	FY1989 H.Con.Res. 268[a]	3	—	—	—	—
101/1	FY1990 H.Con.Res. 106	3	H.J.Res. 280	1	Passed, amended (11-07-1989)	P.L. 101-140 (11-08-1989)
101/2	FY1991 H.Con.Res. 310[b]	5	—	—	—	—
102/1	FY1992 H.Con.Res. 121[c]	6	—	—	—	—
102/2	FY1993 H.Con.Res. 287	5	H.J.Res. 494	1	No action taken	—
103/1	FY1994 H.Con.Res. 64	5	H.J.Res.17 4H.J.Res. 174	1	No action taken	—
103/2	FY1995 H.Con.Res. 218[d]	5	—	—	—	—
104/1	FY1996 H.Con.Res. 67[e]	7	—	—	—	—
104/2	FY1997 H.Con.Res. 178[f]	6	—	—	—	—
105/1	FY1998 H.Con.Res. 84[g]	5	—	—	—	—
105/2	FY1999 H.Con.Res. 284[h]	6	—	—	—	—
106/1	FY2000 H.Con.Res. 68[i]	10	—	—	—	—
106/2	FY2001 H.Con.Res. 290[j]	6	—	—	—	—
107/1	FY2002 H.Con.Res. 83[k]	11	—	—	—	—
107/2	FY2003 H.Con.Res. 353[k]	5	—	—	—	—

Table 1. (Continued)

Congress/ Session	Budget Resolution		Debt-limit Resolution		Senate Initial Disposition (Date of Action)	Final Disposition (Date of Action)
	Fiscal Year and Resolution Number	Number of Public Debt Amounts Specified	Joint Resolution Number	Number of Public Debt Amounts Set Forth		
108/1	FY2004 H.Con.Res. 95	11	H.J.Res. 51	1	Passed without amendment (05-23-2003)	P.L. 108-24 (05-27-2003)
108/2	FY2005 S.Con.Res. 95[l]	5	—	—	—	—
109/1	FY2006 H.Con.Res. 95	6	H.J.Res. 47	1	Passed without amendment (03-16-2006)	P.L. 109-182 (03-20-2006)
109/2	FY2007 H.Con.Res. 376[m]	5	—	—	—	—
110/1	FY2008 S.Con.Res. 21	6	H.J.Res. 43	1	Passed without amendment (09-27-2007)	P.L. 110-91 (09-29-2007)
110/2	FY2009 S.Con.Res. 70	6	H.J.Res. 92	1	No action taken	—
111/1	FY2010 S.Con.Res. 13	6	H.J.Res. 45	1	Passed with amendment (01-28-2010)	P.L. 111-139 (02-12-2010)

Sources: Legislative Information System http://www.congress.gov and *Congressional Record*, various years.

Notes: The Gephardt rule provides for the automatic engrossment of a House joint resolution increasing the public debt limit once Congress agrees to the conference report on a budget resolution. Initially, the rule was codified as House Rule XLIX. The rule was recodified as House Rule XXIII at the beginning of the 106th Congress, and subsequently was repealed at the beginning of the 107th Congress. The rule was restored as a new rule, Rule XXVII, by H.Res. 5 at the beginning of the 108th Congress. Finally, the rule was redesignated as Rule XXVIII during the 110th Congress upon the enactment of the Honest Leadership and Open Government Act of 2007 (S. 1, P.L. 110-81, September 14, 2007).

a.Pursuant to H.Res. 461, the Gephardt rule was suspended because there was no need to increase the public debt limit. See comments by Representative Butler C. Derrick in *Congressional Record*, vol. 134 (May 26, 1988), p. 12529.

b.Pursuant to H.Res. 488, the Gephardt rule was suspended because the House previously had passed and sent to the Senate legislation (H.R. 5355) providing for a long-term increase in the public debt limit. See comments by Representative Derrick in *Congressional Record*, vol. 136 (Oct. 4, 1990), p. 27590.

c.Pursuant to H.Res. 157, the Gephardt rule was suspended because the previous year's reconciliation act (P.L. 101-508) provided a sufficient increase. See comments by Representative Derrick in *Congressional Record*, vol. 137 (May 22, 1991), p. 11856.

d.Pursuant to H.Res. 418, the Gephardt rule was suspended because at the time the current public debt limit was expected to be sufficient until spring or summer 1995. See comments by Representative Anthony C. Beilenson in *Congressional Record*, vol. 140 (May 5, 1994), pp. 9411-9412.

e.Pursuant to H.Res. 149, the Gephardt rule was suspended because some Members wanted the House to have a separate vote on legislation increasing the public debt limit instead of an automatic engrossment of such legislation. See comments by Representative Gerald B. H. Solomon in *Congressional Record*, vol. 14 1 (May 17, 1995), pp. 13275-13276.

f.Pursuant to H.Res. 435, the Gephardt rule was suspended because at the time the current public debt limit was expected to be sufficient until at least October 1997. See comments by Representative Solomon in *Congressional Record*, vol. 142 (May 16, 1996), p. 11477.

g.Pursuant to H.Res. 152, the Gephardt rule was suspended because legislation increasing the public debt limit was contemplated by the balanced budget agreement with the White House in the context of reconciliation legislation. See comments by Representative Solomon in *Congressional Record*, vol. 143 (May 20, 1997), pp. 8904-8905.

h.The House and Senate did not complete action on the FY1999 budget resolution and therefore the automatic engrossment process under the Gephardt rule was not used.

i.Pursuant to H.Res. 131, the Gephardt rule was suspended, presumably because at the time legislation increasing the public debt limit was not necessary due to expected future surpluses. See *Congressional Record*, vol. 145 (March 25, 1999), pp. 567 1-5672.

j.Pursuant to H.Res. 446, the Gephardt rule was suspended, presumably, as in 1999, because at the time legislation increasing the public debt limit was not necessary due to expected future surpluses. See *Congressional Record*, vol. 146 (March 23, 2000), pp. 3442-3443.

k.The Gephardt rule was repealed at the beginning of the 107th Congress by H.Res. 5, adopted on January 3, 2001. See *Congressional Record*, vol. 147 (Jan. 3, 2001), pp. 24-37.

l.The House and Senate did complete action on the FY2005 budget resolution and therefore the automatic engrossment process under the Gephardt rule was not utilized.

m The House and Senate did complete action on the FY2007 budget resolution and therefore the automatic engrossment process under the Gephardt rule was not utilized.

APPENDIX. TEXT OF THE GEPHARDTRULE

(House Rule XXVIII)

STATUTORY LIMIT ON PUBLIC DEBT

1. Upon adoption by Congress of a concurrent resolution on the budget under section 301 or 304 of the Congressional Budget Act of 1974 that sets forth, as the appropriate level of the public debt for the period to which the concurrent resolution relates, an amount that is different from the amount of the statutory limit on the public debt that otherwise would be in effect for that period, the Clerk shall prepare an engrossment of a joint resolution increasing or decreasing, as the case may be, the statutory limit on the public debt in the form prescribed in clause 2. Upon engrossment of the joint resolution, the vote by which the concurrent resolution on the budget was finally agreed to in the House shall also be considered as a vote on

passage of the joint resolution in the House, and the joint resolution shall be considered as passed by the House and duly certified and examined. The engrossed copy shall be signed by the Clerk and transmitted to the Senate for further legislative action.

2. The matter after the resolving clause in a joint resolution described in clause 1 shall be as follows: "That subsection (b) of section 3101 of title 31, United States Code, is amended by striking out the dollar limitation contained in such subsection and inserting in lieu thereof '$_______'.", with the blank being filled with a dollar limitation equal to the appropriate level of the public debt set forth pursuant to section 301 (a)(5) of the Congressional Budget Act of 1974 in the relevant concurrent resolution described in clause 1. If an adopted concurrent resolution under clause 1 sets forth different appropriate levels of the public debt for separate periods, only one engrossed joint resolution shall be prepared under clause 1; and the blank referred to in the preceding sentence shall be filled with the limitation that is to apply for each period.
3. (a) The report of the Committee on the Budget on a concurrent resolution described in clause 1 and the joint explanatory statement of the managers on a conference report to accompany such a concurrent resolution each shall contain a clear statement of the effect the eventual enactment of a joint resolution engrossed under this rule would have on the statutory limit on the public debt.

   (b) It shall not be in order for the House to consider a concurrent resolution described in clause 1, or a conference report thereon, unless the report of the Committee on the Budget or the joint explanatory statement of the managers complies with paragraph (a).
4. Nothing in this rule shall be construed as limiting or otherwise affecting—
   (a) the power of the House or the Senate to consider and pass bills or joint resolutions, without regard to the procedures under clause 1, that would change the statutory limit on the public debt; or
   (b) the rights of Members, Delegates, the Resident Commissioner, or committees with respect to the introduction, consideration, and reporting of such bills or joint resolutions.
5. In this rule the term "statutory limit on the public debt" means the maximum face amount of obligations issued under authority of chapter 31 of title 31, United States Code, and obligations guaranteed as to principal and interest by the United States (except such guaranteed obligations as may be held by the Secretary of the Treasury), as determined under section 3101(b) of such title after the application of section 3101(a) of such title, that may be outstanding at any one time.

End Notes

[1] For more information on the debt limit, see CRS Report RL31967, *The Debt Limit: History and Recent Increases*, by D. Andrew Austin and Mindy R. Levit.

[2] For more information on these alternative procedures, see CRS Report RS21519, *Legislative Procedures for Adjusting the Public Debt Limit: A Brief Overview*, by Bill Heniff Jr.

[3] For the consideration in the House, see *Congressional Record*, vol. 125 (September 26, 1979), pp. 26337-26350. The Senate passed H.R. 5369 by a vote of 49-29 on September 28, 1979. For the consideration in the Senate,

see *Congressional Record*, vol. 125 (September 28, 1979), pp. 26669-2669 1. The President signed the legislation into law on September 29, 1979.

4 *Congressional Record*, vol. 125 (September 26, 1979), p. 26342.

5 See *Congressional Record*, vol. 129 (June 23, 1983), pp. 17162-17164.

6 U.S. Congress, Constitution, Jefferson's Manual, and Rules of the House of Representatives of the United States, One Hundred Tenth Congress, 109th Cong., 2nd sess., H.Doc. 109-157 (Washington: GPO, 2007), p. 981.

7 *Congressional Record*, vol. 129 (June 23, 1983), p. 17163.

8 See *Congressional Record*, vol. 145 (January 6, 1999), pp. 206-208; or U.S. Congress, House Committee on Rules, *The Recodification of the Rules of the House of Representatives*, committee print, 106th Cong., 1st sess. (Washington: GPO, 1999), pp. 172-174.

9 It was repealed by H.Res. 5, adopted on January 3, 2001. See *Congressional Record*, vol. 147 (January 3, 2001), pp. 24-37.

10 Section 2(t) of H.Res. 5, which was agreed to by the House on January 7, 2003. See *Congressional Record*, vol. 149 (January 7, 2003), pp. 7-21.

11 For a recent example of such a statement, see U.S. Congress, Committee of Conference, *Concurrent Resolution on the Budget for Fiscal Year 2008*, conference report to accompany S.Con.Res. 21, 1 10th Cong., 1st sess., H.Rept. 110- 153 (Washington: GPO, 2007), p. 133.

12 For each of these cases, a brief explanation regarding the rule's suspension is provided in the notes at the end of **Table 1**.

13 The House and Senate also did not agree to a conference report on the budget resolution in 2002, but the rule had been repealed at the beginning of the 107th Congress.

14 Specifically, during the second session of the 99th Congress, the Senate passed, as amended, the joint resolution (H.J.Res. 668) automatically engrossed by the House and requested a conference with the House, but no further action was taken (as indicated in **Table 1**).

15 From 1980 to 2010 (through March 18, 2010), a total of 47 public-debt limit changes were signed into law as independent measures or as part of other legislation. For a listing of 46 of the 47 changes, see Table 7.3 in Office of Management and Budget, *Historical Tables, Budget of the U.S. Government, Fiscal Year 2011* (Washington: GPO, 2010), pp. 136-139. The most recent change in the public-debt limit was signed into law (P.L. 111-139, Feb. 12, 2010) after the President's FY20 11 budget was submitted to Congress.

In: The U.S. National Debt: Background, Issues, Significance ISBN: 978-1-61761-767-6
Editor: Charlotte G. Wilson and Emily O. Brown

Chapter 5

INTEREST PAYMENTS ON THE FEDERAL DEBT: A PRIMER

Thomas L. Hungerford

SUMMARY

Of the three broad categories of federal spending, the only category that cannot be reduced by legislative action is net interest payments. Net interest payments accounted for about 7% of federal spending between 1962 and the late 1970s. With the high interest rates in the late 1970s and the large budget deficits in the 1980s, net interest payments eventually rose to 15% of federal spending. The low interest rates combined with budget discipline in the 1990s reduced net interest payments back down to 7% of federal outlays by 2003. Low interest rates kept net interest payments low to 2009. However, net interest payments are projected to increase dramatically over the next 10 years.

Federal spending is divided into three broad categories. First, discretionary spending is provided and controlled by the annual appropriations acts and includes such things as defense and education spending.[1] Discretionary spending currently accounts for about 35% of federal outlays. Second, direct or mandatory spending is provided and controlled by laws other than appropriation acts and includes spending for such programs as Social Security and Medicare.[2] Mandatory spending accounts for over half of federal outlays. Lastly, net interest payments are interest payments on federal debt held by the public and currently account for almost 5% of federal outlays. The Congressional Budget Office (CBO) in their baseline projection has net interest payments growing to almost 14% of federal outlays by FY2020.

In February 2010, President Obama created the bipartisan National Commission on Fiscal Responsibility and Reform. The Commission's task is to identify policies that will improve the fiscal situation in the medium term and achieve fiscal sustainability in the long term. The policies could involve changes to the growth of entitlement spending, increases in revenues, and decreases in other spending. The recommendations of the Commission could serve as a basis for legislation to reduce federal deficits by increasing taxes and reducing spending. The only category of federal spending that cannot be reduced by legislative action (barring default on the public debt) is net interest payments.

While Congress cannot affect current net interest payments, congressional actions on the budget will affect future interest payments. This chapter examines net interest payments and the mechanisms through which Congress can affect net interest payments.

FEDERAL DEBT

Federal debt is composed of debt issued by the Treasury (Treasury securities) and debt securities issued by other federal agencies (agency securities). At the end of 2009, total federal securities amounted to more than $12 trillion, of which only $23.5 billion (less than 0.2%) were agency securities. Federal debt is held either by the public (that is, private investors) or in government accounts. Currently, about 36% of federal debt is held in various government accounts. For example, the two Social Security trust funds currently hold about $2.5 trillion in Treasury securities. The rest of the federal debt is held by the public (foreign and domestic), including individuals, pension funds, banks, and other investors.

Figure 1 shows the level of total federal debt and debt held by the public since 1962 as a percentage of gross domestic product (GDP). Both measures of debt fell as a proportion of GDP between 1962 and the mid-1970s. Beginning in 1981, total federal debt began to climb as tax cuts, increases in defense spending, and a recession increased budget deficits. Total debt continued growing relative to GDP until the mid-1990s. As budget deficits gave way to budget surpluses after 1997, and as the economy expanded, federal debt fell as a percentage of GDP. The mild recession and the tax cuts in 2001 moved the federal budget back into deficit and federal debt consequently increased.

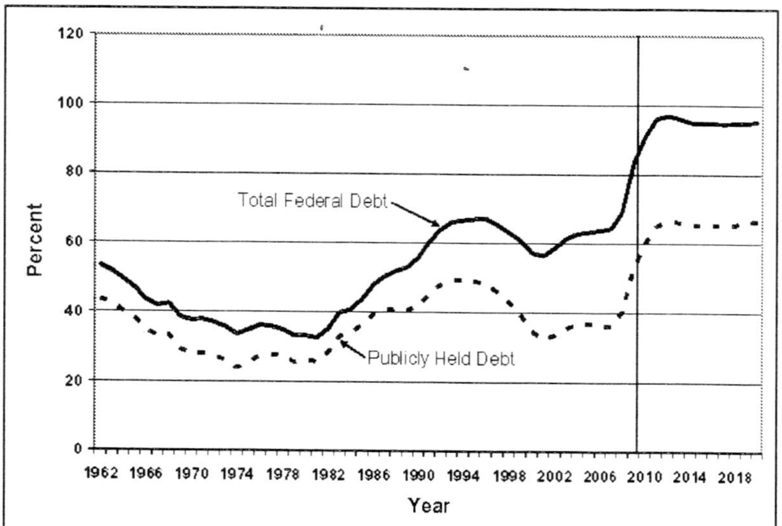

Source: OMB and CBO.

Figure 1 . Total U.S. Federal Debt and Debt Held by the Public, FY1962-FY2020 (as a percentage of GDP)

Between 1962 and 1982, total federal debt and debt held by the public followed roughly parallel trends. After the mid-1980s, however, trends in total federal debt and debt held by the public began to diverge. This was mainly due to changes in the Social Security program enacted in 1983 which increased revenues and reduced the growth in benefit payments. As a result, the Social Security program began to run surpluses (surplus monies are invested in Treasury securities), increasing the share of federal debt held in government accounts. CBO's baseline projection indicates that total federal debt and debt held by the public will continue to diverge over the next 10 years.[3]

INTEREST PAYMENTS ON THE FEDERAL DEBT

In FY2009, total or gross interest on Treasury debt securities amounted to about $383 billion— about 11% of federal outlays. However, not all of this flowed from the Treasury to the public— about $200 billion was credited to government accounts such as the Social Security trust funds. The interest payments on the Treasury securities held in government accounts do not represent funds or real resources available for spending. Rather these interest payments are merely a bookkeeping entry transferring funds from one government account to another.[4]

The upper line in Figure 2 shows the evolution of gross interest payments since 1962. Gross interest payments remained at about 7% to 8% of outlays until the late 1970s. After 1978, interest payments rapidly increased to reach almost 18% of outlays by 1997. After 1997, gross interest payments fell as a percentage of outlays as interest rates fell and the federal budget moved from deficit to surplus. When federal budget deficits reappeared in 2002, gross interest payments began rising.

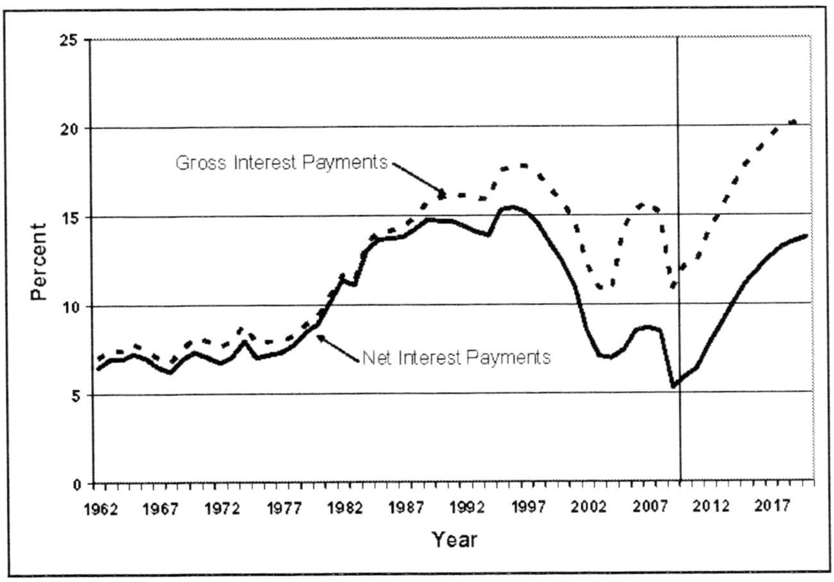

Source: OMB and CBO.

Figure 2. Gross and Net Interest on Treasury Debt Securities, FY1962-FY2020 (as a percentage of federal outlays)

Net interest payments are the component of gross interest payments that involves a transfer of funds or real resources from the government to the public. The lower line in Figure 2 shows the evolution of net interest payments since 1962. For the most part, net interest payments followed the same basic trend as gross interest payments. However, the gap between gross and net interest payments widened after the mid-1980s.[5] As with gross interest payments, net interest payments fell as a percentage of federal outlays when federal debt declined in the late-1990s. Net interest payments began to increase in 2004 but leveled out because of falling interest rates. Additionally, net interest payments fell dramatically in 2009 due to very low interest rates. Large budget deficits in 2009 and 2010, however, will lead to rising net interest payments for the next five to six years.[6] CBO projects that, under plausible scenarios, net interest payments could continue rising indefinitely.[7]

DETERMINANTS OF NET INTERESTPAYMENTS

The primary determinants of net interest payments are (1) the interest rate or yield on U.S. Treasury securities, and (2) the level of debt held by the public. Figure 3 shows the evolution of net interest payments, debt held by the public, and the interest rate since 1967. The interest rate is the yield on five-year constant maturity U.S. Treasury bonds. Both net interest payments and debt held by the public are expressed as a percentage of GDP, and are indexed so that the value in 1967 is equal to one.[8]

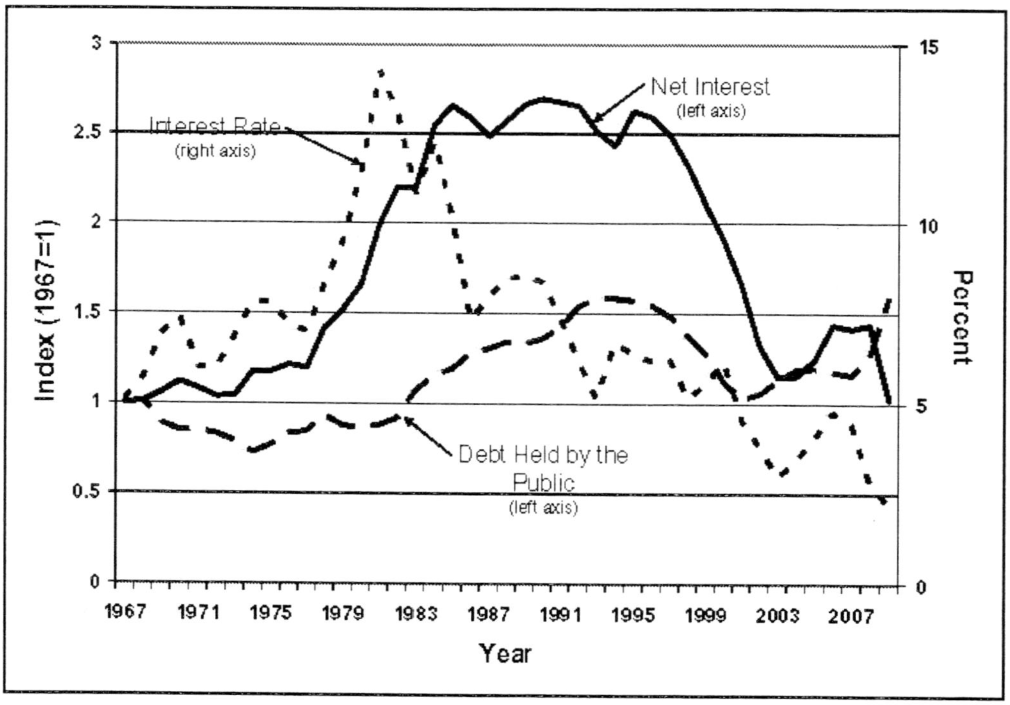

Source: OMB and Federal Reserve Board.

Figure 3. Interest Rate, Net Interest Payments, and Debt Held by the Public, FY1967- FY2009

Net interest payments increased rapidly beginning in 1977 at about the same time that interest rates increased dramatically (see Figure 3). Net interest payments continued to increase after interest rates fell in the early 1 980s because of the increase in debt held by the public. The increase in debt held by the public was due to the large budget deficits in the first years of the Reagan Administration and counteracted the effect of falling interest rates on net interest payments. As both interest rates and debt held by the public fell after 1997, net interest payments fell as a percentage of GDP and as a proportion of federal outlays.

The government can, to some extent, control the effective interest rate paid on its debt by varying the maturity of its securities. The federal government issues both short-term and long-term debt. The yield on Treasury securities varies with the maturity of the securities. Typically, short-term securities have a lower yield than longer-term securities, and the yield curve, therefore, is upward sloping.[9] Occasionally, the yield curve will invert with longer-term securities having a lower yield than short-term securities, but this happens neither often nor for extended periods.

A primary goal of debt management is to obtain the lowest borrowing cost over time.[10] Over the past 30 years, the mean maturity of marketable Treasury securities held by private investors has varied between about three years and six years. Since 2000, the range has narrowed to between five and six years. However, this apparent stability masks changes in the types of securities issued. In 2001, for example, the Treasury stopped issuing 30-year bonds.[11] Although shorter- term Treasury securities tend to have lower yields than longer-term securities, they also are more volatile. Consequently, the financing costs of short-term securities can change dramatically over fairly short periods. This volatility and uncertainty complicate efforts to obtain the lowest borrowing costs over time.

Congressional actions affecting the budget deficit will affect federal debt, which, in turn, affects future net interest payments. Budget deficits and federal debt can also affect the interest rates on Treasury securities.[12] Increasing federal debt will increase the supply of Treasury securities. This will tend to push down the price and increase the yield of these securities.[13] Recent studies have estimated that increasing debt held by the public by one percent of GDP will increase future interest rates by two to six basis points (0.02 to 0.06 percentage points).[14] Thus budget deficits increase federal debt and future interest rates, which in turn increase future net interest payments.

End Notes

[1] For more information on discretionary spending see CRS Report RL34424, *Trends in Discretionary Spending*, by D. Andrew Austin and Mindy R. Levit.

[2] For more information on mandatory spending see CRS Report RL33074, *Mandatory Spending Since 1962*, by D. Andrew Austin and Mindy R. Levit.

[3] CBO's baseline projection starts with Congress's most recent budgetary decisions and then assumes that no policy changes will be made over the projection period. For entitlement programs CBO assumes that current laws will continue unchanged and by law assumes that discretionary spending will grow at the rate of inflation throughout the projection period. For revenues, CBO assumes that the provisions in the 2001 and 2003 tax cuts will expire on schedule, and that more individuals will be subject to the alternative minimum tax (AMT). Furthermore, the baseline projection does not include the budgetary effects of any new stimulus legislation. CBO's baseline is not intended to be a prediction of future budgetary outcomes. See CBO, *The Budget and Economic Outlook: Fiscal Years 2010 to 2020*, January 2010.

[4] In essence, the interest payments are used to purchase more Treasury securities. While not representing real resources available for current spending, the government will eventually have to find real resources (by raising taxes or reducing spending) for the redemption of these securities, under current law.

[5] The widening of this gap is due, in part, to the increases in the Social Security trust fund resulting from the 1983 amendments to the Social Security Act. These amendments led to increasing revenues to the Social Security program, and reduced the growth in benefits.

[6] CBO projects that the deficit will be more than $1,300 billion in 2010 and $980 billion in 2011. See CBO, *Budget and Economic Outlook*, January 2010.

[7] See CBO, *The Long-term Budget Outlook*, June 2010.

[8] The index is created by dividing the value in each year by the value in 1967. This is done so that both series fit on the same graph.

[9] The yield curve is the relationship of the yield on securities and the maturity of those securities.

[10] See CRS Report RL34682, *Federal Debt Management: Concepts, Options, and Policies (1945-2008)*, by James M. Bickley.

[11] Treasury began issuing 30-year bonds again in February 2006.

[12] The strength of the economy, inflation expectations, and the actions of the Federal Reserve Board also have an important effect on interest rates.

[13] There is an inverse relationship between the price of a bond and the yield of the bond.

[14] See Eric Engen and R. Glenn Hubbard, *Federal Government Debts and Interest Rates*, National Bureau of Economic Research, Working Paper no. 10681, August 2004; William G. Gale and Peter R. Orszag, "Budget Deficits, National Saving, and Interest Rates," *Brookings Papers on Economic Activity*, vol. 2004, no. 2 (2004), pp. 101-187; and Thomas Laubach, *New Evidence on the Interest Rate Effects of Budget Deficits and Debt*, Board of Governors of the Federal Reserve System, Finance and Economics Discussion paper no. 2003-13, May 2003.

In: The U.S. National Debt: Background, Issues, Significance ISBN: 978-1-61761-767-6
Editor: Charlotte G. Wilson and Emily O. Brown

Chapter 6

FOREIGN HOLDING OF FEDERAL DEBT

Justin Murray and Marc Labonte

SUMMARY

This chapter presents current data on estimated ownership of U.S. Treasury securities and major holders of federal debt by country. Federal debt represents the accumulated balance of borrowing by the federal government. To finance federal borrowing, U.S. Treasury securities are sold to investors. Treasury securities may be purchased directly from the Treasury or on the secondary market by individual private investors, financial institutions in the United States or overseas, and foreign, state, or local governments. Foreign investment in federal debt has grown in recent years, prompting questions on the location of the foreign holders and how much debt they hold.

SELECTEDSTATISTICS ON FOREIGN HOLDINGS OF FEDERALDEBT

Federal debt represents, in large measure, the accumulated balance of federal borrowing of the U.S. government. The portion of gross federal debt held by the public consists primarily of investment in U.S. Treasury securities.[1] Investors in the United States and abroad include official institutions such as the U.S. Federal Reserve, financial institutions such as private banks, and private individual investors. Table 1 provides December 2009 data, available as of March 2010, on estimated ownership of U.S. Treasury securities by type of investment and the percentage of that investment attributable to foreign investors.[2]

As the table shows, during the past five years, foreign holdings of debt increased by nearly $1.8 trillion to more than $3.6 trillion from December 2004 to December 2009. During the same period, total privately held debt increased by approximately $3.3 trillion to $7 trillion.

Table 1. Estimated Ownership of U.S. Treasury Securities (in billions of dollars)

End of Month	Total Public Debt Held by All Private Investors	Total Debt Held by Foreign Investors	Foreign Holdings as a Share of Total Privately Held Public Debt
Dec. 2009	$7,034.5	$3,614.0	51.4%
Dec. 2008	$5,893.4	$3,076.3	52.2%
Dec. 2007	$4,395.7	$2,352.9	53.5%
Dec. 2006	$4,122.1	$2,105.0	51.1%
Dec. 2005	$3,970.6	$2,036.0	51.3%
Dec. 2004	$3,690.6	$1,853.4	50.2%

Source: Table OFS-2: Estimated Ownership of U.S. Treasury Securities from the March 2009 *Treasury Bulletin.* See link for "Ownership of Federal Securities" tables at http://www.fms.treas.gov/bulletin /index.html.

Notes: Table data represent estimated figures current as of March 22, 2010. For the most current data, connect to the link listed above. Percentage shares calculated by CRS.

Although gross federal debt is the broadest measure of the debt, it may not be the most important one. The debt measure that is relevant in an economic sense is debt held by the public. This is the measure of debt that has actually been sold in credit markets and has influenced interest rates and private investment decisions. This table reflects that portion of public debt held by all private investors in federal securities and the portion of that debt held by foreign investors. See CRS Report RL31590, *The Federal Government Debt: Its Size and Economic Significance*, by Brian W. Cashell.

Table 2. The Top 10 Foreign Holders of Federal Debt, by Country (data current as of March 9, 2010)

Country	Amount Held ($ in billions; as of Dec. 2009)	Percentage of all foreign holdings in federal debt	Country	Amount Held ($ in billions; as of Dec. 2004)	Percentage of all foreign holdings in federal debt
Mainland China	$894.8	24.3%	Japan	$689.9	37.3%
Japan	$765.7	20.8%	Mainland China	$222.9	12.1%
Oil Exporters	$207.4	5.6%	United Kingdom	$95.8	5.2%
United Kingdom	$178.0	4.8%	Taiwan	$67.9	3.7%
Brazil	$169.3	4.6%	Oil Exporters	$62.1	3.4%
Hong Kong	$148.7	4.0%	Korea	$55.0	3.0%
Russia	$141.8	3.8%	Carribean Banking Centers	$51.1	2.8%
Carribean Banking Centers	$128.2	3.5%	Germany	$50.3	2.7%

Table 2. (Continued)

Country	Amount Held ($ in billions; as of Dec. 2009)	Percentage of all foreign holdings in federal debt	Country	Amount Held ($ in billions; as of Dec. 004)	Percentage of all foreign holdings in federal debt
Taiwan	$116.5	3.2%	Hong Kong	$45.1	2.4%
Switzerland	$89.7	2.4%	Switzerland	$41.7	2.3%
Total Top 10 Countries of Foreign Investors in Federal Debt	$2,840.1	77.0%	Total Top 10 Countries of Foreign Investors in Federal Debt	$1,381.8	74.9%
Total All Foreign Investment in Federal Debt	$3689.0	100%	Total All Foreign Investment in Federal Debt	$1,849.3	100%

Source: Treasury Department International Capital System (TIC), at http://www.treas.gov/tic /mfhhis01.txt.

Notes: Data, including estimated foreign holders of federal debt historically by month, in these Treasury Department tables are periodically adjusted. Current monthly estimates are available at http://www.treas.gov/tic/ mfh.txt. Aggregate data totals in Table 1 vary slightly from aggregate data totals in Table 2 because of minor valuation differences of a few securities for a few of the countries in the complete list of International Financial Statistics data used by the TIC data. Percentage approximations calculated by CRS. Percentages may vary slightly due to rounding.

In December 2004, total foreign investment in U.S. federal debt was approximately $1.9 trillion (50.2%) of the total of approximately $3.7 trillion in privately held debt. By December 2009, total foreign investment in U.S. federal debt grew by 1.2 percentage points to $3.6 trillion (51.4%) of the total of approximately $7 trillion in debt held by private investors.[3]

Data on major foreign holders (investors) of federal debt by country are provided in Table 2. According to the data, the top three estimated foreign holders of federal debt by country, ranked in descending order as of December 2009, are China ($894.8 billion), Japan ($765.7 billion), and oil-exporting countries ($207.4 billion). Based on these estimates, China holds approximately 24.3% of all foreign investment in U.S. privately held federal debt; Japan holds approximately 20.8%; and the oil-exporting countries hold approximately 5.6%.[4]

Foreign holdings as estimated by the Treasury Department can be divided into official (governmental investment) and private sources. Figure 1 provides data on the current breakdown of estimated foreign holdings in U.S. federal debt. As the figure shows, 73.3% of foreign holdings in U.S. federal debt are held by governmental sources. Private investors hold the other 26.7%.

FOREIGNINVESTMENT IN U.S. FEDERALDEBT: WHY IS IT AN ISSUE OF CONCERN?

Foreign ownership of federal debt has become a growing concern among some Members of Congress because of the nation's large and rising trade deficit. During the past three decades, U.S. national saving has not been adequate to finance its capital investment needs, and borrowing from abroad has covered the gap. For foreigners to invest in the U.S. economy on net, the United States must import more than it exports (run a trade deficit). When the government runs a budget deficit, as it has done since 2002, it reduces the national saving rate. This implies that domestic investment must fall, unless private saving rises or borrowing from abroad increases.[5]

As seen in Table 1, as the national debt has increased, foreign ownership of U.S. Treasuries has followed closely, suggesting that the budget deficit has been financed, in part, through borrowing abroad. By June 2004, foreigners held more than 50% of the public debt held by private investors for the first time. Although this percentage has no particular economic significance, it may have other significance.

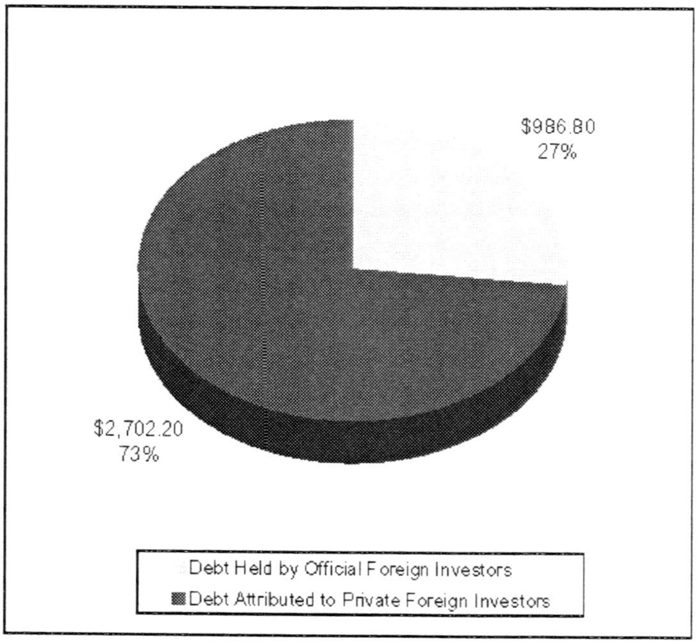

Source: Treasury Department International Capital System, http://www.treas.gov/tic/mfhhis01.txt.

Notes: Data in the chart represent estimated figures current as of March 9, 2010. Figures are in billions of dollars. Data in the Treasury Department tables are periodically adjusted. For the most current estimates, click on the URL address listed above.

The estimated combined total of all foreign holdings for December 2009 was $3,689.0 billion. Data consist of reported December 2009 figures from the Treasury Department International Capital System http://www.treas.gov/tic/mfh.txt. The breakdown between estimated official and private holdings is not publically available on a country-by-country basis. Approximate percentages calculated by CRS.

Figure 1. Breakdown of Official vs. Private Foreign Holdings of U.S. Federal Debt

Since 2002, some observers have been concerned that the nature of foreign purchases of U.S. Treasuries has changed. Beginning in that year, a significant fraction of the trade deficit was financed through official purchases of U.S. assets, such as purchases by foreign central banks. Although no direct data on official purchases of Treasuries by country exist, it can be inferred that the Treasuries may have been purchased by certain Asian and oil-producing countries because they were the only countries that had large increases in their foreign reserves during that period. Although the effect on the U.S. economy of official purchases of Treasuries is the same as private purchases, the motivations behind the purchases are different. Whereas private purchases are typically motivated by the profit incentive, official purchases may be motivated by a country's desire to keep its exchange rate constant or mitigate its rise against the dollar.[6] Many observers are concerned that the large fraction of national debt held by foreigners has the potential to be harmful to the U.S. economy. Specifically, they fear that if foreigners suddenly decided to stop holding U.S. Treasury securities or decided to diversify their holdings, the dollar could plummet in value and interest rates would rise. Others are concerned that China's accumulation of hard currency assets will allow it to undertake activities in the foreign affairs and military realms that are not in the U.S. interest. Some economists argue that foreign borrowing at current levels is unsustainable and could cause problems for the U.S. economy down the road.[7]

When foreigners purchase U.S. Treasuries, or any other U.S. asset, the interest rate is lower than when borrowing is financed domestically out of national saving. Thus, when overall interest rates are lower as a result of net capital inflows, more interest-sensitive spending is undertaken. Interest-sensitive spending includes capital investment (e.g., production plants and equipment), residential investment (e.g., new homes), and durable consumption goods (e.g., automobiles and appliances). On the other hand, U.S. foreign borrowing induces a trade deficit by reducing exports and import-competing production. The trade deficit occurs because foreigners must first purchase U.S. dollars before purchasing U.S. assets. When the demand for dollars increases, the dollar appreciates, making U.S. exports and import-competing goods relatively more expensive. Thus, foreign borrowing shifts production out of the trade sector and into the interest-sensitive sector.[8]

Since the financial turmoil began in August 2007, the supply of Treasury securities has risen sharply, as a result of the increase in federal borrowing to finance spending on economic and financial recovery.[9] At the same time, the demand for Treasury securities has risen as there has been a "flight to quality" caused by greater investor preference for Treasury securities compared with riskier private securities. Thus, although an increase in the supply of Treasury securities would be expected to cause Treasury yields to rise, they instead fell relative to pre-crisis levels. Likewise, although the financial turmoil originated in U.S. markets, after the turmoil deepened in September 2008, net capital inflows pushed up the value of the dollar.

End Notes

[1] Figures on federal debt held by the public are available on the Department of Treasury Bureau of Public Debt website, "The Debt to the Penny and Who Holds It," at http://www.treasurydirect.gov/NP/BPDLogin?application=np.

[2]This chapter discusses foreign holdings of U.S. federal debt. Foreign investors also hold U.S. private securities. For data on foreign holdings of U.S. private securities, see "Survey of Foreign Holdings of U.S. Securities," at http://www.ustreas.gov/tic/shlhistdat.html, produced by the Treasury Department International Capital System.

[3] Data are excerpted from Table OFS-2 in the March 2010 *Treasury Bulletin*. Table OFS-2 presents the estimated ownership of U.S. Treasury securities. Information is primarily obtained from the Federal Reserve Board of Governors Flow of Funds data, Table L209. State, local, and foreign holdings include special issues of nonmarketable securities to municipal entities and foreign official accounts. They also include municipal, foreign official, and private holdings of marketable Treasury securities.

[4] Foreign holdings are estimated by the Treasury Department based on the location of the holdings, not the nationality of the holder. For certain countries, such as the Carribean Banking Centers, many of the holdings are likely owned by third country citizens.

[5] CRS Report RS21409, *The Budget Deficit and the Trade Deficit: What Is Their Relationship?*, by Marc Labonte and Gail E. Makinen.

[6] See CRS Report RS2195 1, *Financing the U.S. Trade Deficit: Role of Foreign Governments*, by Marc Labonte.

[7] See CRS Report RL33186, *Is the U.S. Current Account Deficit Sustainable?*, by Marc Labonte.

[8] CRS Report RL31032, *The U.S. Trade Deficit: Causes, Consequences, and Cures*, by Craig K. Elwell.

[9] For details on the liquidity crisis in financial markets starting in August 2007, see CRS Report RL34182, *Financial Crisis? The Liquidity Crunch of August 2007*, by Darryl E. Getter et al.

In: The U.S. National Debt: Background, Issues, Significance ISBN: 978-1-61761-767-6
Editor: Charlotte G. Wilson and Emily O. Brown

Chapter 7

DEBT MANAGEMENT: TREASURY WAS ABLE TO FUND ECONOMIC STABILIZATION AND RECOVERY EXPENDITURES IN A SHORT PERIOD OF TIME, BUT DEBT MANAGEMENT CHALLENGES REMAIN

United States Government Accountability Office

WHY GAO DID THIS STUDY

This chapter is part of GAO's requirement, under the Emergency Economic Stabilization Act of 2008, to monitor the Department of the Treasury's (Treasury) implementation of the Troubled Asset Relief Program and submit special reports as warranted from oversight findings. It evaluates Treasury's borrowing actions since the start of the crisis, and how Treasury communicates with market participants in the context of the growing debt portfolio and the medium- and long-term fiscal outlook. GAO analyzed market data; interviewed Treasury, the Federal Reserve Bank of New York, and market experts; and surveyed major domestic holders of Treasury securities.

WHAT GAO RECOMMENDS

GAO recommends that the Secretary of the Treasury should continually review methods for collecting market information and consider conducting a periodic survey of end-users and broadening the TBAC. The Secretary of the Treasury should also continue to reduce the amount and term to maturity of CMBs and consider increasing the number of TIPS auctions and distributing them more evenly throughout the year, and study the effect of the recent increase in direct bidding on Treasury's overall cost of borrowing, including options to promote transparency and foster competition.

Treasury agreed with GAO's findings, conclusions, and recommendations.

WHAT GAO FOUND

The economic recession and financial-market crisis, and the federal government's response to both, have significantly increased the amount of federal debt. While the composition of Treasury's debt portfolio changed in response to this increase, Treasury has taken a number of steps in the past year to return the composition of the debt portfolio to pre–market crisis structure. One action Treasury has undertaken has been to reduce its reliance on cash management bills (CMB). While CMBs provided Treasury with needed borrowing flexibility immediately following the financial market crisis in 2008, Treasury paid a premium for its sustained use of CMBs in 2008 and 2009. In recent months, Treasury also has begun to stabilize shorter-term bill issuance and increase issuance of longer-term coupons. Given the medium- and long-term fiscal outlook, Treasury will continue to be presented with the challenge of raising significant amounts of cash at the lowest costs over time. This makes evaluating the demand for Treasury securities increasingly important.

Sufficient information from market participants on their demand for Treasury securities, including the type of information that GAO received from its survey of the largest domestic holders of Treasury securities, will be critical as Treasury moves forward to meet these challenges. In GAO's survey, investors reported increased demand for Treasury Inflation Protected Securities (TIPS) and suggested ways for Treasury to further improve TIPS liquidity and thereby lower borrowing costs. Treasury receives input from market participants through a variety of formal and informal channels, but overall satisfaction with these communication channels varies by type of market participant. Market participants suggested to GAO a number of changes including increasing investor diversification on the Treasury Borrowing Advisory Committee (TBAC) and regular collection of information from end-investors. Primary dealers, who are satisfied with their communication, raised concerns about the recent increase in direct bidding and its effect on Treasury auctions.

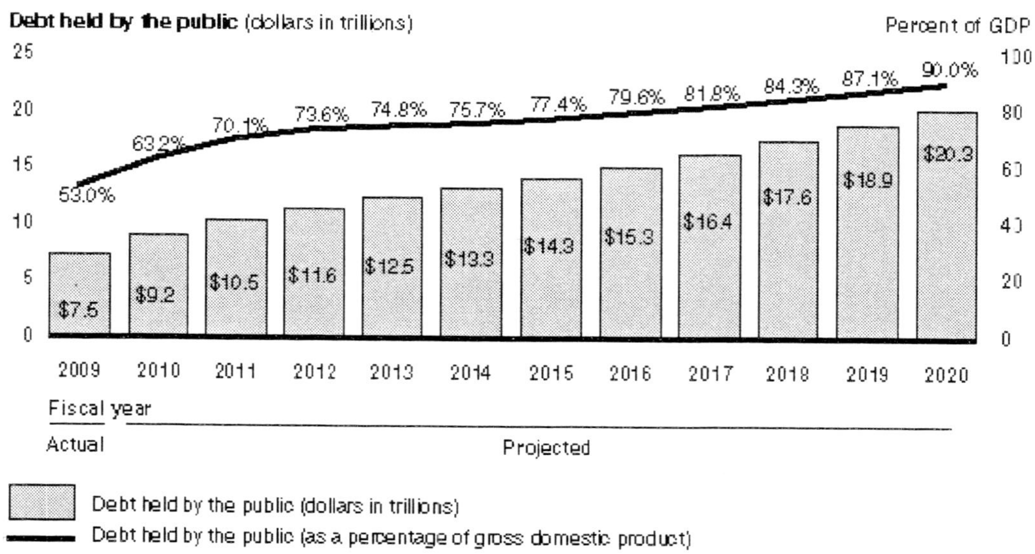

Source: CBO data.

Congressional Budget Office Estimate of Debt Held by the Public and Percent of GDP, Based on President's Budgetary Proposals, 2009 to 2020

ABBREVIATIONS

CBO	Congressional Budget Office
CMB	cash management bill
CME	Chicago Mercantile Exchange Group
Federal Reserve	Board of Governors of the Federal Reserve System
FRBNY	Federal Reserve Bank of New York
GDP	gross domestic product
NTAAPS	New Treasury Automated Auction Processing System
ODM	Department of the Treasury's Office of Debt Management
Recovery Act	American Recovery and Reinvestment Act of 2009
SFP	Supplementary Financing Program
SIFMA	Securities Industry and Financial Markets Association
TARP	Troubled Asset Relief Program
TBAC	Treasury Borrowing Advisory Committee
TIPS	Treasury Inflation Protected Securities
Treasury	Department of the Treasury

May 18, 2010
Congressional Committees

As part of the Emergency Economic Stabilization Act of 2008, GAO is required to monitor the United States Department of the Treasury's (Treasury) implementation of the Troubled Asset Relief Program (TARP) and, under subsection 116, submit special reports as warranted from oversight findings. This chapter examines new debt management challenges that Treasury faces and the efforts that Treasury has undertaken to borrow more than $3.082 trillion over the 2-year period beginning December 2007. Treasury's borrowing financed regular government needs, as well as federal government actions related to both the financial-market crisis and the recession, including TARP investments in financial institutions, housing support through purchases of mortgage-backed securities, support of the Board of Governors of the Federal Reserve System's (Federal Reserve) actions taken to stabilize financial markets, and the American Recovery and Reinvestment Act of 2009 (Recovery Act). The current rapid and substantial increase in federal debt since 2008 takes place in the context of the medium- and long-term fiscal outlook that will present Treasury with continued financing challenges long after the return of financial-market stability and economic growth.

In this chapter, we describe Treasury's borrowing actions since the start of the crisis and the challenges of managing its growing debt portfolio in the context of the medium- and long-term fiscal outlook by answering the following questions: (1) What actions did Treasury take between December 2007 and December 2009 to borrow funds for TARP-related disbursements, the Supplementary Financing Account Program (SFP), the Recovery Act, and other cash needs, and (2) What changes should Treasury make, if any, to better gauge end-investor demand and increase auction participation?[1]

To identify the actions that Treasury has taken to borrow funds for TARP-related disbursements and other cash needs, we analyzed the scale, timing, term-to-maturity, and composition of Treasury's borrowing between December 2007 and December 2009, using data and information obtained from Treasury and the Federal Reserve. We also interviewed market experts, primary dealers and end-investors of Treasury securities, and Treasury and Federal Reserve Bank of New York (FRBNY) staff and officials on Treasury debt management challenges. To describe the cost of the use of cash management bills (CMB) during this time period, we estimated the differential between CMB yields and the yields on outstanding Treasury bills of similar maturity at the time of auction using data from Treasury's Bureau of the Public Debt and the *Wall Street Journal*. We also replicated the analysis estimating the differential between CMB yields and the yields on Treasury auctions that most closely matched the CMB auction in terms of issue date and maturity using data from Treasury's Bureau of the Public Debt. See appendix I for a detailed description of the methodologies that we used to estimate the cost to Treasury of the use of CMBs.

In order to evaluate what changes Treasury should make, if any, to better gauge end-investor demand and increase auction participation, we analyzed Treasury's communication with investors and identified possible actions. In June 2009, we conducted 12 structured interviews with the two largest holders of Treasury securities in each of the following sectors: mutual funds; commercial banks; life insurance companies; property casualty insurance companies; state and local government retirement funds; and private pension funds. In addition, in August 2009 we conducted a Web-based survey that was sent to 66 of the largest domestic holders of Treasury securities in each of these sectors except private pension funds.[2] The survey addressed topics similar to those covered in our structured interviews, including: Treasury auctions and holdings, Treasury Inflation Protected Securities (TIPS), risk exposure, and Treasury's information sources. On October 15, 2009, we briefed Treasury on the findings from the survey, which are discussed and expanded upon in this chapter. See appendix II for our detailed survey methodology and appendix III for a copy of the survey. Because the sample of holders of Treasury securities was not drawn randomly, the survey is not generalizable to the broader population of organizations in the sectors we included in the survey.

To assess the reliability of data used in this study, including publicly available data from Treasury and the Federal Reserve, we examined the data to look for outliers and anomalies and addressed such issues as appropriate. We chose data that are commonly used by Treasury, researchers, and other market analysts to examine Treasury markets and auction performance. Where possible and appropriate, we corroborated the results of our data analysis with other sources, such as analyses done by other market experts or testimonial evidence. On the basis of our assessment we believe the data are reliable for the purpose of this review. We conducted our review from December 2008 to May 2010 in accordance with generally accepted government auditing standards. Those standards require that we plan and perform the audit to obtain sufficient, appropriate evidence to provide a reasonable basis for our findings and conclusions based on our audit objectives. We believe that the evidence obtained provides a reasonable basis for our findings and conclusions based on our audit objectives

Background

Congress has assigned to Treasury the responsibility of borrowing the funds necessary to finance the gap between the money that the government receives, primarily tax revenues, and the money that the government spends. Government expenditures include regular withdrawals for programs such as Medicare and Social Security as well as extraordinary withdrawals for programs such as TARP. Treasury also makes interest and principal payments for outstanding debt and debt that is maturing on a continual basis. Treasury's primary debt management goal is to finance the government's borrowing needs at the lowest cost over time, subject to a statutory limit.[3] To meet this objective, Treasury issues debt through auctions across a wide range of securities mainly in a "regular and predictable" pattern based on a preannounced auction schedule, which it releases on a quarterly basis. Treasury does not "time the market"—or take advantage of low interest rates—when it issues securities. Instead, Treasury is able to lower its borrowing costs by relying on regularly scheduled auctions because investors and dealers value transparency, stability, and certainty of large liquid supply.

Market participants often characterize Treasury securities as the premium risk-free asset. Investors, traders, banks, and foreign central banks actively use them for hedging, liquidity, capital requirements, and reserve purposes. Treasury securities are also a popular investment for end-investors seeking liquidity and low risk. Treasury's "regular and predictable" auctions are for nominal marketable securities that range in maturity from 4 weeks to 30 years and for TIPS that are issued with 5-, 10-, and 30-year maturities.[4] TIPS offer a variety of benefits to Treasury, and inflation protection to investors, who are willing to pay a premium for this protection in the form of an interest rate on TIPS that may be lower than a comparable nominal issuance over the life of the instrument.[5]

Treasury responds to increases in borrowing needs in a traditional manner by: (1) increasing the issuance size of existing securities; (2) increasing the frequency of issuances; and (3) introducing new securities to its auction calendar as necessary. Treasury announces upcoming changes during quarterly refundings so that the market is not surprised. In some instances, Treasury supplements its "regular and predictable" auction schedule with flexible securities called cash management bills (CMB). Because of the nature of CMBs, Treasury does not publish information about CMBs on its quarterly auction schedule as it does for other securities. Instead, Treasury announces CMB auctions anywhere from 1 to 4 days ahead of the auction. Treasury also indicates whether it might issue CMBs over the upcoming quarter in quarterly refunding statements. The term to maturity—or length of time the CMB is outstanding—varies according to Treasury's cash needs. Treasury generally uses CMBs to finance intramonth funding gaps due to timing differences of large cash inflows and outflows.[6] Treasury also uses CMBs to meet sudden and unexpected borrowing needs, such as those that arose from the government's responses to the financial market crisis and economic downturn in 2008 and 2009.

The outstanding mix of Treasury securities can have a significant influence on the federal government's interest payments. Longer-term nominal securities typically carry higher interest rates (which translate to increased cost to the government), primarily due to investor concerns about the uncertainty of future inflation. However, longer-term securities offer the government the certainty of fixed interest payments over a longer period and reduce the amount of debt that Treasury needs to refinance in the short term.[7] In contrast, shorter-term securities generally carry lower interest rates but add uncertainty to the government's interest costs and require Treasury to conduct more frequent auctions to refinance maturing debt, which also poses rollover risk. Among Treasury's short-term securities, those that are issued on a "regular and predictable" schedule generally carry the lowest interest rates.

Two groups, (1) the primary dealers and (2) the Treasury Borrowing Advisory Committee (TBAC) of the Securities Industry and Financial Markets Association (SIFMA) provide regular input to Treasury debt management decisions.[8] The primary dealers are a group of banks and securities broker/dealers, selected by the Federal Reserve Bank of New York (FRBNY), that trade in U.S. government securities with the FRBNY on behalf of the Federal Reserve in order to implement monetary policy. They are also required by the FRBNY to participate in all Treasury auctions. On a quarterly basis, Treasury surveys the primary dealers and also meets with half of them in person. Treasury also meets quarterly with TBAC, an advisory committee that is governed by federal statute and comprised of senior level officials who are employed by primary dealers, institutional investors, and other major participants in the Treasury market. Treasury also monitors market trends via regular contact with the Markets Group at FRBNY, subscriptions to all major investment houses' fixed income research publications, attending fixed income conferences, and meeting with large foreign investors and reserve managers.

THE COMPOSITION OF TREASURY'SDEBT PORTFOLIO CHANGEDSUBSTANTIALLYFOLLOWING THE 2008 FINANCIAL MARKETCRISIS BUT HAS BEGUN TO TRANSITION BACK TO PRE–MARKETCRISIS STRUCTURE

The Size and Composition of Treasury's Debt Portfolio Changed Substantially Due in Part to Borrowing for TARP, the SFP, and the Recovery Act

The borrowing associated with the actions that the federal government took in response to the financial-market crisis and recession including TARP, the SFP, and the Recovery Act, substantially altered the size and composition of Treasury's outstanding debt portfolio. Since the onset of the recession in December 2007, Treasury's total outstanding debt has increased by $3.082 trillion, and marketable debt increased by $2.735 trillion. At the end of December 2009, total outstanding debt was $12.311 trillion, and total outstanding marketable securities stood at $7.272 trillion.[9] According to Treasury, in fiscal year 2009, Treasury held a record 291 auctions in 251 business days and issued nearly $7 trillion in gross marketable securities, a significant portion of which was used to roll over, or refinance, existing debt.

The mix of securities Treasury issued in 2008 and 2009 substantially shortened the average maturity of its debt portfolio and increased the debt maturing in the next 12 months. As seen in figure 1, when looking at Treasury's outstanding marketable securities during the period December 31, 2006, to December 31, 2009, the percentage of securities maturing within a year peaked in December 2008. Reflecting the same trend, the average term to maturity of outstanding marketable securities reached its lowest point of 49 months in

December 2008. As we reported in September 2009, these changes were in accordance with what Treasury described to us as its normal operating procedures. Our September report included specific details about Treasury's debt issuance between December 2007 and June 2009.[10]

Treasury Initially Began to Transition the Composition of Its Debt Portfolio Back to Pre–Market Crisis Structure by Stabilizing Bill Issuance and Increasing Coupon Issuance

The changes to Treasury's debt portfolio, as discussed above, were not intended to be permanent, and Treasury has already started to transition back to pre-financial-market crisis levels of average maturity and composition of the debt portfolio in a manner that, according to Treasury, was as rapid and as prudent as possible. During the November 2009 TBAC press conference, Treasury officials announced that the transition has begun with a shift of bill issuances to nominal note and bond issuance and TIPS issuance. This shift will allow Treasury to retain flexibility in meeting uncertain financing needs in the future. Flexibility is retained by increasing the borrowing capacity that Treasury has available for shorter-term securities, which are used when unexpected financing needs arise. During the February 2010 TBAC press conference Treasury indicated a shift in the transition with the announcement that nominal note and bond issuance will stabilize in the next year and perhaps even decrease. In February, Treasury stated that nominal auctions sizes were at levels that give Treasury the flexibility to address a broad range of potential financing scenarios. Market participants we spoke with anticipated the stabilization of note and bond issuance, but cautioned that any decrease in the amount of nominal note and bond issuance would depend on tax receipts.

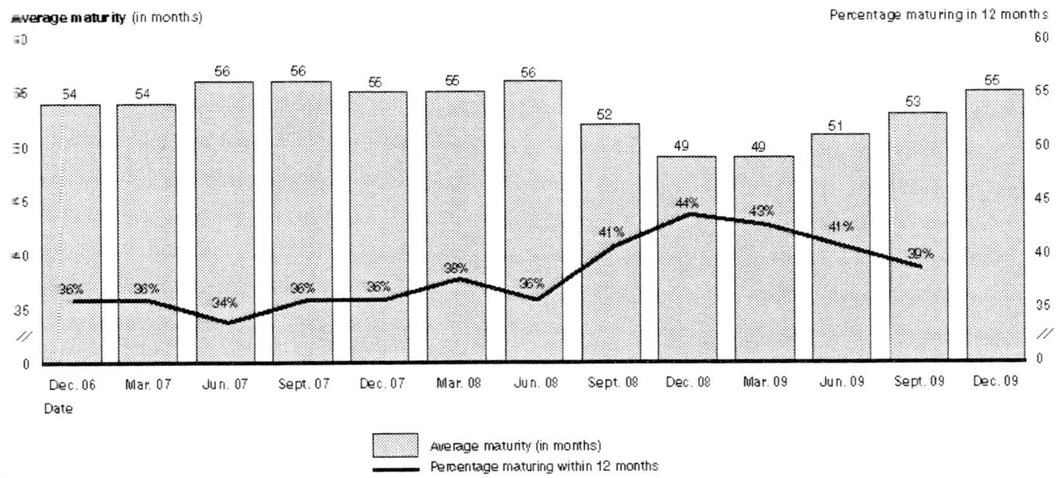

Source: Treasury.

Note: As of March 31, 2010 Treasury had not yet released the percentage of debt maturing in the next 12 months as of the end of December 2009.

Figure 1. Average Maturity of Treasury Outstanding Marketable Securities and Percentage Maturing in Next 12 Months (December 31, 2006, to December 31, 2009)

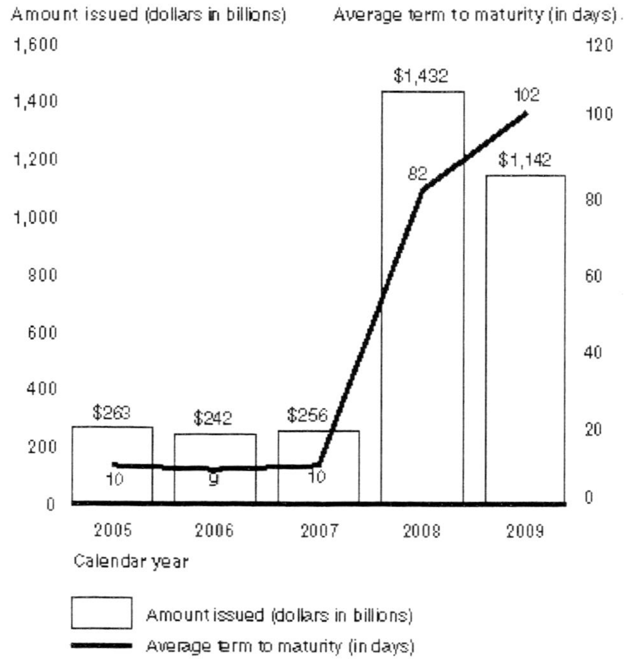

Source: GAO analysis of Treasury data.

Note: On a fiscal-year basis, Treasury issued the following CMB amounts and with the following average term to maturity: 2005—$268 billion (10 days); 2006—$252 billion (9 days); 2007—$259 billion (10 days); 2008—$725 billion (35 days); and 2009—$1.82 trillion (119 days).

Figure 2. Cash Management Bills Annual Issuance Amounts and Average Term to Maturity (2005 to 2009)

Treasury has said that it expects the average term to maturity of outstanding marketable debt to approach the historical average of 5 years (or 60 months) by the end of fiscal year 2010 and could perhaps exceed it in the next 3-5 years. Treasury officials have indicated the changes they are making to the overall debt portfolio will bring short-term bill levels closer to historical averages while stabilizing or perhaps even decreasing nominal note and bond issuance. Treasury has emphasized the importance of making these changes in a gradual, transparent, and incremental manner. Some market participants have expressed concern about a reduction in bill supply. Investors use bills to invest their funds temporarily in a safe and highly liquid asset. Bills are also used by institutional investors that are required to buy financial assets maturing in a year or less. Treasury recognizes the importance of adequate bill supply and said that it will continue to monitor the bills market for any disruptions that the decrease in bill supply may cause.

Treasury's Issuance of CMBs and the Average Maturity of CMBs Increased Dramatically in 2008 and 2009

Shortly after the start of the financial-market crisis in the fall of 2008, Treasury borrowed an unprecedented $1.1 trillion in under 18 weeks largely by issuing CMBs, which are intended for unexpected and immediate cash needs. Treasury's use of CMBs was substantial and continued well after the beginning of the financial-market crisis. The sustained increase was due in part to the Supplementary Financing Program (SFP), a temporary program created in September 2008 to provide cash for use in Federal Reserve initiatives intended to address heightened liquidity pressures in the financial markets.[11]

In 2008 and 2009, Treasury's gross issuance of CMBs was $1.432 trillion and $1.142 trillion respectively (of which $785 billion and $835 billion were issued for the SFP in 2008 and 2009). This compares to average issuance of about $254 billion annually from 2005 to 2007. (See figure 2) To issue $1.432 trillion worth of CMBs in 2008, Treasury held 47 auctions (of which 21 were issued for the SFP), compared to an average of 18 auctions annually from 2005 to 2007.

CMBs that were issued in 2008 and 2009 also departed from historical norms in that their terms to maturity increased significantly. Prior to 2008, Treasury typically used CMBs to fund intramonth funding gaps and, in certain instances, to provide Treasury borrowing flexibility when it was approaching the debt limit.[12] Between 2002 and 2007, CMBs typically had a term to maturity of less than 2 weeks. During 2005, 2006, and 2007, the average term to maturity of CMBs was 10 days, 9 days, and 10 days respectively. In contrast, in 2009, the average term to maturity of CMBs was 109 days or 15.6 weeks. Removing those CMBs that were used for the SFP (debt issued for the SFP does not pay for government expenditures), the average term to maturity of the remaining CMBs was 99 days in 2008 and 198 days in 2009. During its February 2008 quarterly refunding process, Treasury announced its plans to issue longer-dated CMBs. This was a change to Treasury's recent practice of not issuing CMBs with maturities greater than 21 days and according to Treasury was necessary in order to spread the extraordinary financing needs away from the front end of the bill market. Treasury stated that longer-dated maturities would be issued because of seasonal fluctuations in cash balances, volatility associated with the timing of tax refunds, and the increased use of electronic payments versus check payments. On February 13, 2008, Treasury auctioned a 63-day CMB, which had a longer maturity than any other CMB issued in the previous 3 fiscal years. Treasury issued additional CMBs with terms to maturity of greater than 300 days during both fiscal years 2008 and 2009. Longer-dated CMBs were also, in many instances, reopenings of existing Treasury bills. Twenty of the 37 non-SFP CMBs issued in 2008 and 2009 were reopenings of outstanding Treasury bills. Treasury officials told us that they consulted with market participants and decided that longer-dated CMBs, for example 9-month bills, were a prudent, short-term mechanism to raise cash and approximately the length of time that it would take for coupon issuance to "catch up" and shoulder a bigger share of Treasury's financing needs.

Treasury Paid a Premium for the Sustained Use of CMBs in 2008 and 2009

While CMBs provided Treasury with needed borrowing flexibility immediately following the start of the financial market crisis in 2008, Treasury paid a premium for its sustained use of CMBs in 2008 and 2009. We reported in 2006 that Treasury had paid a premium for its use of CMBs during the period of 1996 to 2005.[13] During that period, Treasury paid a higher yield on most CMBs than outstanding Treasury bills of a similar maturity paid in the secondary market. In the low-interest-rate environment during 2008 and

2009, all debt, but particularly short-term debt, was relatively inexpensive for Treasury; however, since the dollar amount of CMBs issued in 2008 was 5.6 times greater than the amount issued in 2007, even a small premium could be costly.

Our analysis shows that of the 37 CMBs not issued for the SFP in 2008 and 2009, most had a higher yield when compared with outstanding Treasury bills of a similar maturity in the secondary market. The difference between these CMB yields and similar maturing outstanding bills—known as the yield differential—was positive for the second half of 2008 and all of 2009, averaging 2.7 basis points higher (or $184 million based on the amount issued) than outstanding bills of a similar maturity.[14] CMBs play an important role in Treasury debt management, and it is likely that Treasury will always need to use CMBs, but Treasury could achieve savings by limiting the amount of CMBs it issues.

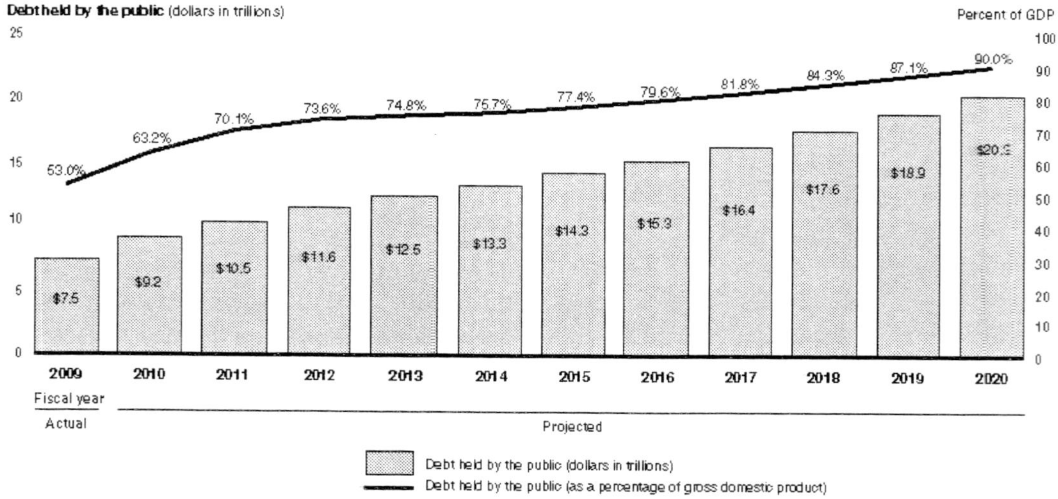

Source: CBO data.

Figure 3. CBO's Estimate of Debt Held by the Public and Percent of GDP, Based on the President's Budgetary Proposals, 2009 to 2020

Treasury has already begun its transition out of CMBs that are not linked to the SFP.[15] As part of that transition, it has extended the average term to maturity of outstanding marketable securities by stabilizing short-term debt issuances and transitioning to nominal note and bond issuances. In February 2010, Treasury officials said that they planned to stabilize nominal note and bond issuance in the first half of 2010 and perhaps reduce nominal note and bond issuance in the second half of 2010. As of September 2009, 28.5 percent of Treasury's debt portfolio was in bills. If Treasury does not alter its current pattern of issuance, Treasury projects this share will decline to 19 percent by September 2010 and to 16 percent by September 2011. Continuing to transition out of CMBs could reduce Treasury's borrowing costs, increase Treasury's borrowing capacity on the short end of the yield curve, and extend the average term to maturity of the debt portfolio.

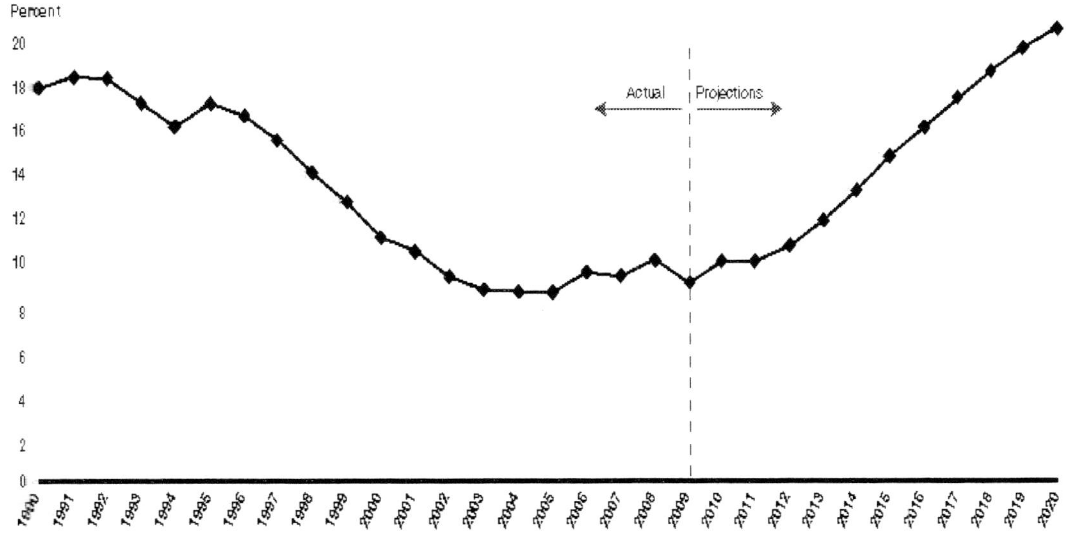

Source: GAO analysis of CBO data.

Figure 4. Net Interest Payments as a Percentage of Total Revenues, 1990 to 2020

The Medium- and Long-Term Fiscal Outlook Will Continue to Present Debt Management Challenges

The actions that Treasury has taken to increase borrowing in response to the recession and financial-market crisis take place within the context of the already-serious longer-term fiscal condition of the federal government. As seen in figure 3, the Congressional Budget Office (CBO) projects that under the President's fiscal year 2011 budget proposals, the debt held by the public will increase from $9.2 trillion in fiscal year 2010 to $20.3 trillion in 2020. Over this same period, CBO projects that debt held by the public will increase from 63 percent of gross domestic product (GDP) in fiscal year 2010 to 90 percent by the end of fiscal year 2020. Our long-term simulations show growing deficits and debt, underscoring that the long-term fiscal outlook is unsustainable.[16]

According to CBO, interest rates and the size of debt held by the public will increase in the medium term, leading to higher interest costs for the government. One way to measure the affordability of debt held by the public is to compare interest payments with expected revenues. As seen in figure 4, according to CBO, net interest payments as a percentage of total revenues will increase from 9.9 percent in fiscal year 2010 to 20.7 percent in fiscal year 2020.[17]

Treasury says its existing suite of securities will leave Treasury well-positioned to meet federal government borrowing needs in fiscal year 2010. Looking beyond 2010, sustained increases in debt in the medium and long term mean that communication with all types of investors to accurately gauge market demand will become increasingly important for Treasury.

TREASURY AND INVESTORS COMMUNICATE THROUGH BOTH FORMAL AND INFORMAL CHANNELS; MARKET PARTICIPANTS IDENTIFIED CHALLENGES AND SUGGESTED IMPROVEMENTS TO BOTH

Treasury and Investors Communicate through Both Formal and Informal Channels

Sufficient information from market participants, including their likely demand for Treasury securities, is critical for debt management decisions. Treasury receives market information through multiple formal and informal channels. (See figure 5) Formal communication channels are quarterly meetings with TBAC and with the primary dealers held as part of Treasury's quarterly refunding process. TBAC is currently comprised of primary dealers, investment managers, hedge funds, and a small broker dealer. According to Treasury officials, TBAC was once more weighted towards primary dealers than it is now. Buy-and-hold investors of Treasury securities are currently underrepresented. TBAC quarterly meetings serve as a forum for Treasury officials to discuss economic forecasts and the federal government's borrowing needs with knowledgeable market participants. Treasury officials pose questions on specific debt management issues in advance and TBAC members present their observations to Treasury on these issues and economic conditions. While TBAC meetings are closed due to the sensitivity of the matters under discussion, Treasury releases TBAC meeting minutes at a press conference 1 day after each meeting and announces the details of its quarterly refunding and any changes to its auction calendar or to debt management policies. Treasury officials told us that Treasury seeks to promote market stability by reserving the release of any new information for the formal quarterly announcements.

Treasury also surveys all 18 primary dealers quarterly and meets with half of them one quarter and the other half the following quarter. Primary dealers are those banks and securities broker-dealers that are designated by FRBNY and maintain active trading relationships with FRBNY. Primary dealers are also required by FRBNY to participate in all Treasury auctions. Primary dealers account for a majority of purchases at auction, some of which they purchase for themselves and some of which they purchase for their customers. Treasury meets with half of the primary dealers before each quarterly refunding to obtain estimates on borrowing, issuance, and the federal budget deficit, as well as input on a variety of debt management discussion topics, posed in advance. The only information about these meetings that is released to the public is the agenda.

Treasury officials also receive information from FRBNY's Markets Group, which has approximately 400 staff engaged in market surveillance. FRBNY provides morning and afternoon briefings, hosts a daily afternoon conference call, and provides a daily report on delivery fails in the secondary market for Treasury securities.[18] FRBNY will also conduct specific market research at the request of Treasury. According to Treasury officials, the Office of Debt Management (ODM) relies on FRBNY for some of its market information.[19] FRBNY is able to carry out large data-collection operations because of its greater resources, which supplements market data Treasury already collects.

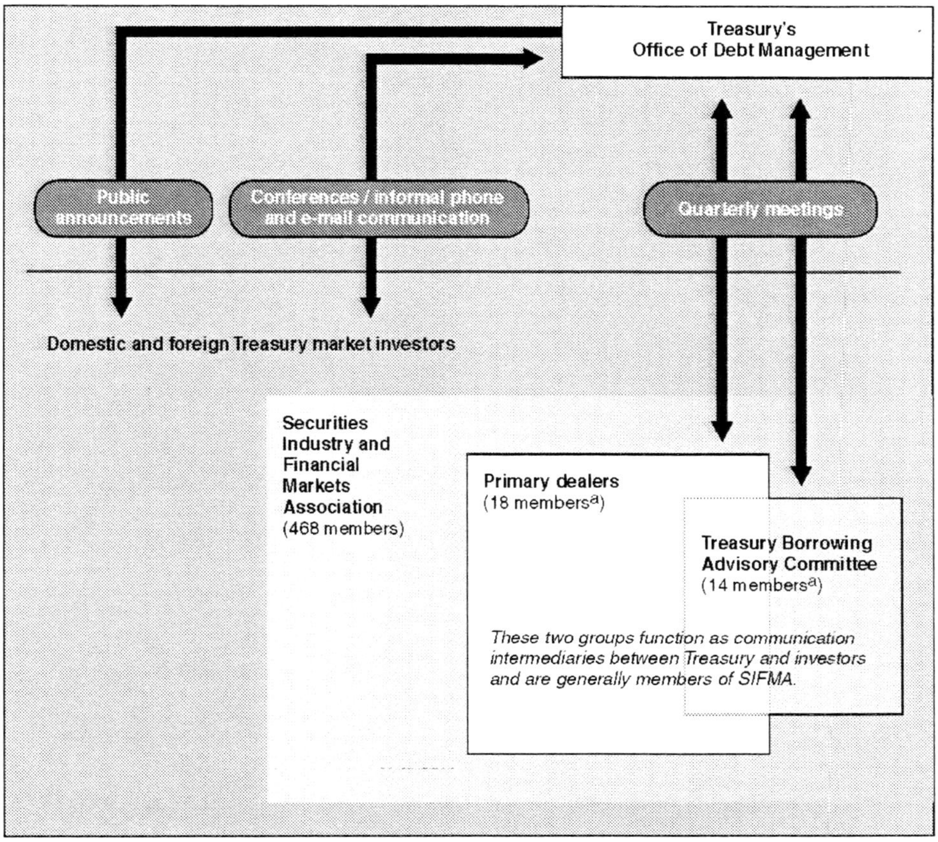

Source: GAO.

[a]There are five common members among TBAC and the primary dealers.

Figure 5. Treasury's Office of Debt Management's (ODM) Market Information Channels

In addition to its formal communication with the market, Treasury continually collects information through informal channels, but this communication is not conducted or logged in a systematic manner. ODM's informal communication includes both ad hoc and regular telephone and e-mail contact between six ODM officials and staff and approximately 500 foreign and domestic financial organizations. Treasury also has seven market-room staff who maintain continuous contact with market participants. Treasury also maintains regular informal contact with representatives of foreign central banks. In addition, Treasury regularly contacts primary dealers to discuss operational issues in the Treasury debt market as well to gather information about what they expect to occur in the Treasury debt market on a given day. Treasury staff and officials also reach out to investors by speaking at and attending conferences sponsored by market participants and meeting with large investors globally.

Investors Reported Mixed Satisfaction with Treasury's Receipt of Information from End-Investors

Responses to our survey of the largest domestic holders of Treasury securities indicate that their views vary on the extent to which Treasury receives sufficient information and input from end-investors. Overall, survey responses suggested room for improvement in Treasury's practices for gathering market information.

Our survey asked respondents the extent to which they believed Treasury receives sufficient information and input from end-investors. They were presented with five response categories that included very great extent, great extent, moderate extent, some extent, and little or no extent, as well as a no basis to judge response choice.[20] Seventeen of the 38 respondents who answered this question on our survey (see figure 6), answered either some extent or little or no extent. This compares with only 10 respondents who answered very great extent or great extent.

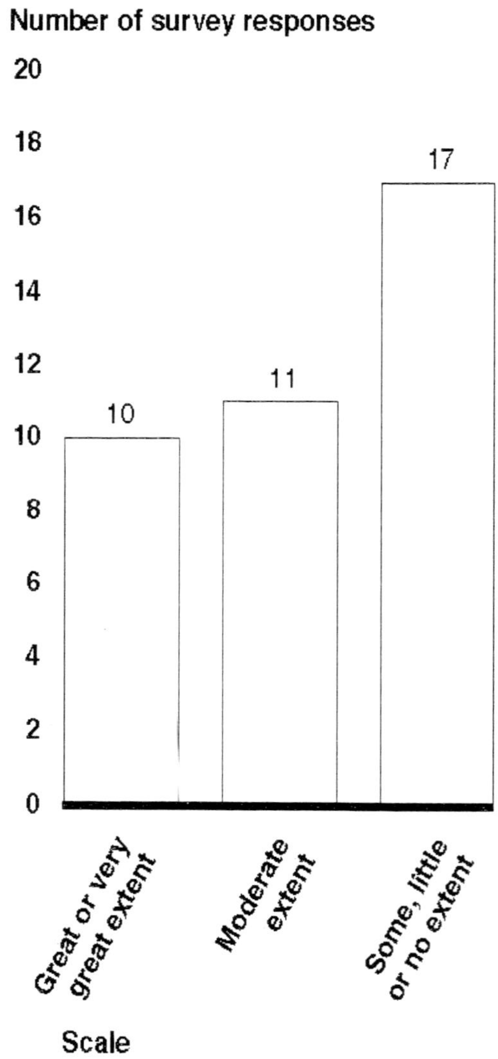

Source: GAO.

Figure 6. Extent to Which Survey Respondents Believe Treasury Receives Sufficient Information from End-Investors

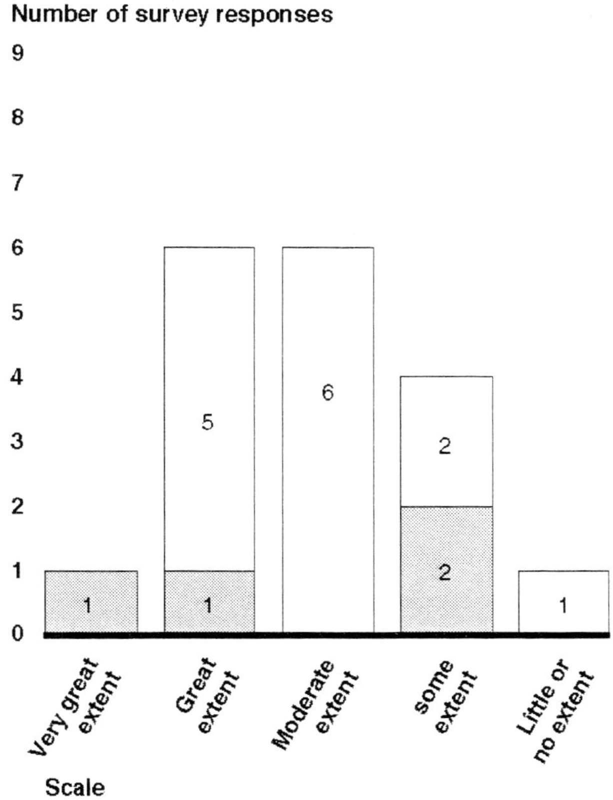

Source: GAO.

Figure 7. Extent to Which Commercial Banks and Mutual-Fund Respondents Believe Treasury Receives Sufficient Information from End-Investors

Survey responses varied by market sector. Commercial banks and mutual funds expressed a greater belief that Treasury receives sufficient information and input from end-investors than did other sectors we surveyed. (See figure 7) At the time of our survey, the mutual-funds sector, the sector with the largest amount of Treasury holdings in our survey, held over $201 billion in Treasury securities. The commercial-banking sector held $125 billion.[21]

In contrast to the mostly positive responses of mutual funds and commercial banks, respondents from the remaining sectors—life insurance companies, property casualty insurance companies, and state and local government retirement funds—were more likely to respond negatively.[22] As shown in figure 8, 12 of 20 respondents from life insurance companies, property casualty insurance companies, and state and local government retirement funds answered some or little or no extent when asked whether they believe Treasury currently receives sufficient information from end-investors. Both of the life insurance companies that completed our survey chose little or no extent. Treasury officials have agreed that they could receive better input from end-investors and have made it a priority to improve investor outreach.

The survey findings were consistent with information we received during interviews with investors conducted in June 2009 that indicated that many investors in liability-driven sectors, such as life insurance and pension funds, both lack formalized means of communication with

Treasury and believe such contact would be beneficial. These investors may have a different demand portfolio than those in other market sectors with whom Treasury maintains closer contact. For example, there may be greater interest in these sectors in buy-and-hold securities like TIPS. With debt levels predicted to continue to rise in the medium and long term, the importance of good information from a range of investors in all sectors increases in importance.

Market Participants and Experts Suggested Ways for Treasury to Improve Its Collection of Information from End-Investors

Respondents to our survey of the largest domestic holders of Treasury securities suggested ideas for improving Treasury's collection of information from end-investors. The most frequently suggested ideas involved increasing the range of investors from whom Treasury obtains information. Survey respondents told us that they thought Treasury could better gauge market demand for securities if a broader range of investors were represented on TBAC. Survey respondents suggested changes such as broadening membership or rotating membership more frequently. Multiple survey respondents told us that some types of end-investors, particularly liability-driven investors such as insurance companies and pensions funds, have limited formal means of communicating their views to Treasury.

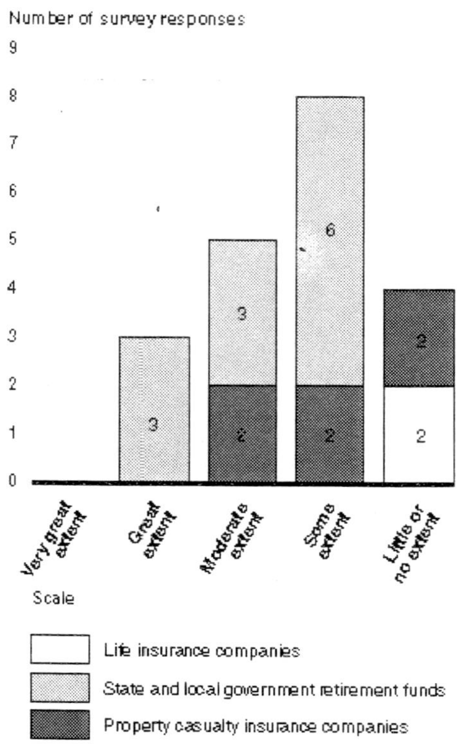

Source: GAO.

Figure 8. Extent to Which Life Insurance, Property Casualty Insurance, and State and Local Government Retirement Funds Believe Treasury Receives Sufficient Information from End-Investors

Survey respondents also suggested that Treasury could better gauge market demand through a periodic collection of market data from a broad range of end-investors. They suggested that the periodic data collection could be in the form of a survey, interviews, focus groups, or additional data reporting by market participants. These responses echoed what market experts told us, that Treasury could benefit from periodic "temperature-taking" of the market through surveys or interviews and from changes to the organization or composition of the groups from which Treasury routinely receives market information and advice. Several survey respondents told us that a good model for a future Treasury survey might resemble the survey we conducted. While Treasury has not conducted a survey of end-investors in the past, similar surveys have been conducted by organizations like SIFMA.

Treasury staff and officials agree that more inclusive representation on TBAC would be desirable, but they also said that increasing the number of members (to even the TBAC charter limit of 20 members) could impede optimal committee functioning. Treasury staff told us that if the committee were to become too large, it might be difficult to allow enough time for members to provide feedback and contribute to discussions. Treasury staff and officials told us that they could broaden TBAC membership to include one or more representatives of buy-and-hold investors such as insurance companies or endowments. Treasury staff and officials also told us that one of Treasury's priorities is to improve investor outreach and to collect information more systematically. Treasury officials told us that improvements to how Treasury communicates with investors are likely to be a priority for ODM in 2010 and beyond.

Investors Reported Increased Demand for TIPS and Suggested Actions for Treasury to Take That Could Improve the TIPS Market

Investors and Market Experts Reported an IncreasedDemand for TIPS

As previously noted, one challenge for Treasury will be to gauge investor demand for Treasury securities in order to finance historically large deficits expected in the medium and long term. Faced with this challenge, communication with investors becomes essential. When we surveyed major domestic holders of Treasury securities in August 2009, many survey participants indicated that their demand could increase for TIPS. As seen in table 1, as of July 31, 2009, survey respondents reported holding $143 billion in TIPS—which represented approximately 26 percent of the total marketable TIPS outstanding. This amount also constituted approximately 21 percent of the survey respondents' total portfolio of Treasury securities. This share allocated to TIPS may indicate that our survey respondents already viewed TIPS favorably. According to Treasury data, TIPS generally represent a much smaller percentage of total outstanding Treasury securities. At the time of our survey in August 2009, TIPS constituted only 8 percent of all Treasury marketable securities outstanding.

Even though the survey respondents were already heavily invested in TIPS, they indicated that they planned to greatly increase their TIPS purchases over the next 17 months. From August 2009 through the end of December 2010, our survey respondents said that they planned to purchase an additional $29 billion in TIPS.

Table 1. Survey Respondents' Reported Treasury Securities Holdings and Future Purchases

Dollars in billions			
	Treasury securities (as of Dec. 31, 2008)	Treasury securities (as of July 31, 2009)	Anticipated purchases (Aug. 1, 2009–Dec. 31, 2010)
Bills	280	247	26
Notes	153	189	50
Bonds	73	62	6
TIPS	139	143	29
STRIPS	25	27	1
Total	**670**	**668**	**112**

Source: GAO.

Note: Not all survey respondents were able to provide figures for anticipated purchases of Treasury securities due to constant changes in the value of Treasury securities relative to other investment options.

The increased investor interest in TIPS, as reported through our survey, corroborates information we received from individual interviews we conducted earlier with large domestic holders of Treasury securities. The investment managers we interviewed at public and private pension funds, mutual funds, insurance companies, and commercial banks expressed continued or growing interest in TIPS during 2009.

At the start of 2009, financial-market experts were recommending that investors purchase TIPS and other inflation-protected investments. Over the course of the year, mutual funds began reporting large inflows into inflation-protected funds, which consist mostly of TIPS. During 2009, the five largest inflation-protected bond mutual funds increased their total net assets by almost 70 percent.[23] The largest of these funds saw its net assets increase by an average of almost $1 billion per month in 2009. Also during 2009, one of the largest fixed income managers introduced three new mutual funds designed to protect investors against inflation.[24] One of those new funds is intended to provide a hedge against inflation but also provide tax-efficient income by allocating at least half of its investments to municipal bonds.[25] The other two new funds are intended to produce monthly income payments that consist of both inflation-adjusted interest and principal. These two funds consist primarily of investments in TIPS and have initial target maturity dates of 2019 and 2029.

Recent Changes to TIPS Suggest That Treasury Is Responding to InvestorConcerns about the Liquidity of TIPS

GAO and others have recommended that Treasury take action to improve the liquidity of TIPS, which could lower Treasury's cost of borrowing.[26] Prior to 2009, holdings of Treasury securities by sectors that we surveyed had been in decline for nearly two decades. (As seen in figure9.) By the onset of the financial crisis in 2008, the share of Treasury securities relative to each sector's total assets was less than half their historical averages for the preceding two decades. By the end of 2007, no sector reported holding more than 5-½ percent of its total assets in Treasury securities.

In 2009, Treasury decided to increase TIPS issuance, reversing the trend of the past few years. As we previously reported, Treasury reduced the annual gross amount of TIPS issuance by 19 percent from 2006 to 2008. Treasury then gradually increased total TIPS issuance in 2009 by 4 percent to $58 billion. During the August 2009 TBAC press conference, Treasury officials stated that they are committed to the TIPS program and to issuing TIPS in a regular and predictable manner across the yield curve. Further, during the November 2009 and February 2010 TBAC meetings, Treasury officials announced that they planned to gradually increase TIPS issuance and would consider making changes to the TIPS auction calendar by increasing the number of TIPS auctions. These changes, which are meant to improve TIPS liquidity, are based on Treasury's own analysis and on input that Treasury received from market participants and GAO. At the time of this chapter, Treasury had already begun to increase TIPS issuance. The size of the 10-year TIPS auction held in January 2010 was $10 billion—an increase of 25 percent over the previous 10-year TIPS auctions that held in July 2009.

If investors continue to express and demonstrate interest in TIPS, Treasury may be able to issue a greater amount of TIPS at a lower cost than in past years. Survey respondents who anticipated a change in their demand for TIPS said that any reallocation into TIPS would most likely be drawn from holdings of nominal Treasury securities or non-Treasury assets. Investments into TIPS were less likely to come from an overall increase in total assets. As previously reported, if Treasury has to increase the supply of nominal securities substantially to fund larger deficits, yields may have to rise in order to attract enough buyers due to the saturation of the nominal Treasury market.[27] Therefore, issuing TIPS may make sense since a substantial shift in the composition of Treasury issuance into TIPS from nominal Treasuries could also lead to lower interest rates paid on the remaining nominal Treasury issuance. The most common reasons cited by our survey respondents for this specific anticipated shift into TIPS were inflation protection and TIPS' valuation relative to other investments—the same reasons most often cited for a general interest in TIPS. Compared to other sectors that we surveyed, mutual fund companies and state and local government retirement funds also responded that some of their investments in TIPS were dedicated based upon active allocation decisions made by clients.

Treasury has also responded to investor concern about the maturity of TIPS issued across the yield curve by reintroducing the 30-year TIPS. At the November 2009 TBAC meeting, there was general consensus to eliminate the 20-year TIPS and replace it with the 30-year TIPS. TBAC members thought this change may allow Treasury to lower its cost of borrowing while it would create a TIPS issue that could be better compared to the 30-year nominal issuance point. Following the TBAC meeting, Treasury announced that it would discontinue the auctions of the 20-year TIPS and reintroduce the 30-year TIPS starting in February 2010.[28]

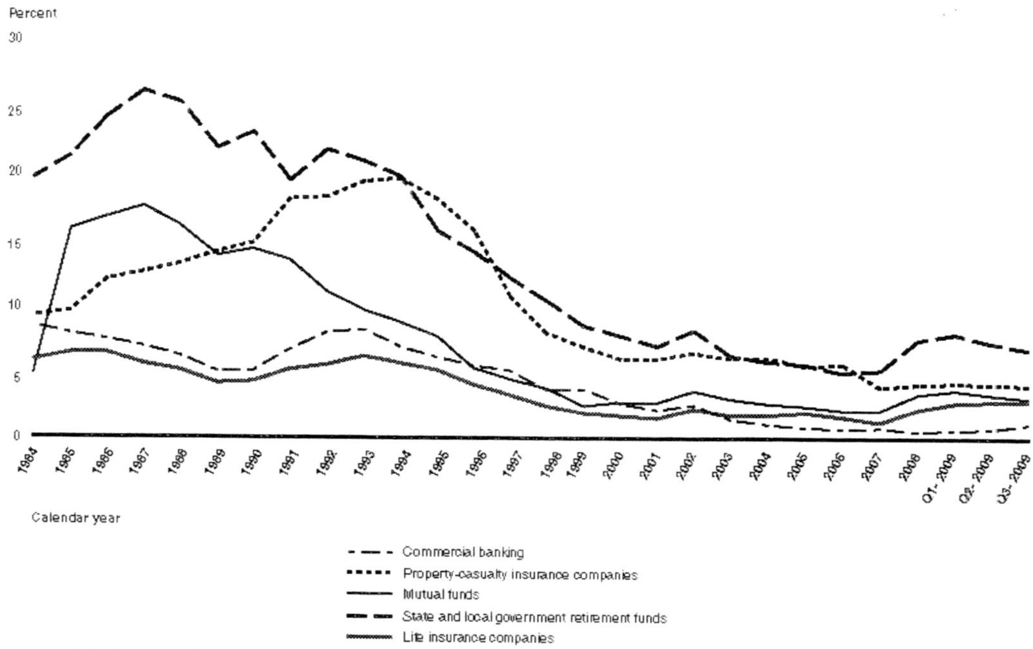

Source: GAO analysis of Federal Reserve data .

Figure 9. Percentage of Total Financial Assets in Treasury Securities by Sector (1984 to 2009)

Options Exist to Improve TIPS Auction Participation, WhichCouldImprove TIPS Liquidity

As we reported previously, investors demand a premium for less-liquid TIPS, which increases Treasury's borrowing costs.[29] Through our survey, market participants identified a number of options to improve participation at TIPS auctions, which could improve TIPS liquidity. Most respondents to our survey were more likely to purchase TIPS in the seconcary market rather than at auction. The most common reasons listed for this were infrequency of TIPS auctions, portfolio needs, relative valuation, and liquidity. On average, survey respondents planned to purchase almost 80 percent of their TIPS in the secondary market. Over half of survey respondents said that although they never participate in Treasury auctions, they were active in the secondary market at least monthly.

Survey respondents said that increasing the dollar amount of TIPS issued per auction and increasing the frequency of TIPS auctions could help improve participation during TIPS auctions. Survey respondents also pointed out that a clearer commitment from Treasury to the TIPS program would improve TIPS liquidity. In interviews with us in February 2010, some primary dealers said that Treasury should modify its current TIPS auction schedule to decrease the amount of time between TIPS auctions, thereby staggering the supply of TIPS so that issuance is not as concentrated. Since 2005, Treasury has held eight TIPS auctions every calendar year—two auctions each in January, April, July and October. At the May 2010 TBAC press conference, the Assistant Secretary for Financial Markets, Mary Miller, said that Treasury will be adding a second reopening of the 10-year TIPS, which would lead to six 10-year TIPS auctions a year. According to Treasury, these changes would help improve TIPS liquidity while diversifying its funding sources.

A More Liquid TIPS MarketCould Support a TIPS Futures Market, Which in TurnCouldFurtherEnhance the TIPS Market

The combination of increased TIPS issuance, Treasury's statements of commitment to TIPS, and the reintroduction of the longer-dated 30-year TIPS, could help sustain a viable TIPS futures market.[30] In interviews and in published material, some financial-market experts have noted the lack of a viable futures trading market for TIPS. Some of these experts have speculated that a successful futures contract could bolster the liquidity of

TIPS. In a public discussion with the Chicago Mercantile Exchange Group (CME) in March 2009, Acting Assistant Secretary for Financial Markets KarthikRamanathan explained that futures products help increase the liquidity, depth, and price transparency of the U.S. Treasury market.

According to market experts, however, the lack of liquidity in the current TIPS market would make it difficult to sustain a viable TIPS futures product. In interviews with GAO in February 2010, primary dealers expressed different opinions on the structure of a potential inflation futures contract. We heard preferences for both a cash-settled index as the basis for an inflation futures contract and also an inflation futures contract with a basket of deliverables similar to how futures contracts for nominal securities are structured. Primary dealers told us that if TIPS were to become more liquid, then a TIPS futures contract might succeed, and that this in turn could further increase the liquidity of TIPS.

ONE OF THE MOST IMPORTANT GROUPS THROUGHWHICHTREASURYRECEIVESMARKET INFORMATION HAS EXPRESSEDCONCERNS ABOUT THE INCREASE IN DIRECT BIDDING IN TREASURYAUCTIONS

One of Treasury's important channels of communication is with primary dealers. Primary dealers that we interviewed told us that they are satisfied with their communication with Treasury. They told us they had recently raised concerns about what they see as consequences of the recent increase in direct bidding in Treasury auctions.

Direct bidders are financial institutions that, like primary dealers, can bid for and buy Treasury securities competitively at auction directly from Treasury instead of in the secondary market. Unlike primary dealers, direct bidders are not required to participate in all Treasury auctions. Most Treasury securities are bought at auction by primary dealers. A much smaller, but growing volume of securities is purchased by direct bidders.[31]

In April 2004, Treasury stated that there were 825 "investors" making use of the auction system that allows direct bidding. Three months later, a Treasury press release announcing the new version of TAAPSLink, the communications system through which auction market participants are provided Internet-based access to Treasury auctions, said that over 600 "firms" used the on-line bidding system.[32] This is the most recent information that Treasury has disclosed to the market on the potential number of direct bidders at an auction.

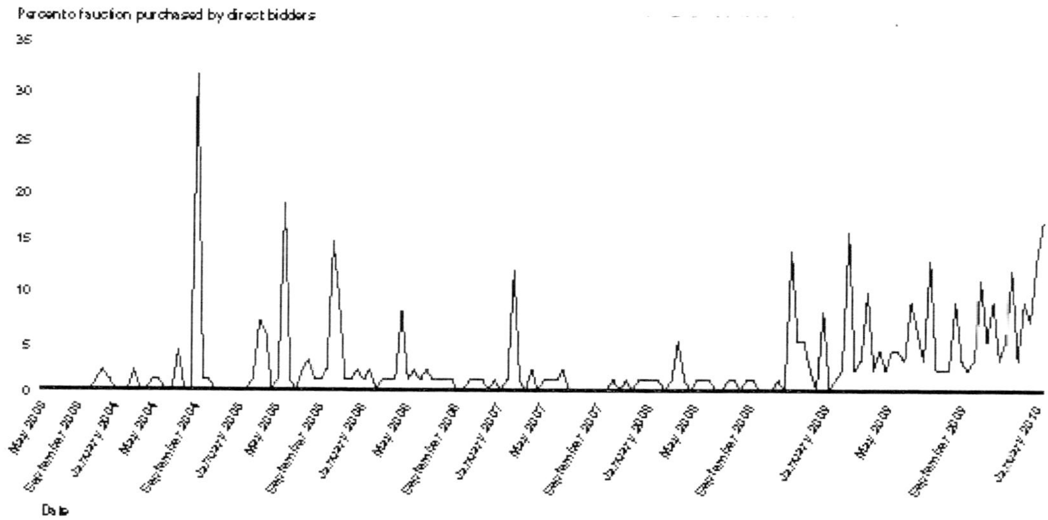

Source: GAO analysis of Treasury data.

Note: The frequency of issuance of the 5- and 10-year notes and 30-year bond varied between May 2003 and January 2010.

Figure 10. Percentage of 5- and 10-year Notes and 30-year Bonds Purchased by Direct Bidders at Treasury Securities Auctions (May 2003–February 2010)

Direct bidding has grown in size and volatility since 2008. Figure 10 illustrates both the overall increase in participation and the volatility of that participation. Direct bidder purchase share in auctions for 5- and 10-year notes and 30-year bonds began to trend upward and show greater variation starting on October 30, 2008, and then hit a 5-year high of almost 30 percent at the March 11, 2010, auction of 30-year bonds. During this period, the average direct-bidder purchase share of 5- and 10-year notes and 30-year bonds was 5.8 percent with a standard deviation of 5.3 percentage points. This contrasts with the period between May 5, 2003, and October 30, 2008, when direct bidders purchased an average of only 1.6 percent of 5- and 10-year notes and 30-year bonds. The standard deviation during this time period was 3.9 percentage points.

Primary dealers have made public statements expressing concerns about both the increase and the unpredictable role of direct bidders in Treasury auctions. Through interviews, we learned that they had expressed their concerns to both Treasury and the FRBNY. Primary dealers said they believe both more direct bidding and the increase in the volatility of direct bidding "dis-incentivizes" primary dealers because it means they have less certainty of information surrounding a particular Treasury auction. For example, if an investor purchases Treasury securities directly at auction instead of going through a primary dealer, a primary dealer could have less information available about the auction. Volatility in direct bidding also increases uncertainty. Increased uncertainty could lead to primary dealers making less aggressive bids, which could lead to increased borrowing costs for Treasury. Some primary dealers also told us that an overall lack of transparency regarding direct bidding potentially contributes to "sloppy auctions." A sloppy auction typically means poor reception or demand for a Treasury auction relative to what was expected and leads to higher yields at the auction. Treasury officials told us that they have not seen any evidence of this and have also stated publicly that Treasury supports broad access to the auction process and that direct bidding fosters competition, therefore helping achieve its goal of the lowest cost of borrowing over time.

According to primary dealers that we interviewed, part of the lack of transparency surrounding direct bidding comes from not knowing the exact number of direct bidders that could potentially bid at each auction and what sectors of the market they represent. One source of information that provides a breakdown of auction results by sector is Treasury's data on Investor Class Auction Allotments, which is released on the 7th business day of each month.[33] Primary dealers that we spoke with said that if Treasury were to provide this data on a more frequent basis it might alleviate some of the uncertainty that currently exists in the market.

CONCLUSIONS

In 2008 and 2009, Treasury successfully raised unprecedented amounts of cash in a very short period of time. However, absent policy changes, the medium- and long-term fiscal outlook means that Treasury will have to continue to raise significant amounts of cash, while achieving its goal of the lowest cost of borrowing over time. Raising significant amounts of cash at the lowest cost of borrowing over time requires sufficient and competitive participation at auctions. Information from market participants on their demand for Treasury securities, including the type of information that we received from our survey of the largest domestic holders of Treasury securities, is critical to this effort.

Treasury initially raised cash to meet TARP and Recovery Act needs by issuing primarily short-term debt, including CMBs, dramatically changing the composition of its debt portfolio. In 2009, Treasury began to take steps to return the composition of its debt portfolio to its pre–market crisis structure. In September 2009 we reported that a more robust TIPS program could benefit Treasury by diversifying and expanding its funding sources and reducing the cost of nominal securities. Treasury reaffirmed its commitment to TIPS and announced plans to gradually increase issuance of TIPS.[34] Through our survey of the largest domestic holders of Treasury securities in August 2009, we found that Treasury can improve the extent to which it receives sufficient information from end-investors. We also found that options exist for Treasury to increase investor participation in TIPS auctions and further improve TIPS liquidity. We briefed Treasury on the findings contained in this chapter in October 2009, December 2009, and March 2010.

RECOMMENDATIONS FOR EXECUTIVE ACTION

The Secretary of the Treasury should continually review methods for collecting market information and consider the following actions to help gauge investor demand in the context of projected sustained increases in federal debt:

- conducting a systematic and periodic survey of the largest holders of Treasury securities in all sectors, and

- increasing the number of representatives on TBAC and ensuring diverse representation by including members that represent end-investors.

The Secretary of the Treasury should continue to reduce the amount and term to maturity of CMBs, when appropriate.

The Secretary of the Treasury should consider increasing the number of TIPS auctions and distributing them more evenly throughout the year in order to improve participation in TIPS auctions.

The Secretary of the Treasury should study whether the recent increase in direct bidding at Treasury auctions has changed Treasury's overall cost of borrowing. As part of this study, Treasury should consider options to promote transparency surrounding direct bidding that would not discourage participation or affect Treasury's goal of fostering competition at auctions, including releasing its data on Investor Class Auction Allotments more frequently.

List of Committees

The Honorable Daniel K. Inouye
Chairman
The Honorable Thad Cochran
Vice Chairman
Committee on Appropriations
United States Senate

The Honorable Christopher J. Dodd
Chairman
The Honorable Richard C. Shelby
Ranking Member
Committee on Banking, Housing, and Urban Affairs
United States Senate

The Honorable Kent Conrad
Chairman
The Honorable Judd Gregg
Ranking Member
Committee on the Budget
United States Senate

The Honorable Max Baucus
Chairman
The Honorable Charles E. Grassley
Ranking Member
Committee on Finance
United States Senate

The Honorable David R. Obey
Chairman

The Honorable Jerry Lewis
Ranking Member
Committee on Appropriations
House of Representatives

The Honorable John M. Spratt, Jr.
Chairman
The Honorable Paul Ryan
Ranking Member
Committee on the Budget
House of Representatives

The Honorable Barney Frank
Chairman
The Honorable Spencer Bachus
Ranking Member
Committee on Financial Services
House of Representatives

The Honorable Sander M. Levin
Acting Chairman
The Honorable Dave Camp
Ranking Member Committee on Ways and Means
House of Representatives

Appendix I. Methodology for the Analysis of the Cash Management Bill YieldDifferential

We analyzed the yield differential for all cash management bills (CMB) issued over a 2-year period beginning on January 1, 2008, and ending on December 31, 2009, removing from our analysis any cash management bills that were used for the Supplementary Financing Program (SFP). We used two methods to analyze the yield differential between CMBs and equivalent regular 4-, 13-, 26-, or 52-week Department of the Treasury (Treasury) bills. First, we compared CMB yields to recently auctioned Treasury bills of similar maturity. Second, we compared CMB yields to average secondary market yields on Treasury bills of similar maturity. There are limitations to both of these yield differential estimates. Neither captures any effect from the announcement of CMBs on yields for similar maturing bills. If the announcement of a CMB increased the yield on similar maturing bills, then our estimate may be understated. Also, in some cases, the surrounding Treasury bills we used could include CMBs that were reopenings of regular Treasury bills. This would also lead to an understatement of the yield differential because the yield on the outstanding securities including CMBs would be higher than outstanding securities that did not include CMBs.

CMB Yields Compared to Recently Auctioned Treasury Bills of Similar Maturity

We compared CMB yields with the yields of similar Treasury bills that were auctioned the same day, or immediately before and after the date of the CMB auction. Once we identified two Treasury bills (one auctioned before and one after each CMB) with a maturity closest to the CMB, we derived a weighted average yield for the two bills. The weights were based on the relative difference in each bill's auction date from that of the CMB, with the Treasury bill having a closer auction date receiving a greater weight and the weights summing to 1. Then, the weighted average Treasury bill yield was subtracted from the CMB auction yield to obtain the yield differential. In the final step, the yield differential was applied to the dollar amount of the CMB to obtain an estimate of the cost of issuing a CMB instead of a regular Treasury bill.

CMB Yields Compared to Average Secondary Market Yields on Treasury Bills of Similar Maturity

Taking a second approach, we also calculated the difference between a CMB's yield and the average secondary market yield on other Treasury bills that are most similar (in terms of maturity) to the CMB on the day of auction.[35] That is, we compared CMB yields with yields on the nearest-maturing Treasury bills—either same day maturity, or one maturing before the CMB and one after. The CMB yields were obtained from the Bureau of the Public Debt while rates on similar-maturity outstanding Treasury bills were obtained from the *Wall Street Journal*. Due to the availability of *Wall Street Journal* data at the time of our analysis, the secondary market yield differential could only be calculated for the second half of 2008, but was calculated for all of 2009. For each Treasury bill, the asked yield was identified. Next, the weighted average yield for the two bills nearest in maturity to the CMB was derived. The weights were based on the relative difference in each bill's maturity date from that of the CMB, with the Treasury bill having a closer maturity date receiving a greater weight and the weights summing to 1. Then, the weighted average Treasury bill yield was subtracted from the CMB auction yield to obtain the yield differential. In the final step, the yield differential was applied to the dollar amount of the CMB to obtain an estimate of the cost of issuing a CMB instead of a regular Treasury bill.

Appendix II. Survey Scope and Methodology

To help achieve our objective of determining what changes the Department of the Treasury (Treasury) could make to better gauge end-investor demand and increase auction participation, we conducted a Web-based survey of domestic institutional investors in Treasury securities.

Population and Sample Design

In June 2009, we conducted 12 structured interviews with the two largest holders of Treasury securities in each of the following sectors: mutual funds; commercial banks; life insurance companies; property casualty insurance companies; state and local government retirement funds; and private pension funds. Based on what we learned in these interviews, in August 2009 we conducted a more comprehensive Web-based survey that was sent to the 12 holders of Treasury securities that we interviewed in June, as well as to additional holders of Treasury securities in each sector, with the exception of private pension funds. Private pension funds were excluded from the Web-based survey because our initial interviews revealed that their funds are managed primarily by external investment management companies represented in other sectors. Neither the structured interviews nor the Web-based survey are generalizible.

We established two criteria for inclusion of a sector in the nonprobability sample for our 12 structured interviews. First, the sector had to have Treasury holdings in the top 20 of all sectors as of the third quarter of 2008, according to table L.209 of the *Flow of Funds Account of the United States*. Second, the sector had to be identified by market experts that we interviewed in February 2009 as having the potential to purchase large quantities of Treasury securities in the future. Both criteria were used to ensure that the sectors have a relevant financial stake in Treasury markets.

The household sector and federal-government retirement funds sector were identified by the criteria, but not included in our sample. The household sector was not included due to the difficulty of identifying, ranking, and contacting individual household investors. In addition, it would have been beyond our ability to survey a sufficient number of households to reach the 50 percent market-share criterion that we later applied to the other sectors. The federal-government retirement funds sector was not included because the Thrift Savings Plan does not invest in nominal Treasury securities and Treasury Inflation Protected Securities (TIPS), and therefore, it was outside the scope of our survey.

Survey Administration and Response Rates

Table 2. Recipients, Respondents, and Treasury Holdings by Sector

Sector	Total recipients of survey	Total completed surveys	Response rate (percent)	Treasury holdings reported in survey (as of July 31, 2009) (dollars in billions)
Mutual fund	27	18	67	473
Commercial banking	7	4	57	32
Property casualty insurance	10	9	90	41
Life insurance	3	2	67	36
State and local government retirement fund	19	16	84	86

Source: GAO.

To identify the organizations within each sector that would receive our Web-based survey, we used rankings of the largest organizations in each sector based on total assets (or an equivalent financial indicator).[36] From these ranked lists, we determined Treasury holdings for each organization, and selected as many organizations as needed to represent at least 50 percent of the total amount of Treasury holdings for that sector (based on table L.209 of the *Flow of Funds Account of the United States*, as of the third quarter 2008).[37]

Analysis of Open-Ended Responses

Several survey questions solicited open-ended responses from respondents. To analyze the responses to these questions, two GAO analysts separately reviewed the responses and identified themes for each item. They then developed a mutual list, which was used to independently code survey responses. Independently coded responses were then compared and successfully coded at 80 percent agreement or higher, with any remaining disagreements reconciled through discussion. At least 80 percent agreement was obtained in all cases The coded responses were then used in two ways: (1) to obtain a sense of the range of perspectives on a given point, and (2) to obtain an idea of the frequency or extent to which a particular viewpoint or perspective was held by our survey respondents.

APPENDIX III. SURVEY INSTRUMENT

Survey Respondent

1. Please provide the following information for the organization and the person primarily responsible for completing this survey in case we need to contact you to clarify a response.

Organization name:	
Contact name *(first and last)*:	
Telephone *(Include area code)*:	
E-mail address:	

Treasury Auctions and Holdings

2. For the following types of Treasury securities that your organization may purchase **at auction**, at what frequency does it usually do so?
(Select one answer in each row.)

	Never	Daily	Weekly	Monthly	At every auction	Other *(Specify below)*
a. **Bills**	○	○	○	○	○	○
b. **Notes**	○	○	○	○	○	○
c. **Bonds**	○	○	○	○	○	○
d. **TIPS**	○	○	○	○	○	○

If you answered "Other" above, please enter the frequency of purchase **at auction** below.

a. Bills:

b. Notes:

c. Bonds:

d. TIPS:

3. For the following types of Treasury securities that your organization may purchase **in the secondary market**, at what frequency does it usually do so?
(Select one answer in each row.)

	Never	Daily	Weekly	Monthly	Other *(Specify below)*
a. **Bills**	○	○	○	○	○
b. **Notes**	○	○	○	○	○
c. **Bonds**	○	○	○	○	○
d. **TIPS**	○	○	○	○	○
e. **STRIPS**	○	○	○	○	○

If you answered "Other" above, please enter the frequency of purchase **in the secondary market** below.

a. Bills:

b. Notes:

c. Bonds:

d. TIPS:

e. STRIPS:

4. What factors influence your organization's choice to purchase Treasury securities **at auction** rather than in the secondary market? ***(Check all answers that apply in each row.)***

	Relative valuation	Amount	Timing of auction	Liquidity	Portfolio needs	Other *(Specify below)*
a. **Nominals**	☐	☐	☐	☐	☐	☐
b. **TIPS**	☐	☐	☐	☐	☐	☐

a. Nominals:	
b. TIPS:	

5. What factors influence your organization's choice to purchase Treasury securities **in the secondary market** rather than at auction? ***(Check all answers that apply in each row.)***

	Relative valuation	Amount	Timing of auction	Liquidity	Portfolio needs	Other *(Specify below)*
a. Nominals	☐	☐	☐	☐	☐	☐
b. TIPS	☐	☐	☐	☐	☐	☐

If you answered "Other" above, please enter the factor(s) influencing your purchase **in the secondary market**.

a. Nominals:	
b. TIPS:	

Treasury Auctions and Holdings - *Continued*

6. What amounts of the following types of Treasury securities did your organization hold as of the following dates and what would you estimate to be the change in the amount of Treasury securities held by your organization between August 1, 2009 and the end of 2010?

(Enter dollars in billions. Use a decimal to show the portion of a billion; for example, 500 million would be entered as 0.5 billion; one-and-a-half billion would be entered as 1.5 billion, etc. For the anticipated changes, please include a minus sign preceding the dollar amount to indicate a decrease.)

Treasury Bills

Amount held as of December 31, 2008	$	billion
Amount held as of July 31, 2009	$	billion
Anticipated change between August 1, 2009 and the end of 2010 *(Please include a minus sign to indicate a decrease.)*	$	billion

Treasury Notes

Amount held as of December 31, 2008	$	billion
Amount held as of July 31, 2009	$	billion
Anticipated change between August 1, 2009 and the end of 2010 *(Please include a minus sign to indicate a decrease.)*	$	billion

Treasury Bonds

Amount held as of December 31, 2008	$	billion
Amount held as of July 31, 2009	$	billion
Anticipated change between August 1, 2009 and the end of 2010 *(Please include a minus sign to indicate a decrease.)*	$	billion

TIPS

Amount held as of December 31, 2008	$	billion
Amount held as of July 31, 2009	$	billion
Anticipated change between August 1, 2009 and the end of 2010 *(Please include a minus sign to indicate a decrease.)*	$	billion

STRIPS

Amount held as of December 31, 2008	$	billion
Amount held as of July 31, 2009	$	billion
Anticipated change between August 1, 2009 and the end of 2010 *(Please include a minus sign to indicate a decrease.)*	$	billion

Treasury Auctions and Holdings - *Continued*

7. To what extent, if at all, do you consider each of the following to be reasons why Treasury securities are an attractive investment option for your organization or clients?
(Select one answer in each row.)

	Very great extent	Great extent	Moderate extent	Some extent	Little or no extent	No basis to judge
a. Liquidity (Ability to buy and sell with little effect on prices)	○	○	○	○	○	○
b. Depth of the Treasury market (Ability to purchase large amounts)	○	○	○	○	○	○
c. Treasuries are used for hedging	○	○	○	○	○	○
d. Treasuries have the backing of the U.S. Government	○	○	○	○	○	○
e. Ability to purchase Treasury securities across the yield curve	○	○	○	○	○	○
f. Treasuries are used to meet investment guidelines	○	○	○	○	○	○
g. Low charge against risk-based capital	○	○	○	○	○	○

	Very great extent	Great extent	Moderate extent	Some extent	Little or no extent	No basis to judge
h. Stability of terms and conditions	○	○	○	○	○	○
i. Inflation protection	○	○	○	○	○	○
j. Macroeconomic outlook	○	○	○	○	○	○
k. Relative valuation	○	○	○	○	○	○
l. Cash management	○	○	○	○	○	○
m. Asset liability matching	○	○	○	○	○	○
n. Other - *Please select an answer and specify below.*	○	○	○	○	○	○
o. Other - *Please select an answer and specify below.*	○	○	○	○	○	○
p. Other - *Please select an answer and specify below.*	○	○	○	○	○	○

If you answered "Other" in rows n through p above, please specify.

Specify entry in "n" above:	
Specify entry in "o" above:	
Specify entry in "p" above:	

Treasury Inflation-Protected Securities (TIPS)

8. If your organization currently invests in TIPS, what percentage of your organization's TIPS purchases is dedicated based on active allocation decisions made by clients? *(Enter percentage below.)*

Percentage dedicated based on active allocation decisions made by clients ______ percent

Please enter any comments you may have relating to your answer to question 8 above.

9. How interested, if at all, would your organization be in purchasing TIPS with the following maturities?
(Select one answer in each row.)

	Extremely interested	Very interested	Moderately interested	Slightly interested	Not interested	No basis to judge
a. 5-year TIPS	○	○	○	○	○	○
b. 10-year TIPS	○	○	○	○	○	○
c. 20-year TIPS	○	○	○	○	○	○
d. 30-year TIPS (if introduced)	○	○	○	○	○	○

10. What are the primary reasons your organization purchases TIPS or plans to purchase TIPS in the future? *(Please list up to five reasons in order of importance.)*

Reason #1:

Reason #2:

Reason #3:

Reason #4:

Reason #5:

11. In your opinion, what effect, if any, would a 30-year TIPS have on demand for TIPS securities with other maturities?

- ○ Would increase demand
- ○ Would have no effect on demand
- ○ Would decrease demand
- ○ No basis to judge

Treasury Inflation-Protected Securities (TIPS) - *Continued*

12. Do you anticipate any change in your organization's demand for TIPS from this year to next year?

- ○ Yes - *Continue with question 13.*
- ○ No (Click here to skip to question 15)
- ○ No basis to judge (Click here to skip to question 15)

13. If you anticipate change in your organization's demand, what do you anticipate the change(s) will be? ***(Check all answers that apply.)***

- ☐ A reallocation into TIPS from nominal Treasury securities
- ☐ A reallocation out of TIPS into nominal Treasury securities
- ☐ A reallocation into TIPS from an increase in total assets
- ☐ A reallocation out of TIPS from a decrease in total assets
- ☐ A reallocation into TIPS from non-Treasury assets
- ☐ A reallocation out of TIPS into non-Treasury assets
- ☐ Other change(s) - *Please specify below.*
- ☐ No basis to judge

If you answered "Other change(s)" above, please specify below.

14. What are the primary reasons behind the change in demand for TIPS from this year to next year? *(Please list up to five reasons in order of importance.)*

Reason #1:

Reason #2:

Reason #3:

Reason #4:

Reason #5:

15. In your estimation, about what percent of your organization's TIPS purchases in the next year will be made through the following means?

a. **Auctions:** ______ percent

b. **Secondary market:** ______ percent

Please enter any comments you may have relating to your answer to question 15 above.

16. Would the following actions by Treasury increase the likelihood that your organization would: 1) participate in a TIPS auction, and 2) buy more securities at each auction? *(Select one answer in each row.)*

	Would increase our participation	Would increase the amount of securities purchased	Would increase both participation and amount purchased	Would do neither	No basis to judge
a. Increase the frequency of TIPS auctions and reopenings	○	○	○	○	○
b. Increase TIPS issuance amounts per auction	○	○	○	○	○
c. Purchase off-the-run TIPS securities	○	○	○	○	○
d. Other - *Please answer and specify below.*	○	○	○	○	○
e. Other - *Please answer and specify below.*	○	○	○	○	○
f. Other - *Please answer and specify below.*	○	○	○	○	○

If you answered "Other" above, please specify other ways to increase participation or amount of securities bought.

Specify entry in d. above:

Specify entry in e. above:

Specify entry in f. above:

17. The liquidity of TIPS has been found to be less than nominal Treasury securities. In your opinion, what actions could Treasury take to enhance the liquidity of TIPS? *(Please list up to five actions in order of importance.)*

Action #1:

Action #2:

Action #3:

Action #4:

Action #5:

Risk Exposure

18. In your opinion, what are the risks that your organization faces as an investor in Treasury markets? *(Please list up to five risks in order of importance.)*

Risk #1:

Risk #2:

Risk #3:

Risk #4:

Risk #5:

19. In your opinion, what actions could be taken to address and mitigate the risks identified in question 18 above? *(Please list up to five actions corresponding to the risks identified in question 18 above.)*

Action #1:

Action #2:

Action #3:

Action #4:

Action #5:

Treasury Information Sources

20. In your opinion, to what extent, if at all, does Treasury currently receive sufficient information and input from end-investors?

- Very great extent
- Great extent
- Moderate extent
- Some extent
- Little or no extent
- No basis to judge

21. How effective, if at all, do you consider each of the following communication channels between your organization and Treasury to be at providing Treasury with sufficient information and input from end-investors?
(Select one answer in each row.)

	Extremely effective	Very effective	Moderately effective	Slightly effective	Not effective	No basis to judge
a. Direct contact with Treasury debt management officials and staff	○	○	○	○	○	○
b. Direct contact with Federal Reserve officials and staff	○	○	○	○	○	○
c. Direct contact with Treasury Borrowing Advisory Committee (TBAC) members	○	○	○	○	○	○
d. Direct contact with Primary Dealers	○	○	○	○	○	○
e. Direct participation in TBAC or Primary Dealer quarterly meetings	○	○	○	○	○	○
f. Other - *Please select an answer and specify below.*	○	○	○	○	○	○
g. Other - *Please select an answer and specify below.*	○	○	○	○	○	○
h. Other - *Please select an answer and specify below.*	○	○	○	○	○	○

If you answered "Other" in rows f through h above, please specify.

Specify entry in "f" above:

Specify entry in "g" above:

Specify entry in "h" above:

22. What actions could Treasury take to ensure that it receives sufficient information and input from end-investors? *(Please list up to five actions in order of importance.)*

Action #1:

Action #2:

Action #3:

Action #4:

Action #5:

Submit Your Responses to GAO

23. **Are you ready to submit your final completed questionnaire to GAO?**
(This is equivalent to mailing a completed paper questionnaire to us. It tells us that your answers are official and final.)

- ○ Yes, my questionnaire is complete - *Click on the "Exit" button below to submit your answers.*
- ◉ No, my questionnaire is not yet complete

You may view and print your completed questionnaire by clicking on the Summary link in the menu to the left.

Print this Page

Exit

End Notes

[1] There is no one-to-one relationship between Treasury securities issued and TARP expenditures and, therefore, our objectives were not to look into this specific relationship. For more information on Treasury debt issuance between December 2007 and July 2009 seeGAO, *Debt Management: Treasury Inflation Protected Securities Should Play a Heightened Role in Addressing Debt Management Challenges*, GAO-09-932 (Washington, D.C.: Sept. 29, 2009).

[2] Private pension funds were excluded from the survey because during our structured interviews we were told that many large private pension funds hired external investment managers and therefore did not manage the funds in-house.

[3] Gross debt of the federal government (excluding some minor adjustments) is subject to a statutory ceiling—known as the debt limit. The current limit—$14,294 billion—was enacted in February 2010. Treasury's authorities are codified in chapter 31 of title 31 of the United States Code.

[4] In November 2009, Treasury announced that it was replacing the 20-year TIPS with the 30-year TIPS. The reinstituted 30-year TIPS auction was held in February 2010.

[5] For additional information on TIPS, see GAO-09-932.

[6] For additional information on securities that are not issued as part of Treasury's "regular and predictable" schedule, see GAO, *Debt Management: Treasury Has Refined Its Use of Cash Management Bills but Should Explore Options That May Reduce Cost Further*, GAO-06-269 (Washington, D.C.: Mar. 30, 2006).

[7] In this chapter we use the term refinance to mean rolling over maturing debt into a new issuance of Treasury securities. In times of federal budget deficits, all maturing debt must be rolled over into a new issuance.

[8] SIFMA is a group that represents the shared interests of participants in the global financial markets. SIFMA was formed by a merger of the Bond Markets Association and the Securities Industry Association in 2006. Membership in SIFMA is open to firms rather than individuals. Broker-dealer firms can be full members while other firms with interest in the financial markets can be associate members. While SIFMA provides limited financial support to TBAC, SIFMA does not participate in TBAC deliberations.

[9] Federal debt includes both debt held by the public as well as debt held by government accounts, which is federal debt held by the federal government itself, or intragovernmental debt. Treasury issues two major types of debt securities to the public: marketable and nonmarketable securities. Marketable securities, which consist of Treasury bills, notes, bonds, and TIPS and can be resold by whoever owns them while nonmarketable securities, such as savings securities and special securities for state and local governments, cannot be resold. Intragovernmental debt is primarily held by trust funds, such as Social Security and Medicare. Most trust funds invest in special U.S. Treasury nonmarketable securities, with a small amount in marketable securities. For the purpose of analyzing the market for U.S. Treasuries, we primarily focus on marketable securities in this chapter.

[10] See GAO-09-932.

[11] Under the SFP, Treasury issued new securities and left the proceeds from the sale of these securities on deposit at the Federal Reserve, increasing its liabilities. For additional information see, Todd Keister and James J. McAndrews, "Why are Banks Holding So Many Excess Reserves?" Federal Reserve Bank of New York, *Current Issues in Economics and Finance*, vol. 15, no. 8 (December 2009).

[12] The debt limit is a legal ceiling on the amount of gross federal debt (excluding some minor adjustments), which must be raised periodically to accommodate additional federal borrowing.

[13] See GAO-06-269.

[14] One basis point is equal to 1/100th of 1 percent. Thus, 2.7 basis points is 0.027 percent. A similar analysis, which compared the auction yields of CMBs with the auction yields of similar maturity Treasury bills that were auctioned before and after the CMBs, found that the yield differential was also positive. During 2008 and 2009, the auction yield differential averaged 2.1 basis points. Our analysis only covers half of 2008 and all of 2009 due to availability of Treasury quote data from the *Wall Street Journal*.

[15] At its height in October 2008, the SFP reached a cash value of $559 billion, funded entirely with CMBs. In September 2009, Treasury announced that it anticipated that the balance in the SFP would decrease to $15 billion, as outstanding SFP bills mature and were not rolled over. In February 2010, Treasury announced that it would increase the balance of the SFP to $200 billion.

[16] See GAO, *The Federal Government's Long-Term Fiscal Outlook: January 2010 Update*, GAO-10-468SP (Washington, D.C.: March 2010). See http://www.gao.gov/special.pubs/longterm/.

[17] See Congressional Budget Office, *An Analysis of the President's Budgetary Proposals for Fiscal Year 2011* (Washington, D.C.: March 2010).

[18] A delivery failure occurs when one party fails to deliver Treasuries to another party by the date previously agreed by the parties.

[19] ODM is responsible for providing the Assistant Secretary for Financial Markets with advice and analysis on matters related to the Treasury's debt management policy, the issuance of Treasury and federal-related securities, and financial markets.

[20] "No basis to judge" responses have generally been excluded from our totals except in cases where large numbers of respondents gave this response.

[21] This figure is the total sector holdings derived from *Flow of Funds Accounts of the United States*, a statistical release compiled by the Federal Reserve. These figures differ from the reported holdings of our survey respondents reported in app. II. The figures in app. II represent only a subset of the sector.

[22] At the time of our survey, life insurance companies had Treasury holdings of $106.2 billion, property casualty insurance companies held $56.0 billion, and state and local government retirement funds held $177.7 billion.

[23] As of December 31, 2009, the five largest inflation-protected bond mutual funds (with their respective total net assets) were: Vanguard Inflation-Protected Securities Fund ($27.4 billion); PIMCO Real Return Fund ($16.8 billion); Barclays TIPS Bond Fund ($18.5 billion); American Century Inflation-Adjusted Bond Fund ($3.1 billion); and Fidelity Inflation-Protected Bond Fund ($2.2 billion).

[24] PIMCO introduced the Real Income Funds on September 8, 2009, and the Tax Managed Real Return Fund on November 9, 2009. The Real Income Funds are designed to provide retirees a steady stream of monthly income that is hedged against inflation, and the Tax Managed Real Return Fund is designed to provide tax-efficient income and a hedge against inflation.

[25] Interest income from municipal bonds is exempt from federal, and in some cases state, taxes.

[26] For additional information on TIPS, see GAO-09-932.

[27] For additional information on TIPS, see GAO-09-932.

[28] The first auction of the reintroduced 30-year TIPS was held on February 22, 2010, and the total issuance amount was $8 billion.

[29] For additional information on TIPS, see GAO-09-932.

[30] In 1997, after Treasury introduced TIPS, the Chicago Board of Trade developed a related futures product but ultimately terminated the contract due to a lack of trading and demand. In 2004, the Chicago Board of Trade introduced a CPI futures contract but again terminated the product for similar reasons.

[31] The Treasury Auction Results statement also defines a third category of competitive bidders in Treasury auctions. Indirect Bidders are defined as customers placing competitive bids through a direct submitter, including foreign and international monetary authorities placing bids through the FRBNY. Auction participants may also bid noncompetitively but will pay whatever price is paid by successful competitive bidders.

[32] TAAPSLink is no longer used as Treasury introduced its New Treasury Automated Auction Processing System (NTAAPS), now called TAAPS, in April 2008.

[33] The Investor Class categories listed in the Auction Allotment Data are: Federal Reserve System, Depository Institutions, Individuals, Dealers and Brokers, Pension and Retirement Funds and Insurance Companies, Investment Funds, Foreign and International, and Other. See http://www.ustreas.gov/offices/domestic-finance/debt-management/investor_class_auction.shtml (downloaded on Mar. 31, 2010).

[34] See GAO-09-932.

[35] This method was used in our previous report on cash management bills issued in 2006. See GAO, *Debt Management: Treasury Has Refined Its Use of Cash Management Bills but Should Explore Options That May Reduce Cost Further*, GAO-06-269 (Washington, D.C.: Mar. 30, 2006).

[36] We used the following listings of organizations for each of the following sectors: (1) Mutual fund sector: Organizations were identified and selected based on a listing provided by the Investment Company Institute of the largest intermediate- and long-term government funds and inflation-protected funds in terms of total assets; (2) Commercial bank sector: Organizations were identified and selected based on a listing made available by the American Bankers Association of the largest bank and thrift holding companies in terms of total assets; (3) Property casualty insurance sector: Organizations were identified and selected based on a listing made available by the National Association of Insurance Commissioners of the largest property casualty insurance organizations in terms of total direct premiums; (4) Life insurance sector: Organizations were identified and selected based on a listing made available by the National Association of Insurance Commissioners of the largest life insurance organizations in terms of total direct premiums; and (5) State and local government retirement fund sector: Organizations were identified and selected based on a listing made available by the National Association of State Retirement Administrators of the largest funds in terms of total assets.

[37] This methodology was the same for the structured interviews mentioned above, except that for the structured interviews we selected and interviewed the two largest organizations in each sector.

In: The U.S. National Debt: Background, Issues, Significance ISBN: 978-1-61761-767-6
Editor: Charlotte G. Wilson and Emily O. Brown

Chapter 8

THE NATIONAL DEBT: WHO BEARS ITS BURDEN?

Marc Labonte

SUMMARY

The United States has been free of a national debt for only two years, 1834 and 1835. In its first year, 1790, the country faced a debt of $75 million. From FY1998 to FY2001, the federal government ran budget surpluses. Since then, the budget has returned to deficit, and the debt had risen to $7.5 trillion by 2009. It rose to a high of 108.6% of gross domestic product (GDP) at the end of World War II; declined to a post-World War II low of 23.8% of GDP in 1974; and, then, rose to another high of 49.5% of GDP in 1993.

The national debt results from borrowing to finance budget deficits. Historically, the major cause of debt accumulation has been war. The United States has financed the extraordinary expenditures associated with war by borrowing rather than by raising taxes or printing money. This pattern was broken by the large budget deficits of the 1980s, the first half of the 1990s, and the period subsequent to 2001, which caused the national debt to rise substantially as a fraction of GDP.

Although economists have long recognized that a national debt imposes an inescapable burden on a nation, they have debated whether the burden is borne by the generation who contracts the debt or is shifted forward to future generations. There has also been some controversy over the nature of the burden.

The current consensus among economists is that the burden of the national debt is largely shifted forward to future generations. However, the burden imposed by the national debt does not arise from debt per se, but from budget deficits that gives rise to a national debt. If an economy is fully employed and the government increases its expenditures, for example, the resultant increase in aggregate demand will cause interest rates to rise and this will reduce or "crowd out" interest-sensitive spending by the private sector. This type of spending is likely to be for capital purposes (e.g., business spending for plant and equipment and household spending for housing and durable goods including automobiles). As a result, the private capital stock inherited by future generations is likely to be smaller and their real income or output will likely be lower. It is the reduction in future output that constitutes the burden of the national debt and it is a burden borne largely by future generations. It is a burden that cannot be decreased by borrowing abroad even though foreign borrowing could leave unchanged the size of the private capital stock.

Crucial to the consensus view (and other views) is the assumption that the economy is fully employed. And the burden discussed must be regarded as a gross burden in the sense that certain intangible gains must be set against it such as freedom from tyranny and domination by a foreign power that might have occurred had the United States lost such a contest as World War II.

BACKGROUND

The United States, from its beginning in 1790 to the present, has been free of a national debt for only two years, 1834 and 1835.[1] The national debt has grown from $75.5 million in 1790 to $5.8 trillion in 2008. The history of the U.S. national debt as a percent of gross domestic product (GDP) since 1940 is shown in **Figure 1**.[2] The national debt reached a high of 108.6% of GDP in 1946. It then began a long decline, reaching a low of 32.5% in 1981. The large budget deficits of the 1980s and 1990s reversed this trend and pushed the percentage to another high of 49.5% in 1993. The federal budget surpluses from FY1998 to FY2001 were used to retire a portion of the publicly held national debt. Between FY1997 and FY2001, the publicly held portion of the debt declined by more than $400 billion. Since FY2002, a return to budget deficits has caused the debt to grow again.

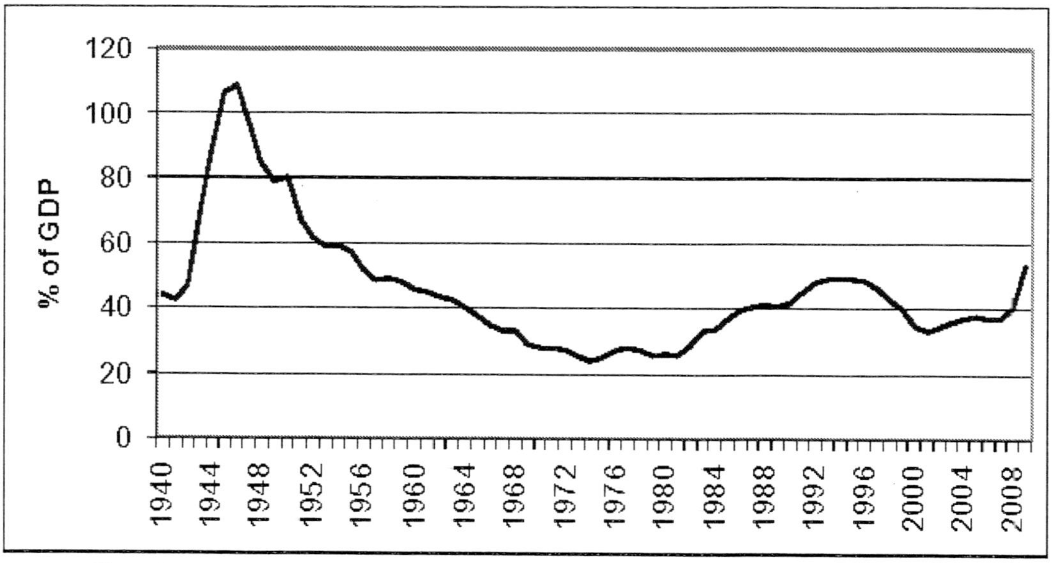

Source: Office of Management and Budget.

Figure 1. Federal Debt as a % of GDP, 1940-2009

When evaluating the burden of the national debt, the gross debt must first be divided into two parts: debt held by the public (including the Federal Reserve), shown in **Figure 1**, and the amount held in accounts called federal trust funds, the principal one being for social security.[3] Because trust fund debt is owed to one part of the government to another, it has no effect on the economy, and does not impose any burden.[4] Thus, it will be neglected in the discussion below. The publicly held debt is often subdivided into that portion that is domestically owned and that portion owned by foreigners. U.S. Treasury securities have become increasingly popular among foreigners. At the end of FY2009, more than half of the privately held federal debt (which excludes debt held in government trust funds and by the Federal Reserve) was owned by foreigners.

The need to finance wars has been the major reason for the growth of a national debt. In common with other major countries, the United States has rarely financed the surge in wartime expenditures exclusively by raising taxes. A large part of wartime expenditures have been bond financed. During the Civil War, from mid-1861 to mid-1865, the national debt grew from about $65 million to $2.7 billion. Between mid-1916 and mid-1919, the increased debt associated with World War I, grew from $1.2 billion to $25.5 billion. And from mid-1941 to mid-1946, the debt associated with World War II, rose from $49 billion to $269 billion. Thus, it has been a common practice of American public finance to increase the national debt during wartime and then reduce the debt, at least as a percentage of GDP, during times of peace. This pattern was broken during the 1980s and early 1990s when the national debt grew both absolutely and relative to GDP. Recently debt has again grown in wartime; however, the recent increase in the debt has greatly exceeded the cost of the war. Growth of the national debt has also occurred during periods of economic contraction.

THE TRADITIONAL VIEW OF THE BURDEN OF A NATIONAL DEBT

Is a national debt a burden on a country? If it is, what is the nature of the burden? Who bears this burden? Questions such as these have perplexed economists at least since the days of Adam Smith. Great Britain in his day had accumulated a large national debt fighting the Seven Years War (the French and Indian War) and was about to add a further considerable sum suppressing the rebellion in its American colonies.

Interestingly, mainstream macroeconomics views the burden of a national debt, not in terms of the debt per se, but in terms of government budget deficits that are the cause of the debt and its growth. Thus, the burden that a national debt imposes on a country is due to the government's budget deficits.[5]

To see clearly the nature of this burden and who bears it, assume that the country's resources are fully employed and that capital (or saving) cannot flow internationally between countries. Also assume that this country now engages in a war with a neighbor and that the increased expenditures associated with the war lead to a budget deficit that is financed by issuing bonds.

The increase in government expenditures increases aggregate demand. In a fully employed economy, in addition to raising prices, the increase in demand will lead to a rise in interest rates.[6] The increase in interest rates is the means by which the government obtains the additional resources to fight the war for the increase will discourage interest-sensitive spending by the private sector. This is primarily business spending for capital goods such as plant, equipment, and structures and spending by households for homes, automobiles, appliances and the like. Thus, the budget deficit "crowds out" private capital and the burden of the growing national debt represented by the bonds issued to finance the war, is the decrease in the private capital stock of the country. The level of output is determined by the capital stock, labor force, and productivity levels. Since the private capital stock inherited by future generations will be smaller, it implies that the level of output enjoyed by them will be lower.[7] The lower level of output is thus the ultimate burden of the debt and it is a burden that is largely shifted forwarded to future generations.[8]

Suppose Capital Can Flow Internationally

It might be thought that a high degree of international capital mobility could moderate the burden of the debt because foreign saving could supplement domestic resources such that the private capital stock need not diminish. Suppose, for example, that as interest rates tended to rise in response to the increased expenditures, foreign capital (or foreign saving) was attracted in sufficient volume to keep domestic interest rates from rising.[9] This would keep the domestic capital stock unchanged. Would this mean that there was no burden from a national debt? Unfortunately, this is not the case. Although it is true that the private capital stock inherited by future generations will remain unchanged, a portion of it will now be owned by foreigners. And the rewards from that capital will not flow to Americans, but will have to be transferred abroad.

Thus, having foreigners supply some or all of the resources for the war effort, as in this example, does not avoid the burden of the debt. Future generations will still have a lower level of income available to them.

Would Financing the Deficit by Issuing Money Eliminate the Burden?

In the preceding discussion, the budget deficit was financed by issuing interest-bearing debt or bonds. The government, however, has available another means for financing its budget deficit. Rather than borrowing the wherewithal it could simply print money (currency) and pay its bills.[10] Might not this method of finance reduce or eliminate the burden the national debt places on future generations? Although the simple answer is basically yes, the explanation is more complicated.

Financing a budget deficit in a fully employed economy by issuing money is inflationary. And inflation is a form of taxation. It is tax on the existing stock of money held by the public in the sense that it reduces the purchasing power of that money. It is by reducing the wealth and purchasing power of the private sector that inflation enables the government to obtain the additional resources to finance the war. Inflation (taxation) thus crowds out private spending, some of which may be spending on capital goods. The majority of that spending, however, is likely to be on current consumption. Because it is, the burden of these additional government expenditures, used in the example above, are almost exclusively borne by the current generation. The private capital stock inherited by future generations is unlikely to be diminished and, hence, they will not suffer much of a decrease in their standard of living. Thus, financing a budget deficit by substituting non-interest-bearing debt (money) for interest-bearing debt (bonds) does not eliminate the burden of the debt; it largely shifts the main burden from future generations to the present generation.[11]

Do All Budget Deficits That Increase the National Debt Impose a Burden?

The preceding analysis is framed in terms of a fully employed economy that experiences an increase in aggregate demand due to an increase in government expenditures. This increase in demand requires an increase in real interest rates to decrease or crowd out private sector spending. Yet there are circumstances under which a government budget deficit can arise or increase with little or no crowding out.

Suppose, for example, that the United States economy is, as it is now, in a recession and either expenditures are increased or taxes cut in an effort to "jump start" an expansion. It is possible in these circumstances for a budget deficit to grow without increasing interest rates. The reason being that the increase in income generated by the increase in demand generates additional saving for financing the deficit. The additional resources represented by the saving make it possible to maintain an undiminished private capital stock in the face of a rising budget deficit.[12] Thus, debt issued during a recession imposes a smaller burden than an equivalent amount issued during an economic expansion; if the recession is serious enough the burden is negligible.[13]

The Role of Interest Payments in the Traditional View

The accumulation of a national debt means that the government budget will contain as an expenditure item the interest payable on that debt. Does this impose a burden on future generations whose taxes will be used for debt service? In the traditional view, the answer depends on whether the debt is internally or externally held. For an internally held debt, the payment of interest is an income transfer from taxpayer to bond holder. In the simple case, if they are the same person, they are left neither poorer nor richer. If they are not the same person, then while the taxpayer is left with less income, the bond owner has a larger income. As a group, however, they are neither richer nor poorer by the payment of interest. The payment of interest is not an additional burden of an internally held debt. That burden, as noted above, is the lower level of output (income) enjoyed by future generations who inherit a reduced private capital stock.

When the national debt is externally held, the payment of interest abroad is a transfer of income from Americans to foreigners. This is not a separate burden from the national debt, however. As noted above, when a national debt is sold abroad, the private capital stock passed on to future generations need not be diminished. But a portion of that capital stock will be foreign owned and a portion of the income generated by that capital will accrue to foreigners. This is the interest or, more properly, debt service paid to them, and it reduces the level of income that accrues to Americans. Thus, the payment of interest to foreigners is how the burden of an externally held national debt is shifted forward to future generations of Americans.

A National Debt and National Interest Rates

It might be thought that a large national debt would have an effect on market interest rates since if the debt is short term, the government must be in financial markets more or less continuously as the debt rolls over frequently. Such is not the case. The rate of interest that prevails in a country over time is determined by saving and investment and these are what economists call flows. The national debt is what they call a stock. And it is the flows that govern the real rate of interest. The refinancing of the national debt when the budget is balanced should not alter the flows. Essentially, refinancing involves replacing maturing securities with ones that come due in the future. Since this makes no new net claim on the nation's saving, it should have no effect on interest rates. If this were not the case, we should observe real national interest rates fluctuating with the size of a nation's national debt. This pattern is not to be found consistently in the data.

There are historical examples in which countries have had difficulties in rolling over their maturing interest-bearing debts. Often these episodes have been attributed to a lack of confidence in the governments in question. When these episodes have occurred, they have often resulted in the monetization of the maturing debt with the result being serious inflation and rising market interest rates as the market rates come to embody expectations of inflation. Thus, a very large debt could increase interest rates by threatening the government's solvency. The U.S. debt is not near this point.

The Retirement of the National Debt

The budget surpluses from FY1998 through FY2001 were used to retire the national debt. By the end of 2001, debt held by the public was some $400 billion below its 1997 peak. What are the effects of debt retirement on the U.S. economy?

In the traditional model, the effect on the economy from retiring an internally held debt is just the reverse of what would happen if the national debt were increased. The budget surpluses augment the national pool of saving, a pool contributed to by the business and household sectors. An increase in the fraction of GDP that is saved leads to lower interest rates. This encourages (or "crowds in") interest-sensitive spending. From the previous discussion, this is business and household spending on capital goods. Thus, the budget surpluses increase the capital stock of the country and, over time, this raises the level of real income and the material well-being of Americans. This, then, is the benefit that comes from reducing the national debt. It is a benefit that comes from budget surpluses and it largely benefits future generations.

In a broader framework in which the U.S. economy is linked to foreign economies through trade and capital flows, the interaction of budget surpluses, retirement of the national debt, and its effect on the U.S. economy, is more complex. Retiring debt that is foreign owned relieves the United States from having to pay interest to foreigners. This raises the fraction of U.S. GDP that is available to Americans and this benefits the current generation as well as those alive in the future. In addition, since the higher saving rate leads to lower interest rates in the United States, some of that additional saving is likely to flow abroad augmenting the capital stock of foreign countries. This, in turn, increases the claims of Americans on foreign output (or decreases the net claim foreigners have on U.S. output) thereby enhancing their material well-being about the same as would have occurred if those resources had been used to augment the domestic capital stock.[14]

Does Implicit Debt Impose the Same Burden?

So far, this chapter has focused on *explicit* national debt, the issuance of U.S. Treasuries to the public. But the recent work of economists in the area of generational accounting has resulted in a better appreciation of the equivalence between explicit and *implicit* national debt. These economists argue that categories of government activity such as "expenditures," "revenues," and "deficits" are economically arbitrary. Instead, the focus should be on the economic incidence of any government policy over time, regardless of its label. They argue that today's explicit budget deficit is paltry compared with the large budget deficits that will accrue in the distant future as implied by current policy. And these implicit deficits currently impose the same burden on future generations as if they were made explicit today through the issuance of U.S. Treasuries.

This can be illustrated by examining the Social Security system. The retirement of the baby boomers means that the current "pay as you go" system will become insolvent in the future under current policy—benefits promised will greatly exceed payroll tax revenues. If it is assumed that all legally promised benefits will be met in the future, then large payroll tax increases will be necessary. Thus, future generations would be forced to consume fewer goods and services because a larger part of their income would be taxed and transferred to Social Security recipients.[15]

Taxing working generations in the future to pay unfunded retirement benefits is not the only way to deal with this problem. There is an alternative that imposes the same burden on future working generations. Imagine that the present discounted value of those future unfunded social security benefits were included as an outlay in this year's budget. Each baby boomer would be given a one-time payment today in lieu of their future unfunded benefits. This added expenditure would increase the size of the present budget deficit, reduce the national saving rate, and would be financed by issuing additional Treasury securities. This would increase interest rates, lower private capital spending, and reduce the size of the economy in the future. As a result, the pre-tax income of future generations would be smaller, but because they would not have to pay higher taxes to fund the additional social security benefits, their after tax income at that time would be the same as it would be in the situation above where the future unfunded benefits were paid for with higher taxes. Thus, an implicit debt imposes the same burden on future generations as an explicit debt because the two concepts are economically equivalent.

CONCLUSION

The current consensus view among economists is that the source of the burden associated with a national debt is the government budget deficit that gives rise to the debt. In a fully employed economy, the deficit "crowds out" private sector spending, especially spending on capital goods. Thus, a smaller private capital stock and a lower level of output are passed along to future generations and it is this lower level of output that is the ultimate burden of the national debt. And, it is a burden that is largely shifted forwarded to future generations. Thus, according to the consensus view, the burden of a national debt is borne by future generations.

Should the debt be sold abroad, there is still a burden since a portion of the output from the unchanged size of the private capital stock will accrue to foreigners.

When the national debt is retired through budget surpluses, the effect on the economy is the reverse of debt increases. Future generations acquire a larger capital stock (or a larger American owned capital stock) and a higher level of output (or increased material well-being).

APPENDIX A. STATISTICAL DATA

Table A-1. Federal Outlays, Receipts and Deficits/SurplusesFY1982-FY2009

Fiscal Year	Outlays		Receipts		Deficit or Surplus	
	$ Billions	% of GDP	$ Billions	% of GDP	$ Billions	% of GDP
2009	3,517.7	24.7	2,105.0	14.8	-1412.7	-9.9
2008	2,982.6	20.7	2,524.0	17.5	-458.6	-3.2
2007	2,728.7	19.6	2,568.0	18.5	-160.7	-1.2
2006	2,655.1	20.1	2,406.9	18.2	-248.2	-1.9
2005	2,472.0	19.9	2,153.6	17.3	-318.3	-2.6
2004	2,292.9	19.6	1,880.1	16.1	-412.7	-3.5
2003	2,159.9	19.7	1,782.3	16.2	-377.6	-3.4
2002	2,010.9	19.1	1,853.1	17.6	-157.8	-1.5
2001	1,862.9	18.2	1,991.1	19.5	128.2	1.3
2000	1,789.0	18.2	2,025.2	20.6	236.2	2.4
1999	1,701.8	18.5	1,827.5	19.8	125.6	1.4
1998	1,652.5	19.1	1,721.7	19.9	69.3	0.8
1997	1,601.1	19.5	1,579.2	19.2	-21.9	-0.3
1996	1,560.5	20.2	1,453.1	18.8	-107.4	-1.4
1995	1,515.8	20.6	1,351.8	18.4	-164.0	-2.2
1994	1,461.8	21.0	1,258.6	18.0	-203.2	-2.9
1993	1,409.4	21.4	1,154.3	17.5	-255.1	-3.9
1992	1,381.5	22.1	1,091.2	17.5	-290.3	-4.7
1991	1,324.2	22.3	1,055.0	17.8	-269.2	-4.5
1990	1,253.0	21.9	1,032.0	18.0	-221.0	-3.9
1989	1,143.7	21.2	991.1	18.4	-152.6	-2.8
1988	1,064.4	21.3	909.2	18.2	-155.2	-3.1
1987	1,004.0	21.6	854.3	18.4	-149.7	-3.2
1986	990.4	22.5	769.2	17.5	-221.2	-5.0
1985	946.3	22.8	734.0	17.7	-212.3	-5.1
1984	851.8	22.2	666.4	17.3	-185.4	-4.8
1983	808.4	23.5	600.6	17.5	-207.8	-6.0
1982	745.7	23.1	617.8	19.2	-128.0	-4.0

Sources: Office of Management and Budget, *Historical Tables. Fiscal Year 2011*, Washington, February 2010, table 1.3.

Table A-2. Federal Debt and Interest OutlaysFY1982-FY2009

Year	Debt Held by the Public		Interest Outlays		
	$ Billions	% of GDP	$ Billions	% of Budget Outlays	% of GDP
2009	7,544.7	53.0	186.9	5.3	1.3
2008	5,803.0	40.2	252.8	8.5	1.7
2007	5,035.0	36.2	237.1	8.7	1.7
2006	4,829.0	36.5	226.6	8.5	1.7
2005	4,592.3	36.9	184.0	7.4	1.5
2004	4,295.5	36.8	160.2	7.9	1.4
2003	3,913.4	35.6	153.1	7.1	1.4
2002	3,540.4	33.6	170.9	8.5	1.6
2001	3,319.6	32.5	206.2	11.1	2.0
2000	3,409.8	34.7	223.0	12.5	2.3
1999	3,632.4	39.4	229.8	13.5	2.5
1998	3,721.1	43.0	241.1	14.6	2.8
1997	3,772.3	45.9	244.0	15.2	3.0
1996	3,734.1	48.4	241.1	15.4	3.1
1995	3,604.4	49.1	232.1	15.3	3.2
1994	3,433.1	49.2	202.9	13.9	2.9
1993	3,248.4	49.3	198.7	14.1	3.0
1992	2,999.7	48.1	199.3	14.4	3.2
1991	2,689.0	45.3	194.4	14.7	3.3
1990	2,411.6	42.1	184.3	14.7	3.2
1989	2,190.7	40.6	169.0	14.8	3.1
1988	2,051.6	41.0	151.8	14.3	3.0
1987	1,889.8	40.6	138.6	13.8	3.0
1986	1,740.6	39.5	136.0	13.7	3.1
1985	1,507.3	36.4	129.5	13.7	3.1
1984	1,307.0	34.0	111.1	13.0	2.9
1983	1,137.3	33.1	89.8	11.1	2.6
1982	924.6	28.7	85.0	11.4	2.6

Scurces:Office of Management and Budget, *Historical Tables, Fiscal Year 2011*, Washington, February 2010, table 7.1 and table 3.1.

APPENDIX B. SELECTIVEVIEWS ON THE BURDEN OF A NATIONAL DEBT

Although economists have long recognized that a national debt imposes an inescapable burden on a nation, they have argued about who bears this burden.[16] In particular, whether the burden is borne by the generation that incurred the debt or whether it is shifted forward to a future generation or, in the language of the time, whether it is a "burden or mortgage on our children." This issue acquired new urgency when the view (since discarded) took hold in the economics profession that mature market economies might be incapable of generating sustained periods of more or less full employment without a continuous government budgetdeficit. If this were the case, the national debt could be expected to grow continuously. And if that debt were a burden on future generations, it would mean that the present generation would enjoy employment only by shifting a burden to future generations.

This appendix provides a flavor of the various arguments advanced by economists about the burden of the public debt, the nature of that burden, and who bears that burden. The arguments summarized in this appendix are all concerned with an internally held debt. It is recognized that an externally held debt must be treated differently.

The "We Owe It to Ourselves" View

As a result of the concern over whether the enjoyment of full employment by the current generation would shift a burden to the future, it became an accepted view during the 1930s, 40s, and 50s, that an *internally held* national debt would impose a burden only on the generation present when it was contracted and would impose no burden on future generations because we "owe the debt to ourselves." The words of Paul Samuelson best express the view that the current generation bears the burden of deficit finance. Drawing on wartime experience, he wrote: "*To fight a war now, we must hurl present-day munitions at the enemy; not dollar bills, and not future goods and services.*" Thus, the alternative use of these resources in the private sector constituted the burden of the national debt and it was a burden borne by the generation that, in this case, fought the war.

That subsequent debt service imposed no burden on future generations can be clearly seen in the simple case where the owners of government bonds, the evidence of the national debt, were also taxpayers. Servicing the government debt would mean taking money from one pocket and putting it into the other. In other words, this is a mere income transfer. It is not a burden. Since future generations would inherit both the bonds and the tax liabilities needed to service the bonds, no burden would be shifted to the future. In a more complex case in which the bond owners and taxpayers were not the same people, the existence of a national debt would imply some income redistribution from the latter to the former. However, this would not be a burden for the society as a whole because there would be no loss of resources for the group as a whole to use.[17] Thus, the burden of an internally held debt, according to this view, is borne by the generation alive when the debt is contracted. And the burden consists of the alternative private sector uses of the resources that are withdrawn for use by the public sector.[18]

Should the national debt be owned by foreigners, this view argued that it would constitute a burden primarily on future generations. The current generation, by borrowing resources from abroad, would have more goods and services to consume than it produced. It thereby gains by incurring a foreign debt. To service this debt a portion of future national output would have to be transferred abroad thereby reducing the income of future generations who, the argument states, would have fewer goods and services to use than it produced. Thus, in the case of an external debt, we would not "owe it to ourselves" but to foreigners. And this was the important distinction as far as who bears the burden was concerned.

The Buchanan View

Prof. James Buchanan, a Nobel Prize winner in the 1980s, attacked the then orthodox view of burden of the debt in his popular text book on public finance first published in 1958.[19] Buchanan's argument is that the burden of an internally held national debt is shifted forwarded to future generations. It is not borne by the generation who contracted the debt. His argument is that when individuals buy government interest-bearing debt, they are making a voluntary decision to give up the current use of resources for a larger future income (larger by the amount of interest they receive on their now larger asset holdings). Since this is a voluntary decision, no burden is imposed on the purchaser (i.e., the generation present when the debt is contracted). In fact, since the purchase would not have been made had a superior alternative been available, the purchaser is actually better off than had an alternative use been made of that income. However, subsequent generations of taxpayers must surrender to the bond holders the wherewithal for debt service. And this necessity is forced on them. In this sense, it is the future generations who will bear the burden of an internally held debt and the burden is the taxes they must pay for debt service. This is not a voluntary decision, but one forced on them by the decisions of an earlier generation. Although Buchanan's view was subject to criticism by some economists, he was soon to get major support from others.[20]

The Bowen, Davis, and Kopf View

Acknowledging that Buchanan's view had stimulated their collective thinking, Professors Bowen, Davis, and Kopf (hereafter BDK) came up with an argument for why an internally held debt imposes a burden on future generations.[21] BDK define burden in terms of the lifetime consumption of a generation (as opposed to the resources that must be given up now to, let us say, fight a war). The generation whose lifetime consumption is reduced is, according to BDK, the generation burdened by a national debt. With this in mind, they argue that the generation that contracts the national debt need not be burdened by it so long as it does not pay the debt off. This is so, because while that generation must decrease its consumption to buy the debt (even if they are forced to do so), it can always sell it to the next generation before its members die and enjoy the added consumption it had to forego when it purchased the debt. This process can go on indefinitely until the debt is retired.[22] The generation that retires the debt, however, has no additional consumption to offset the consumption it gave up when it purchased the debt from the generation before it. Thus, BDK share in common with Buchanan a belief that the national debt is a "burden on our children." It is they who must ultimately retire the debt and, with retirement, undergo a permanent reduction in their consumption.[23]

The Barro View

The most recent, innovative, and serious challenge to the conventional view of the burden of a national debt comes from Prof. Robert Barro.[24] As noted in the body of this chapter, crowding out would not occur and the burden would not be shifted forward to future generations if the current generation would only save an additional amount of resources to match the increased demand for resources represented by the additional government expenditures that are financed by issuing interest-bearing debt. Barro has an ingenious argument for why such behavior could be forthcoming. Suppose, he says, that individuals live forever and that they have as a goal the maximization of consumption over time. To attain this goal, they have to be concerned about the private capital stock for it is an important determinate of income and income governs consumption. As in the standard macroeconomic model, the saving behavior of the publicgoverns the resources available for capital goods purposes. How much of their income they save, and, hence, private investment, will depend on how they value current as opposed to future consumption.

If individuals live forever, Barro argues, they will be indifferent between the government using taxes or the sale of bonds to finance, let us say, additional expenditures related to war. If the additional expenditures are financed through an additional tax, the public, in an effort to keep the private capital stock (the key to its goal of maximizing consumption) unchanged, will reduce current consumption by the amount of the tax. As a result, the burden of the war-related expenditures will be felt when they are incurred.[25]

Alternatively, the government could have chosen to finance the additional expenditures through the sale of bonds or interest-bearing debt. Had this option been chosen, the public would have behaved in the same way. In order to keep the private capital stock at the optimum level over time, it would have to reduce its consumption and save a higher fraction of its income. This additional saving would then be used to buy the bonds and provide the resources to the government for the war.

It might be thought that the necessity to pay interest on the bonds over time (and, perhaps, provide for their redemption) would, by requiring additional taxes, shift a burden forward. This is not the case, for the taxpayer and the bondholder are the same people. Money is simply taken from one pocket as taxes and put back into the other pocket as interest. This is no additional burden. To the extent that the taxpayer and bondholder are different people, some income redistribution could be expected. Thus, if individuals live forever, they would be indifferent between financing these added expenditures through a tax increase or the sale of bonds.[26] And, the burden of the debt is felt in terms of reduced consumption. It is a burden borne at the time the additional expenditures are made.

Barro must deal with the fact that individuals do not live forever. To address this problem, he asks: are there circumstances under which they would behave as if they had eternal life? He argues that this behavior would be forthcoming if individuals treat the well being of their children on a par with their own. Since their children would behave similarly, and so on, individuals in the current generation would behave as if they lived forever. If individuals behaved in the way Barro argues, the conventional argument about the burden of a national debt, is likely to be wrong. Debt financed government expenditures will not crowd out the private capital stock because it will be offset by an equal amount of private sector saving.[27] This behavior is designed to ensure that future generations do not inherit a smaller private capital stock and, hence, a lower level of output and suboptimal consumption. Thus, the burden of the national debt is not shifted to them as the convention view argues.[28]

The attack on Barro's view has been both theoretical and empirical. On the theoretical side, it is argued that individuals for a number of reasons may be reluctant to equate the well-being of their children on a par with their own (this presumes that the individuals under scrutiny have children).[29] On the empirical side, the saving behavior of the private sector does not correlated well with the saving/dis-saving behavior of the public sector. The Barro view implies that this behavior should be highly correlated: on a one-to-one basis. Only in this way is the private capital stock passed on to future generations rendered immune to the public finances of government.

Appendix B. Conclusion

This appendix has provided a flavor of the various arguments advanced by economists about the burden of the public debt, the nature of the burden, and who bears that burden. It has basically been a debate about who bears the burden. According to the various views, the burden, depending on how it is defined, can be borne by the generation that contracted the debt or shifted forward to future generations. The arguments summarized in this appendix are all concerned with an internally held debt. It is recognized that an externally held debt must be treated differently.

End Notes

[1] In 1834 the national debt was $37,733 and in 1835 it was $37,513. It is generally believed that the bonds represented by these sums were lost, misplaced, or destroyed and, thus, would never be presented for payment.

[2] Official data on U.S. GDP are available subsequent to 1929. Finding a consistent series on the national debt prior to 1940 is difficult because the treatment of U.S. Agency debt is not consistent across time. When a somewhat comparable series for gross debt for the period 1929-1939 is used, it is shown to rise from 16.6% of GDP in 1930 to 44.3% in 1934. It then remains in the low 40% range until 1938, rising to 45.5% in 1939. However, the rise from 1930 to 1934 is due mainly to the decline in GDP during the Great Depression. During the period 1934-1938, the national debt grew at about the same rate as GDP.

[3] Traditionally, the national debt of a country has consisted only of its interest-bearing debt. Non-interest-bearing debt or currency, even though a *technical* liability of the government, has been excluded from national debt calculations.

[4] Because of various accounting conventions and practices used by the federal government, it is possible for the gross debt of the United States to rise even as the publicly held portion declines. And, indeed, this occurred from FY1998 to FY2001.

[5] The literature on the burden of a national debt is extensive. It is selectively reviewed in **Appendix B**.

[6] The mechanism by which this occurs is presented in the literature in several ways. Often is it said that the increase in government expenditures and the resultant rise in the budget deficit reduces national saving. The reduction in national saving then causes interest rates to rise to allocate the reduced flow of saving over private investment. Alternatively, the rise in real (or inflation adjusted) interest rates occurs because the government must float additional bonds to cover the deficit. And it is this increased demand for funds in financial markets which raises interest rates. Finally, the increase in real interest rates is said to come from an increased demand for money as income increases in response to the rise in aggregate demand. This increase in money demand, in the presence of a fixed money supply, causes interest rates, the price of money, to rise to restore equilibrium between demand and supply.

[7] If additional resources were made available through additional saving by the public, the increase in government expenditures would not raise real interest rates and crowd out private investment. (This is identified as the Barro view in **Appendix B**.) This would not, however, eliminate the burden of the debt. It would merely shift it forward to the present generation. The consumption of this generation would be reduced by the additional saving.

[8] Some of the burden will be borne by the current generation (or generation present when the debt is contracted) for they will share part of the lower output over their remaining life as well. Of course, this burden must be regarded as a gross burden. Some budget deficits are incurred to increase the stock of social capital such as highways, power grids, water supplies, etc. This capital may perform a very useful and complementary role relative to private capital in increasing output. In addition, offset against the burden of other types of spending may be a large immeasurable gain enjoyed by future generations such as freedom from tyranny and domination by another country.

[9] It should be recalled that foreign capital or saving comes to a country in the form of a trade deficit. It is the trade deficit or excess of imports over exports, that allows a country to use more goods and services than it produces. It is this excess that makes it possible, in this example, to use resources for war and, at the same time, keep the capital stock from falling.

[10] This was the principal means used by the Continental Congress to finance the American Revolution. The Confederacy used this means heavily in the American Civil War. It was used to a lesser degree by the Union government.

[11] Another way of expressing what is occurring is to say that as inflation erodes the real value of the public's money holdings, it must refrain from using income for consumption in an effort to restore it's real money balances. This reduced level of consumption is then the burden of the debt and it is a burden borne by the current generation.

[12] Similarly, a budget deficit that rises as an economy goes into a downturn is unlikely to "crowd out" private investment since it will not force up interest rates. The most that can be said is that the deficit may keep interest rates from falling as much as they would otherwise. In that sense, the deficit reduces the hypothetical capital stock available to future generations.

[13] This part of the traditional view on debt burden seems to be incomplete or based on the implicit assumption that a national debt accumulated in periods when the economy is operating at less than full employment is retired during periods when the economy is operating at full employment. If this is not the case, and the country faces a budget deficit even at full employment, the prospect arises of an ever-growing national debt. A case can be made that should the debt continue to rise relative to GDP the fiscal regime may be unsustainable over the longer run.

[14] It was noted above that in the traditional view, the interest paid on an internally held debt is regarded as an income transfer and not as a burden. When an internally held debt is retired, the interest expenses of the government fall. If the taxes used to pay these expanses are not reduced through a tax cut, but are used instead to purchase goods and services, it increases the size of the government. Thus, a case can be made that some of the decline in the interest expenses in the federal budget from debt retirement should be matched by a tax cut. This argument does not apply to the portion of the interest expenses that are used to service the foreign held component of the national debt.

[15] Returning Social Security to solvency through benefit cuts would create an equivalent burden. Since retirees would receive lower benefits, they would be able to purchase fewer goods and services. Assuming taxes were raised or benefits were cut at the same date, the generational incidence of this burden would be slightly different, however. The burden of higher taxes would be felt by workers from that date forward, while the burden of lower benefits would be felt by retirees from that date forward. Thus, an older generation (retirees at that date) would share in the burden of a benefit cut.

[16] For a more comprehensive review of the burden of a national debt, see *Public Debt & Future Generations*, edited by James M. Ferguson (Chapel Hill: The University of North Carolina Press, 1964) and Randall Holcombe, John D. Jackson, and AsgharZardkoohi, "The National Debt Controversy," *Kyklos*, 34 (1981), pp. 186-202

[17] Notice that this argument neglects the fact that the budget deficit that gave rise to the debt could have crowded out private investment thereby reducing the capital stock inherited by future generations and the lower level of income that this reduction implies. It may well be that this view was substantially influenced by economic conditions during the depressed 1930s when budget deficits were unlikely to have crowded out private investment. It should also be noted that this and other arguments about the burden of a national debt abstracted from the possibility that the taxes to service the debt may have far reaching consequences for the incentives to work, save, invest, and take risks, all of which are important in market economies and that affect the long run level of output.

[18] This view of burden seems to imply that the resources withdrawn for use by the government comes at the expense of private sector consumption. For if private sector investment were curtailed, then some of the burden will be shifted to the future as suggested by the crowding out view discussed above. This view may also have been influenced by U.S. experience during World War II when a large part of crowding out did take the form of a decrease in private consumption. It should be noted that the above view of burden was formulated before economists had developed growth models. Once growth models were developed, they forced economists to think differently about debt burden.

[19] *Public Principles of Public Debt* (Homewood, IL: Richard D. Irwin, 1958).

[20] Prof. James Tobin was an important critic of Buchanan. He was concerned with Buchanan's view of burden. If a person voluntarily does something, it is no burden to that person, according to Buchanan. This suggests to Tobin that a person who voluntarily purchases a good on which an excise tax is levied incurs no tax burden. Yet, there is a whole literature in public finance on the "incidence and effects" of taxes that Buchanan's notion of burden seems to throws away. Perhaps, in reference to the national debt, it would be more appropriate and less troublesome to ask "who bears the incidence of the debt" rather than the burden of the debt.

[21] "The Public Debt: A Burden on Future Generations?" *American Economic Review*, 50 (September 1960), pp. 701-706 and "The Distribution of the Debt Burden: A Reply," *American Economic Review* 51 (March 1961), pp. 141-143.

[22] There is, however, the question of the time distribution of that consumption. Consumption is given up early in the life of the current generation to be recouped at a later period when the debt is sold to the next generation. But consumption at a later date is unlikely to be of equal value to the consumption given up when the bonds are purchased. Because it is not, individuals must be rewarded for postponing consumption until later. And this is the role of interest in the BDK model. It is the reward paid to bond holders for postponing current consumption until later. The present discounted value of those interest payments and the principal, should be equal in value to the consumption that could be enjoyed today if the bonds were not purchased. From that perspective, the lifetime consumption of the current generation is not reduced. However, paying interest involves having to pay taxes, and taxes reduce the lifetime ability of any generations to consume. Thus, on balance, debt financing reduces the net lifetime consumption of every generation which means that part of the burden of debt is spread across all generations including the generation present when the debt was contracted.

[23] BDK were careful to remind the reader that there is nothing inherently undesirable with debt financing of government. For example, if such government spending was for capital goods that benefitted future generations, a case could be made that they should be burdened by their cost (or a sort of pay-as-you-use system).

[24] "Are Government Bonds Net Wealth?" *Journal of Political Economy*, 82 (November-December 1974), pp. 405-14.

[25] If individuals do not live forever, and it will be shown later that this isn't crucial to Barro's argument, it could be said that the burden of the war expenditures were felt by the generation alive when they were incurred.

[26] This taxpayer indifference between bond or tax financed government expenditures has been attributed to a founder of modern political economy, David Ricardo. It has been shown that this so-called Ricardian Equivalence is not the true view of Ricardo. On the contrary, Ricardo argued that the taxpayers would not be indifferent, but would generally prefer to finance such expenditures by selling bonds rather than paying additional taxes.

[27] Technically speaking, the current generation need not save a precisely offsetting sum from current income. This is because the current generation can always leave a bequest to the next generation.

[28] Barro further argues that if the current generation wanted to ensure that their children inherited a smaller private capital stock, they have a simple means to do so: they could save a smaller portion of their disposable income. They don't need a government budget deficit for that purpose. Thus, in the presence of a budget deficit, they are, according to Barro, likely to offset it with a higher saving rate. The opposite is supposed to occur when it is faced with a budget surplus.

[29] For a more complete theoretical critique of Barro, see James Tobin, *Asset Accumulation and Economic Activity* Chapter III,(Chicago: University of Chicago Press, 1980), pp. 49-96.

In: The U.S. National Debt: Background, Issues, Significance ISBN: 978-1-61761-767-6
Editor: Charlotte G. Wilson and Emily O. Brown

Chapter 9

How Treasury Issues Debt

Mindy R. Levit

Summary

The U.S. Department of the Treasury (Treasury), among other roles, manages the country's debt. The primary objective of Treasury's debt management strategy is to finance the government's borrowing needs at the lowest cost over time. To accomplish this Treasury adheres to three principles: (1) to issue debt in a regular and predictable pattern, (2) to provide transparency in the decision-making process, and (3) to seek continuous improvements in the auction process.

Specifically, the Office of Debt Management (ODM) makes all decisions related to debt issuance and the management of the United States debt portfolio. When federal spending exceeds revenues, the ODM directs the Bureau of Public Debt (BPD) to borrow the funds needed to finance government operations by selling securities to the public and government agencies via an auction process. BPD manages the operational aspects of the issuance of Treasury securities, including the systems related to and the monitoring of the auction process.

During the mid-1970s, Treasury faced a period of rising nominal federal budget deficits and debt requiring unanticipated increases in issuances of securities. At that time, debt management was characterized by an ad-hoc, offering-by-offering survey of market participants. Due to the lack of transparency in such a process and the potential for market related volatility, a new strategy was implemented in order to provide greater transparency and regularity to the debt management process. The purpose of this new strategy was to modernize the Treasury securities market, to realize the benefits of predictability in an environment of large deficits, and to use this predictability to induce policymakers to alter the practices of the institutions they managed. Treasury auctions became a key part of the new strategy focusing on regular and predictable debt management.

Most of the debt sold by the federal government is marketable, meaning that the securities can be resold on the secondary market. Currently, Treasury offers four types of marketable securities: Treasury bills, notes, bonds, and inflation protected securities (TIPS), sold in over 250 auctions per year. A small portion of debt held by the public and nearly all intragovernmental debt (debt held by government trust funds) is nonmarketable.

Investors examine several key factors when deciding whether they should purchase Treasury securities, including price, expected return, and risk. Treasury securities provide a known stream of income and offer greater liquidity than other types of fixed-income securities. Because they are also backed by the full faith and credit of the United States, they are often seen as one of the safest investments available, though investors are not totally immune from losses. Prices are determined by investors who place a value on Treasury securities based on these characteristics.

Legislative activity can affect Treasury's ability to issue debt and can impact the budget process. Congress sets a statutory limit on federal debt levels in an effort to assert its constitutional prerogatives to control spending and impose a form of fiscal accountability. The statutory limit on the debt can constrain debt operations, which, in the past, has hampered traditional practices when the limit was approached. The accounting of asset purchases in the federal budget has created differences between how much debt Treasury has to borrow to make those purchases and how much the same purchases will impact the budget deficit. If budget deficits continue to rise, thereby causing more resources to be devoted to paying interest on the debt, there will be fewer funds available to spend on other federal programs, all else equal.

INTRODUCTION

The U.S. Department of the Treasury (Treasury) performs three main duties, which are key to the functioning of the United States government and economy. Treasury manages federal obligations by collecting tax revenue and issuing debt when necessary. It also disburses payments of government benefits to eligible recipients. Finally, Treasury acts as a centralized account holder for other federal agencies. As part of these functions, Treasury also advises the President on economic and financial issues, works to maintain stability in financial institutions, and sustains economic growth. It accomplishes these goals by working with other federal agencies and foreign institutions.[1]

The Treasury, among other roles, manages the country's debt. The primary objective of Treasury's debt management strategy is to finance the government's borrowing needs at the lowest cost over time. To accomplish this Treasury adheres to three principles: (1) to issue debt in a regular and predictable pattern, (2) to provide transparency in the decision-making process, and (3) to seek continuous improvements in the auction process.

Specifically, the Office of Debt Management (ODM) makes all decisions related to debt issuance and the management of the United States debt portfolio. When federal spending exceeds revenues, the ODM directs the Bureau of Public Debt (BPD) to borrow the funds needed to finance government operations by selling securities to the public and government agencies via an auction process. BPD manages the operational aspects of the issuance of Treasury securities, including the systems related to and the monitoring of the auction process.

Recent economic instability and concerns over the long-term fiscal outlook of the United States bring prominence to the role of the Department of the Treasury in financing the obligations of the country. In addition, long-term obligations resulting from the retirement of the Baby Boom generation and rising health care costs, in the absence of policy changes, will likely lead to an unsustainable rise in future federal debt. Given these longer term challenges, the ability to maintain efficient and stable debt markets to ensure confidence and liquidity will remain an issue going forward.

As the amount of money owed by the United States to holders of Treasury securities rises, interest payments can become a greater burden on taxpayers. If investors choose to purchase Treasury securities, less money is available to finance other types of investments such as those in the private sector. To the extent that these securities are held by foreign governments or individuals abroad, those investors will be the beneficiaries of the interest payments.

Understanding how Treasury issues debt illustrates how this agency works to provide financial security and minimize costs incurred by taxpayers during a time of rapid debt issuance as well as addressing future concerns going forward. This chapter examines Treasury's debt management practices, focusing on the auction process, how prices and interest rates of securities are determined, and the role of market participants in the process. It also addresses the impact of debt on the federal budget.

An Overview of Debt Management Practices

Congress holds the authority to issue debt on behalf of the United States through power granted in Article I, Section 8 of the Constitution. This power was delegated to the Secretary of the Treasury in 1789. However, Congress retains ultimate control over spending, via the budget and appropriations process, and revenue levels, via tax legislation. If spending exceeds revenues, Treasury determines what type of debt instruments will be used to finance the borrowing.

The primary objective of Treasury's debt management strategy is to finance the government's borrowing needs at the lowest cost over time. Beyond providing financing to the federal government, the success of Treasury's debt management strategy also affects the global economy due to the influential role of the United States around the world. Treasury adheres to three debt management principles: (1) to issue debt in a regular and predictable pattern, (2) to provide transparency in the decision-making process, and (3) to seek continuous improvements in the auction process.[2] Adherence to this strategy is important to help secure growth and efficiency in both the domestic and global capital markets.

Development of modern debt management dates to the passage of the Second Liberty Bond Act of 1917, as amended, which designated the Treasury Secretary as the principal authority to determine the types of issues, terms, and techniques most appropriate to manage public debt. Prior to this measure, interest rates and maturity periods of bonds were set by legislation and Congressional authority.[3] Further refinements in debt management policy came when Treasury established the Bureau of Public Debt within the Office of Fiscal Service in June 1940. In the late 1980s, ODM, formerly known as the Office of Market Finance, became the central office responsible for the decision making behind Treasury's borrowings. The Bureau of Public Debt now oversees the operational aspects of the borrowing process of the federal government, accounts for and services federal debt, and provides reimbursable support services to federal agencies under the authority of the Treasury Franchise Fund.[4] It also conducts auctions of Treasury securities to allow individuals, institutions, and financial professionals to invest in Treasury bills, notes, bonds and inflation-protected securities (TIPS).

The Federal Reserve (Fed) works alongside the Treasury in the debt management process acting as Treasury's fiscal agent. Created in 1913 to institute stability in the banking sector following a time of financial panic, the Fed's role was primarily to oversee the money supply and supervise the banks during a time when the need for borrowed funds increased as the United States sought ways to finance World War I expenses.[5] For the first several decades of its existence, the Fed worked closely with Treasury to implement fiscal policy goals. Since the early 1950s, however, the Fed has operated independently from Treasury and uses its open market operations to manage the amount of money and credit in the economy via monetary policy. The Fed also provides banking services to the federal government by maintaining deposit accounts for Treasury, paying U.S. government checks drawn on the Treasury, and issuing and redeeming savings bonds and other government securities.[6]

How Treasury Sells Debt

During the mid-1970s, the economy experienced a period of rising nominal federal budget deficits, which increased the level of debt issuance and resulted in market disruptions. At that time, Treasury decided that it needed to implement a new strategy in order to provide greater transparency and regularity in debt management.[7] The purposes of the new strategy were to modernize the Treasury securities market, to realize the benefits of predictability in an environment of relatively large budget deficits, and to use this predictability to induce policymakers to alter the practices of the institutions they managed.[8] As a result of the implementation of this regular and predictable schedule, Treasury was able to raise large amounts of money with a minimal impact on the financial markets. These policies also extended the average maturity of the national debt and produced a better defined yield curve.[9]

Auction Process

Auctions are the cornerstone of Treasury's regular and predictable debt management strategy.[10] Dates and offering amounts for each auction are scheduled and announced in advance. Bidders in Treasury auctions may be either foreign or domestic individual or institutional investors, or government entities at the federal, state, or local level. Treasury securities can be bought via a web-based account using the department's Treasury Direct system. Purchases of Treasury bills, notes, bonds, TIPS, and savings bonds can be made through this system.

The yield-to-maturity, interest coupon rate, and the discount or premium on a Treasury security are key terms in understanding the auction process. The yield-to-maturity is the rate of return anticipated on a security if it is held until the maturity date and is what is specified by a competitive bidder at the auction. The interest (or coupon) rate is set at the highest yield level, in increments of one-eighth of one percent, that does not result in a price greater than

100% of principal.[11] If the price of a Treasury security, as determined at auction, is less/greater than the face value of the security, then the security was purchased at a discount/premium.

Auction bids for Treasury securities may be submitted as noncompetitive or competitive. With a noncompetitive bid, a bidder agrees to accept the discount rate (or yield) determined at auction and is guaranteed to receive the full amount of the bid. With a competitive bid, a bidder specifies the yield that is acceptable.[12] A bid may be accepted in a full or partial amount if the rate specified is less than or equal to, respectively, the discount rate set by the auction.

Once the auction closes, all noncompetitive bids are accepted and competitive bids are ranked based on yield, from lowest to highest. Competitive bids are accepted, starting at the lowest yield, until the offering amount has been exhausted. The highest accepted yield becomes the "stop". A competitive bid will not be accepted if the rate specified in the bid is higher than the yield set at the auction. Though interest payments received by successful bidders may vary based on the yield specified in their auction bids, all securities in an auction are sold for a single price, computed based on the "stop" yield.[13]

Marketable Securities

Most of the debt sold by the federal government is marketable, meaning that securities are sold via the auction process and can be resold on the secondary market. Currently, Treasury offers four types of marketable securities, Treasury bills, notes, bonds, and inflation protected securities, sold in approximately 200 auctions per year.[14] If Treasury borrowing requirements or financing policy decisions change, the types of securities, the length of maturity periods, and offering amounts could be altered.

Treasury Bills

Treasury bills (T-bills) are short-term securities that mature in one year or less. T-bills are sold at a discount from their face value. The interest rate determines the discount from face value and the price paid at auction. When the bill reaches maturity, the investor receives the face value. T-bills are currently being offered with maturities of 4, 13, 26, and 52-weeks. Auctions for T-bills take place weekly on Tuesdays (4-week bills) and Mondays (13 and 26-week bills). Every 4 weeks, 52-week bills are auctioned on Tuesdays as well. The timing from the announcement of the auction, to its execution, to issuance of the purchased security is generally between 7 and 10 days.[15]

Treasury Notes

Treasury notes are interest-bearing securities, offered in multiples of $100, currently being offered in 2, 3, 5, 7, and 10-year fixed maturities. The relationship between yield to maturity and the interest rate determines the price at auction. If the yield-to-maturity is greater than/equal to/less than the interest rate, the price will be less than/equal to/greater than par (face) value. Treasury notes pay interest on a semi-annual basis and the investor receives the face value when the note matures. Treasury notes are currently being auctioned on a monthly basis (2, 3, 5, and 7- year notes) and quarterly (10-year notes).[16]

Treasury Bonds

Treasury bonds are interest-bearing securities, offered in multiples of $100, with maturities over 10 years. The price, yield, and interest rate of a Treasury bond are determined at auction in the same way as a Treasury note. Treasury bonds pay interest on a semi-annual basis and investors receive face value when the bond matures. Treasury bonds are currently auctioned quarterly. [17]

Treasury Inflation-Protected Securities (TIPS)

TIPS are interest-bearing securities that protect investors from inflation. TIPS are offered in multiples of $100, with maturity periods of 5, 10, and 20 years. The TIPS principal adjusts based on the movements in the consumer price index (CPI-urban, non-seasonally-adjusted) with a 3- month lag. These adjustments in the principal of the security form the basis for the interest payments, paid semiannually at a fixed rate. If inflation/deflation occurs, the interest payment increases/decreases. However, when a TIPS matures, the investor is paid the inflation-adjusted principal or original principal, whichever is greater. TIPS are currently being offered in April (5- year), January and June (10-year), and January (20-year).[18]

Nonmarketable Securities

Nonmarketable debt is composed of approximately 9% of publicly held debt and nearly all intragovernmental debt. Publicly held debt that is nonmarketable is primarily the state and local government series and savings bonds. [19]Intragovernmental debt is largely composed of debt owed by Treasury to the Social Security, Civil Service Retirement and Disability, and Medicare trust funds.[20]

The main purpose of publicly-held nonmarketable debt is to protect the bearers from market risk. The state and local government series was created in 1972 to restrict state and local governments from earning arbitrage profits by investing any tax-exempt bond proceeds in investments that may generate higher yields, thereby risking the returns. This program sells Treasury securities to state and local governments to help them comply with this requirement. Savings bonds provide a means for the small investor to participate in government financing. Savings bonds have been sold continuously since 1935 when they were introduced to encourage broad public participation in government financing by making federal bonds available in small denominations.[21]

U.S. government trust funds, which compose intragovernmental debt, contain revenues designated by law for a specific purpose. When revenues in the trust funds exceed benefit payments, the unspent monies must remain in the trust fund for future use. However, this excess cash is transferred to the Treasury's General Fund and is used to finance other activities which fall outside the specific purpose of the trust fund. In exchange, the trust fund is issued a Treasury "special issue" security to be redeemed at face value at any time in the future when the funds are needed.[22] "Special issue" securities are available only to trust funds and are designated as nonmarketable, earning interest on a semi-annual basis. The interest rate is determined by formula, based on the average yield of certain marketable securities.[23] Securities of this type protect the trust fund investments from market fluctuations.

Role of Federal Reserve and Primary Dealers

The Federal Reserve serves as Treasury's fiscal agent. In this role, it is responsible for the primary dealer relationships which are used not only for Treasury auctions but other open market operations to conduct monetary policy. In addition, the Federal Reserve plays an important role in the operational aspects of the auction process and payments mechanism. The Federal Reserve is not responsible for making debt issuance decisions – this responsibility rests solely within Treasury's ODM to ensure the independence of the two institutions.

In addition, the Fed is a holder of Treasury securities. It is involved in the purchase and resale of these securities to the secondary market through its open market operations. These operations help keep the federal funds rate close to a target rate that is set by the Federal Open Market Committee. Its holdings of Treasury securities amounted to nearly $500 billion as of December 2008.[24] Any profits earned by the Fed through the sale of Treasury securities and other activities are remitted to Treasury and recorded as revenues in the federal budget.[25] The Federal Reserve banks also act as fiscal agents and depositories for Treasury accounts by accepting deposits of federal taxes and other federal agency receipts and processing checks and electronic payments drawn on the account.

The Fed's monetary policy actions can affect interest rates on Treasury securities in the short run. The Fed conducts its monetary policy by setting a federal funds rate, the price at which banks buy and sell reserves on an overnight basis, based on the supply and demand for bank reserves. Monetary actions by the Fed generally affect short-term nominal interest rates. If the Fed lowers the federal funds rate, resulting in a lower short-term interest rate, long-term interest rates are likely to fall also, though they may not fall as much or as quickly.[26]

Primary dealers are securities brokers and dealers who are registered to operate in the government securities market and have a trading relationship with the Federal Reserve Bank of New York.[27] Primary dealers are the largest purchasers of Treasury securities sold to the public at auction.[28] In many cases, auction purchases by primary dealers are later sold on the secondary or "when- issued" markets (see discussion in the next section).

In addition to their role in the auction process, the primary dealers also work closely with the Fed to execute its monetary policy. These primary dealers are large financial institutions who the Fed relies on to act as intermediaries through which Treasury securities are bought and sold and then resold on the secondary market in order to increase or decrease the money supply. They are expected to maintain trading relationships with the Fed's trading desk and provide the trading desk with market information and analysis that may be useful to the Fed in the formulation and implementation of monetary policy. The primary dealers also use this system to help them meet their liquidity needs by swapping securities with the Fed on an overnight basis. This type of securities lending has no effect on general interest rates or the money supply since it does not involve cash, but can affect the liquidity premium of the securities traded.

Other Purchasers of Treasury Securities

Along with the primary dealers and the Fed, individual investors, other dealers and brokers, private pension and retirement funds, insurance companies, investment funds, and foreign investors (private citizens and government entities) also purchase Treasury securities through the auction process and on the secondary market. Treasury releases a variety of data on purchasers of Treasury securities following each auction. The data are arranged into two categories. The bidder category data show purchases by primary dealers, direct bidders, indirect bidders, and noncompetitive bidders by bill type. The investor class data show purchases by different types of investors described in the previous paragraph.[29]

However, limitations on data do exist. For example, until a marketable security matures, ownership can change, meaning that the composition of ownership can be different from what it was at the time of auction. This is particularly true of primary dealers who purchase large amounts of securities and then resell them on the secondary market.

Secondary and Repurchase Markets

Participants in the secondary market play an indirect role in determining the price of Treasury securities. Once an auction is announced by Treasury, dealers and market participants start trading securities on a "when-issued" basis, meaning that once a security is purchased and issued, it will be immediately resold to the secondary market purchaser. Because trading starts in the secondary market before the actual auction takes place, "when-issued" market participants effectively determine the yield or discount rate of Treasury securities based on what they are willing to pay. [30]

Transactions of Treasury securities between investors and companies or dealers on the repurchase (repo) market play a role in the effective functioning of the credit markets. In the repo market, transactions take place between two parties who exchange Treasury securities, often on a very short term basis, for cash. The company or dealer pays the investor an agreed upon rate of interest for use of the funds with the expectation that the Treasury security will be repurchased at the mutually agreed upon future date. This process provides the company or dealer with the liquidity needed to meet immediate obligations.

Recently, the repo market has shown volatility as some investors were unable or unwilling to return the Treasury securities, thus affecting market liquidity. In the fall of 2008, failures in this market spiked to nearly $2.7 trillion, half of the market's total value, due to the general market panic caused by the bankruptcy of Lehman Brothers. These settlement fails were the highest ever recorded. Treasury took the unprecedented response of reopening four securities in October 2008 to renew market functioning.[31] In addition, the Treasury Market Practice Group, a private sector group sponsored by the Federal Reserve Bank of New York, suggested new guidelines to lower the level of future failures. Their recommendations resulted in the implementation of a three percentage point fee on failed repo transactions. However, since the interest rates on repo transactions generally remain close to the rates in the federal funds market, which are currently low, this fee may result in negative interest rates. Essentially, this means that investors will pay for owning the Treasury security that they have exchanged for cash and may be less likely to enter the repo market, potentially hurting liquidity.[32] Some analysts feared that that these negative interest rates will impact the broader Treasury security market, but, to date, volumes and trading activity remain robust.

MANAGING FEDERAL FINANCIAL FLOWS

The Secretary of the Treasury manages revenue, works to improve public credit, provides for on- time revenue collection and payment of debts.[33] If federal government finances are not correctly managed, financial stability and economic growth could be at risk. Throughout the year, the balance held by Treasury can fluctuate significantly as a result of higher or lower revenue collections or issuance of more or less debt during certain periods. As a result, Treasury must ensure that adequate funds are available, either via revenue streams or borrowing, to finance obligations. In order to finance the government's obligations while minimizing borrowing costs, Treasury must accurately project what cash requirements will be needed on a daily basis to cover government payments especially given these variations.[34]

Treasury's financing needs generally follow a predictable seasonal pattern. **Figure 1** shows the month-to-month growth in the public debt during fiscal year (FY) 2008. This varied from a low (or decline in debt held by the public) of -1.7% in April, due to the filing of personal income tax returns paid during that month, to a high of 6.0% (or increase in debt held by the public) in September, as a result of the need to meet obligations due at the end of the fiscal year.

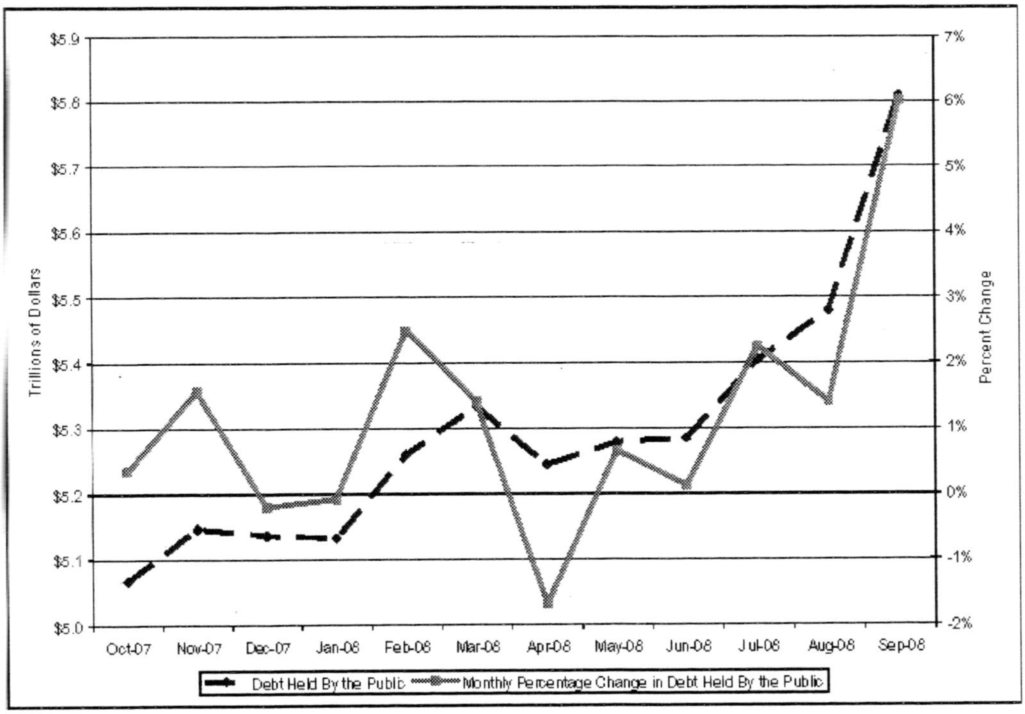

Source: U.S. Department of the Treasury, *Monthly Statement of the Public Debt*, October 2007 to September 2008, available at http://www.treasurydirect.gov/govt/reports/pd/mspd/mspd.htm.

Figure 1. Seasonality of Debt Held By the Public, FY2008

The total amount of debt issued over the fiscal year depends in large part on the decisions made by Congress and the priorities it chooses in its annual budget and appropriations process. Recently, Treasury has issued increasing amounts of debt as a result of activities related to the economic downturn and resulting decline in tax revenues. Over the longer term, these priorities may change as the economy recovers and decisions on how to finance the promises to retirees for healthcare and other benefits may increase the demands on Treasury's debt issuance.

In addition to funding the needs of the government, Treasury manages the accounts of government agencies through the Financial Management Service (FMS). Loans are provided to Departments or Agencies in order to meet obligations, such as payments owed to eligible beneficiaries of social service programs. FMS disburses payments to individuals and businesses, collects federal revenue, and issues government-wide financial reports.

How Much Debt is Outstanding?

Gross federal debt is composed of debt held by the public and intragovernmental debt. Debt held by the public, issued through the Bureau of Public Debt, is the total amount the federal government has borrowed from the public and remains outstanding. This measure is generally considered to be the most relevant in macro-economic terms because it is the amount of debt sold in credit markets. Intragovernmental debt is the amount owed by the federal government to other federal agencies, primarily in the Social Security, Medicare, and Civil Service Retirement and Disability trust funds, to be paid by Treasury.[35]

The Bureau of Public Debt and the FMS provide various breakdowns of debt figures. The most up-to-date data on federal debt can be found on the "Debt to the Penny" section of the Bureau's Treasury Direct website.[36] The Daily Treasury Statement (DTS) and Monthly Treasury Statement (MTS) provide greater detail on the composition of federal debt, including the operating cash balance, the types of debt sold, the amount of debt subject to the debt limit, and federal tax deposits.[37] The Monthly Statement of the Public Debt (MSPD) includes figures from the DTS as well as more detailed information on the types of Treasury securities outstanding.[38] The Office of International Affairs provides figures on the amount of debt held by foreigners through the Treasury International Capital System (TIC).[39] The TIC data reflect estimates of who holds Treasury securities at a given period of time, which may be different from who purchased these securities at auction.

Levels of federal debt change on a daily basis. On July 31, 2009, for example, gross federal debt totaled $11 .669 trillion, intragovernmental debt totaled $4.334 trillion, and debt held by the public totaled $7.336. By the next business day, August 3, 2009, gross federal debt fell to $ 11.649 trillion, followed by $11 .660 trillion on August 4, 2009.[40]

Treasury also estimates who owns federal securities. Because marketable Treasury securities can be and are often sold on the secondary market, ownership will change over time. As of March 2009, the latest period for which such estimates are available, gross debt totaled $11.1 27 trillion, of which, $4.785 trillion was owned by the Federal Reserve and Intragovernmental Holdings. U.S. savings bonds accounted for $0. 194 trillion and foreign and international holdings accounted for $3 .267 trillion. The remainder of the debt was held in depository institutions (i.e., commercial banks), pension funds, insurance companies, mutual funds, state and local governments, and other investors (i.e., individuals and corporations).[41]

FACTORS AFFECTING SUPPLY AND DEMAND FOR TREASURY SECURITIES

Investors examine several key factors when deciding whether they should purchase Treasury securities. As with all types of investments, price, expected return, and risk play a role in this process. Treasury securities provide a known stream of income and offer greater liquidity than other types of fixed-income securities. Prices are determined by investors who place a value on Treasury securities based on the characteristics of safety and liquidity afforded by this investment option.[42] Because they are also backed by the full faith and credit of the United States, they are often seen as one of the safest investments available, though investors are not totally immune from losses. The behavior of the market can lead to price changes, changes in interest rates, or inflation, which does create some investment risk. Despite the current economic conditions and financial market volatility, Treasury securities have remained attractive to investors.

Yield Curve

The yield curve shows the relationship between the interest rate (cost of borrowing) and the maturity of debt (i.e., U.S. Treasury securities) at a given time. In other words, the yield represents the rate of return an investor would earn if a security was held to maturity. The yield curve typically changes on a daily basis as interest rates move. Generally, yield curves are upward sloping (i.e., the longer the maturity, the higher the yield), with diminishing rates of increase over time.

Two opposing forces affect the slope and shape of the yield curve. First, investors must be compensated for choosing to invest now even though they may be able to achieve higher interest rates if they invested at a future point in time. This pushes interest rates up. Opposing this increase in interest rates is the fact that the longer the period to maturity, the greater the likelihood that interest rates will fall. This increases the risk to the lender (i.e., Treasury), as they could save on interest costs if they decided to wait before borrowing money. Generally speaking, the first effect will outweigh the second, leading to an upward sloping yield curve. An upward sloping yield curve also illustrates expectations for future economic growth and rising short-term interest rates. A downward sloping curve implies that investors expect short-term interest rates to rise above long-term rates.[43] These yield curves have frequently occurred before recessions.[44]

Yields can change for the same maturities from auction to auction and can vary on a daily (business day) basis. Treasury's Office of Debt Management generates the official daily yield curves to calculate a rate of constant maturity on Treasury securities in order to provide a meaningful measure of the yield on a security with a 10-year maturity, for example, even if no outstanding security has exactly 10 years remaining to maturity.[45] All securities with the same length to maturity must have the same yield, even if they were originally issued with different maturities or coupon rates. Yields are equalized through price changes.

Figure 2 shows the Treasury constant maturity rates for selected maturities since 1962. Rates on securities with different maturities generally track each other. This is because securities with similar maturity periods tend to have similar rates because they offer fixed interest payments over essentially the same period of time. Given that securities with longer maturities tend to reflect expectations about the future path of the interest rates of short-term securities, short-term rates generally provide a picture of the path of their longer-term counterparts. Therefore, over history, movements in constant maturity rates have generally tracked each other, regardless of length of maturity. [46]

Despite declines over the past year, long-term interest rates have recently begun to increase, approaching levels not seen since latter part of 2008 and generating some concern in the financial market. In June 2009 the rate on a 10-year Treasury securities briefly rose to nearly 4%, which is low by historical standards (as seen in **Figure 2**), but up from 2.5% in January 2009. The increase came in spite of the Fed's program to purchase Treasury securities in an attempt to keep interest rates low. At a June 2009 hearing before the House Budget Committee, Federal Reserve Chairman Ben Bernanke explained that the increase in Treasury and mortgage yields reflected other causes, including greater optimism about the economic outlook, a reversal of flight-toquality flows, and technical factors related to the hedging of mortgage holdings.[47]

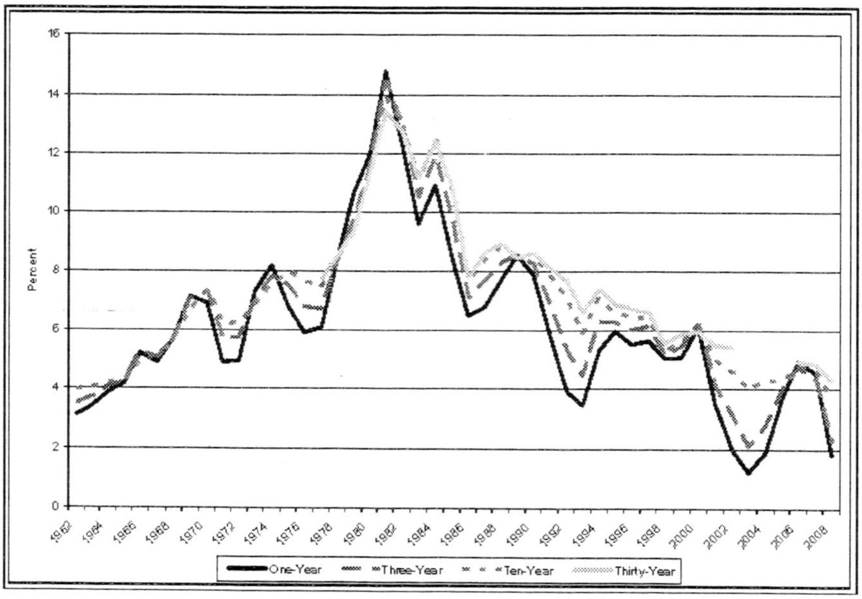

Source: Federal Reserve Board, *Federal Reserve Statistical Release*, H.15 Selected Interest Rates, U.S. Government Securities – Annual Series, available at http://www.federalreserve.gov/releases /h15/data.htm.

Notes: Treasury began issuing 30-year Treasury securities in February 1977 and did not issue these securities between February 18, 2002 and February 9, 2006. The Office of Debt Management also calculates constant maturity rates for securities with other maturity periods in addition to calculating rates for inflation-indexed securities (i.e., TIPS).

Figure 2. Selected Treasury Nominal Constant Maturity Rates (annual rates, 1962-2008)

Determining Maturity Mix

Newly issued Treasury securities, sold to finance the operations of the federal government, are offered at a mix of maturities in order to satisfy the provisions of the regular and predictable debt management strategy and to minimize interest payments over time. The profile of securities is also important due to its influence on liquidity. In addition, Treasury must make sure that it has adequate cash balances available to pay federal obligations. Balancing all of these objectives leads to a strategy which offers a mix of short- and long-term securities.

Longer-term securities generally command higher interest rates compared to shorter-term securities because investors demand greater compensation for incurring risk over a longer period of time. Generally, a strong economy will be accompanied by higher interest rates. If Treasury issues long-term debt during this time, they are committing to paying higher interest rates for a longer period and may decide to purchase shorter-term securities. However, this leads to uncertainties over the longer term, since the interest rate will likely change. During periods of economic downturn and low interest rates, Treasury may decide to finance at shorter maturities to take advantage of lower borrowing costs. This, however, may lead to more volatile and uncertain yearly interest payments because Treasury has to enter the market more often. Figure 3 shows the average length of marketable interest-bearing public debt securities held by private investors between 1969 and 2008, as of the end of each fiscal year.

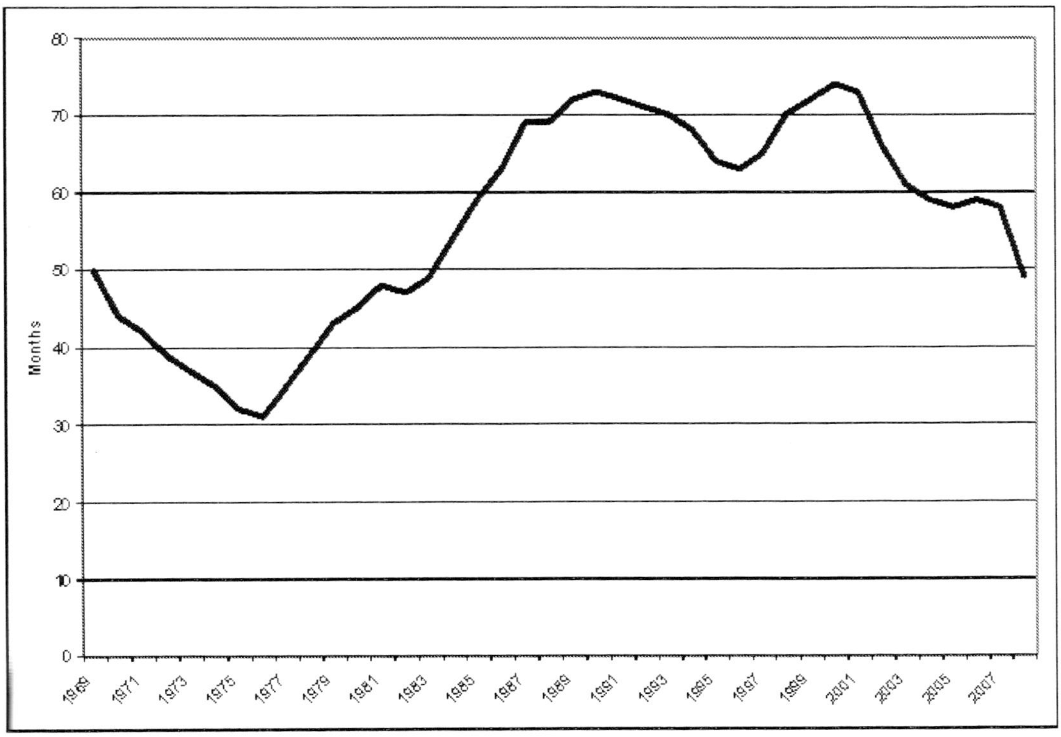

Source: Council of Economic Advisors, *Economic Report of the President*, January 2009, Table B-88, available at http://www.gpoaccess.gov/eop/tables09.html.

Figure 3. Average Maturity of Marketable Interest-Bearing Public Debt Securities Held by Private Investors, 1969-2008 (maturity period in months)

Since 1969, the average maturity period of Treasury securities reached its minimum point in FY1976 at 31 months and its peak in FY2000 at 74 months. In the mid-1970s, prior to the initiation of the regular and predictable debt management strategy, the average maturity of Treasury securities declined due to the rapid increase in the deficit during FY1975. In order to meet the unexpected financing needs, numerous debt offerings took place. However, Treasury officials were generally reluctant to offer longer-term securities because they were unsure of investor demand. In contrast, during the surplus years of the late 1990s and the resulting decline in federal debt levels, Treasury did not have immediate financing needs and did not auction new securities as older ones matured. This effectively increased average maturity since more longer term bonds remained outstanding.

Despite recent increases in the amount of Treasury securities due to the federal government's economic recovery activities, average maturity of the debt continues to decline. Given the nature of current borrowing requirements, coupled with expected future demands on borrowing needs due to long-term obligations related to Medicare and Social Security, Treasury's Borrowing Advisory Committee recommended that Treasury increase the size of issues across the maturity spectrum in order to allow the Treasury to meet its financing needs over the short to intermediate term and reduce the uncertainty surrounding interest rates over the long-term.[48] Effectively, this should reduce risk and ensure adequate financing over the long term, while increasing average maturity.

Current Economic Conditions

Current economic conditions as well as actions taken by the federal government to intervene in the housing and financial markets have raised concerns over Treasury's ability to raise money to finance obligations due to the large amount of funding needed. In order for Treasury to sell debt, buyers must have confidence in the value of U.S. currency and the ability of the government to pay back its obligations. In order to sell enough debt to finance spending in FY2009 and beyond, Treasury initiated more frequent auctions, new maturity terms, reopenings, and raised the overall amount of regular weekly and monthly securities issued. Further changes may be announced in the future.[49]

The new debt issued by Treasury will also face competition with debt being issued for similar purposes by other countries. With this competition, investor demand for U.S. securities may fall, at a time when issuance is relatively high, if foreign securities offer the prospect of better returns or are viewed as a safer investment. Alternatively, investors may decide to buy U.S. securities but only at higher interest rates if the market is flooded with supply, potentially increasing the cost of debt over the long term. The U.S. government faces a greater risk from competition because, compared to other countries, it has sold a relatively large amount of debt to foreigners. Despite this, demand for U.S. debt thus far had remained solid as indicated by the fall in interest rates.[50]

As a result of the Fed's actions during the financial crisis, there has been a large and unprecedented increase in the monetary base.[51] Though inflation levels remain low and are currently holding down interest rates, some investors have expressed concern that the Fed's actions will lead to inflation, thereby diluting the value of their investment, especially over the long term. If these fears become dominant, investors would demand a higher yield on Treasury securities.

BUDGETARY IMPACTS

Legislative activity can affect Treasury's ability to issue debt and can impact the budget process. The statutory limit on the debt can constrain debt operations, which, in the past, have hampered traditional practices when the limit was approached. The accounting of asset purchases in the federal budget has created differences between how much debt Treasury has to borrow to make those purchases and how much the same purchases will impact the budget deficit. If budget deficits continue to rise, thereby causing more resources to be devoted to paying interest on the debt, there will be fewer funds available to spend on other federal programs, all else equal.

Some economists have expressed concerns that long-term deficits could drive up interest rates, making it more expensive for the government, businesses, and consumers to borrow money. The government cannot add infinitely to the national debt without facing market consequences or hindering future ability to borrow. A portion of the current increase in the debt is attributed to financing the purchase of assets or loans to stabilize the financial sector. These investments are expected to yield some return in the future, while loans are expected be repaid, at least in part. In recent testimony to Congress, Federal Reserve Chairman Ben Bernanke warned that addressing the government's growing debt and annual deficits must begin or the country would risk facing further economic problems in the coming years. Though the country is dealing with rising levels of federal debt related to the current economic crisis, dealing with entitlement costs and related increases in the nation's debt as a result of obligations due to rising health care costs will likely become a concern once the economy recovers.[52]

Constraints of the Debt Limit

Congress sets a statutory limit on federal debt levels in an effort to assert its constitutional prerogatives to control spending and impose a form of fiscal accountability. At times, the debt limit has restricted the Treasury's ability to manage the federal government's finances. Standard methods of financing federal activities or meeting government obligations can be hobbled when federal debt nears its legal limit. If the limit prevents the Treasury from issuing new debt to manage short-term cash flows or to finance an annual budget deficit, the government may be unable to obtain the cash it needs. Because the law requires that the government's legal obligations be paid, the debt limit may prevent it from issuing the debt that would allow it to do so. While the debt limit has never caused the federal government to default on its obligations, at times it has added uncertainty to Treasury operations.[53]

Accounting of Recent Debt Increases

In 1990, the Federal Credit Reform Act (FCRA; Title V of P.L. 101-508) revamped the way that federal credit (direct loans and loan guarantees) was accounted for in the budget process. Prior to the creation of this law, asset purchases were recorded on a purchase price or net cash flow basis. If a subsequent sale led the government to recoup some of their investment, that would be recorded in a later fiscal year as negative outlays. Beginning in FY1992, asset purchases were recorded on an accrual basis, which reported the budgetary cost of a credit program equal to the estimated subsidy costs at the time the credit is provided. The subsidy cost was defined as "the estimated long-term cost to the government of a direct loan or a loan guarantee, calculated on a net present value basis, excluding administrative costs."[54]

Accounting under FCRA has become a more prominent issue due to recent federal financial interventions and resulting loans and asset purchases made by the federal government to stabilize the economy. Because the ultimate value of these assets once they are sold is not knowable, the ultimate increase in the federal debt as a result of these interventions is also unknown. Asset purchases financed under the Troubled Asset Relief Program (TARP) require outlays equal to the purchase price, which increase the debt held by the public by the same amount. In the future, the government will likely sell the assets and the proceeds from the sale will return to the Treasury's General Fund.

However, the budgetary impact is somewhat different. The TARP law contained a provision which required budgetary accountability for these asset purchases to follow the provisions of FCRA with an additional adjustment for market risk. This means that for budgetary purposes, the cost of these purchases was recorded on a subsidy basis, which takes into account the asset's expected return. What the government paid to purchase the assets led to an increase in the debt held by the public, in the amount of the purchase price, that exceeded the increase in the budget deficit, the amount of the subsidy.

Interest and the Debt

Interest paid on the federal debt increases the overall cost of borrowing. Interest costs can be affected by various conditions, including legislative activity and the economy, as well as actions taken by the Treasury and the Fed, as discussed earlier. The level of budget deficits, hence the need to borrow, and federal debt can also affect the interest rates on Treasury securities. If interest rates are low, interest payments on Treasury securities may also be low, thereby making debt less costly. However, increased borrowing will increase the supply of Treasury securities, which generally leads to higher interest rates and future net interest payments.[55]

Despite the recent increases in federal borrowing due to federal financial interventions, stimulus legislation, and financial turmoil, the economic downturn and the actions of the Fed have kept interest rates near zero. Therefore, borrowing costs to the Treasury currently remain low. Interest payments are projected to match historically low levels both as a percentage of gross domestic product and as a percentage of total outlays even as overall debt is increasing.

Over the long term however, borrowing costs are projected to grow, likely leading to increasing interest payments.

CONCLUSION

Part of Treasury's mission is to secure America's economic and financial future. In part, this is achieved by maintaining a regular and predictable debt management strategy as well as ensuring global trust and confidence in U.S. currency. However, Treasury's actions are affected by several outside actors, including Congress, the Fed, and different types of investors, as well as economic conditions. As long as the United States continues to issue Treasury securities to finance government operations, the actions of the Treasury will continue to play a key role in maintaining stability in the financial and credit markets and the U.S. economy.

End Notes

[1] U.S. Department of the Treasury, "Duties & Functions of the U.S. Department of the Treasury," available at http://www.treas.gov/education/duties/.

[2] U.S. Department of the Treasury, Office of Domestic Finance, Office of Debt Management Overview, available at http://www.treas.gov/offices/domestic-finance/debt-management

[3] Tilford C. Gaines, *Techniques of Treasury Debt Management* (New York: The Free Press of Glencoe, 1962), pp. 19, 21, 154.

[4] The Treasury Franchise Fund provides common administrative support services to other parts of Treasury as well as other government agencies on a competitive and fully cost-reimbursable basis. The collection of delinquent debt owed to the U.S. government is collected by the Financial Management Service. Department of the Treasury, Bureau of Public Debt, *Strategic Plan: Fiscal Years 2009-2014*, available at http://www.publicdebt.treas.gov/whatwedo/ bpdstrategicplan09-14.pdf.

[5] The Federal Reserve Bank of Minneapolis, *Born of Panic: Forming the Fed System*, August 1988, http://www.minneapolisfed.org/publications_papers/pub_display.cfm?id=3816.

[6] History of the Federal Reserve, available at http://www.federalreserveeducation.org/fed101/history/. For more information, see CRS Report RS20826, *Structure and Functions of The Federal Reserve System*, by Pauline Smale.

[7] Previously, debt was issued on an offering-by-offering survey of the market, whereby Treasury officials made decisions on what type of maturities to offer and when they should be offered based on anticipated needs. Auctions were used during this time for certain types of securities and some predictability did exist.

[8] Treasury bills had been issued on a regular basis for decades. With the new strategy, Treasury began issuing notes and bonds on a schedule as well. Garbade, Kenneth D., *The Emergence of "Regular and Predictable" as a Treasury Debt Management Strategy*, FRBNY Economic Policy Review, March 2007, pp. 54-55.

[9] Garbade, Kenneth D., *The Emergence of "Regular and Predictable" as a Treasury Debt Management Strategy*, p. 65.

[10] Though auctions were the main component of the new strategy, Treasury had tried to institute an auction based system in 1935 and 1963. Both of these earlier attempts failed.

[11] There are no coupon rates for Treasury bills – bills are sold on a discount basis.

[12] For bills and TIPS auctions, the bids are offered in terms of a discount rate rather than a yield.

[13] Garbade, Kenneth D. and Jeffrey F. Ingber, *The Treasury Auction Process: Objectives, Structure, and Recent Adaptations*, FRBNY Current Issues in Economics and Finance, February 2005, pp. 2-3.

[14] Cash Management bills are occasionally offered in order to meet short- and medium-term cash needs as determined by Treasury. These bills mature on dates determined by Treasury based on need, generally a few days from issue. Occasionally, Treasury also offers reopenings of previous auctions where additional amounts of a previously issued security are sold at the same coupon interest rate and maturity, but with a different issue date and price.

[15] U.S. Department of the Treasury, Treasury Bills, available at http://www.treasurydirect.gov/instit/marketables/tbills/ tbills.htm.

[16] Initial offerings of 10-year notes are currently auctioned in February, May, August and November. Each initial offer is followed by two reopenings of the same issue in January, March, April, June, July, September, October, and December. In a security reopening, the U.S. Treasury issues additional amounts of a previously issued security. The reopened security has the same maturity date and interest payment date as the original security, but has a different issue date and usually a different price. U.S. Department of the Treasury, Treasury Notes, available at http://www.treasurydirect.gov/instit/marketables/tnotes/tnotes.htm.

[17] Initial offerings of 30-year bonds are currently auctioned in February, May, August, and November. Each initial offer is followed by two reopenings in the two months following the initial auction. U.S. Department of the Treasury, Treasury Bonds, available at http://www.treasurydirect.gov/instit/marketables/tbonds/tbonds.htm.

[18] U.S. Department of the Treasury, Treasury Inflation-Protected Securities, available at http://www.treasury direct.gov/ instit/marketables/tips/tips.htm.

[19] U.S. Department of the Treasury, Bureau of Public Debt, *Monthly Statement of Public Debt*, March 2009, Tables I and III, available at http://www.treasurydirect.gov/govt/reports/pd/mspd/2009/opdm032009.pdf.

[20] U.S. Department of the Treasury, Financial Management Service, *Monthly Treasury Statement*, June 2009, Table 6 – Schedule D, available at http://fms.treas.gov/mts/mts0609.pdf.

[21] Such offerings of Treasury securities dated back to 1776. Between 1776 and 1935, these securities were marketable and subjected the investor to market fluctuation. Particularly during World War I, small investors incurred significant losses if they were forced to sell their bonds prior to maturity.

[22] The trust funds now hold only special issues, but they have held public issues in the past.

[23] The specifications for securities issued to each type of trust fund are listed in separate places in the U.S. Code. Specifications for the Social Security Trust Fund can be found in 42 USC §40 1. Specifications for the Civil Service Retirement and Disability Fund can be found in 5 USC § 8348.

[24] Currency, not Treasury securities, is the Fed's primary liability. Treasury securities are assets to the Fed.

[25] For more information on the Fed's recent activities, see CRS Report RL34427, *Financial Turmoil: Federal Reserve Policy Responses*, by Marc Labonte.

[26] The federal funds rate is linked to the interest rates that banks and other financial institutions charge for loans – or the provision of credit. Thus, while the Fed may directly influence only a very short term interest rate, this rate influences other longer term rates. However, this relationship is far from being on a one-to-one basis since the longer term market rates are influenced not only by what the Fed is doing today, but what it is expected to do in the future and what inflation is expected to be in the future. For more information, see CRS Report RL30354, *Monetary Policy and the Federal Reserve: Current Policy and Conditions*, by Marc Labonte.

[27] A list of current primary dealers can be found at http://www.newyorkfed.org/markets/pridealers_listing.html.

[28] Purchases by primary dealers can be found at http://www.treasurydirect.gov/instit/annceresult/auctdata/ auctdata_stat.htm.

[29] Auction results are available at http://www.treasurysecurities.gov/RI/OFGateway and http://www.treas.gov/ offices/ domestic-finance/debt-management/investor_class_auction.shtml. For an analysis of bidder category and investor class data, see Fleming, Michael J., *Who Buys Treasury Securities at Auction?*, FRBNY Current Issues in Economics and Finance, January 2007.

[30] Garbade, Kenneth D. and Jeffrey F. Ingber, *The Treasury Auction Process: Objectives, Structure, and Recent Adaptations*, FRBNY Current Issues in Economics and Finance, February 2005, p. 2.

[31] Data on Treasury fails back to July 1990 are available on the FRBNY's website at http://www.newyorkfed.org/ markets/pridealers_failsdata.html. Settlement fails are reported on a cumulative basis. For example, if a dealer fails to deliver $50 million in securities on the agreed upon date, but makes the delivery one day late, the fail is recorded at $50 million. However, if the $50 million is delivered 4 days late, the fail is valued at $200 million ($50m x 4). For more information, see Fleming, Michael J. and Kenneth D. Garbade, *Explaining Settlement Fails*, FRBNY Current Issues in Economics and Finance, September 2005.

[32] Fleming, Michael J. and Kenneth D. Garbade, *Explaining Settlement Fails*, FRBNY Current Issues in Economics and Finance, September 2005, pp. 4-5.

[33] U.S. Department of the Treasury, available at http://www.treas.gov/education/fact-sheets/history/act-congress.shtml.

[34] U.S. Department of the Treasury, *Strategic Plan: Department of the Treasury, Fiscal Years 2007-2012*, p. 15.

[35] For additional historical analysis of federal debt levels, see CRS Report RL34712, *Ebbs and Flows of Federal Debt*, by Mindy R. Levit.

[36] See http://www.treasurydirect.gov/NP/BPDLogin?application=np. Debt information typically lags the current business day by one to two business days.

[37] Current issues of the DTS and MTS, respectively, can be found at http://fms.treas.gov/dts/index.html and http://fms.treas.gov/mts/index.html.

[38] The current issue of the MSPD can be found at http://www.treasurydirect.gov/govt/reports/pd/mspd/mspd.htm.

[39] Data on major foreign holders of Treasury securities by country is available at http://www.treas.gov/tic/ ticsec2.shtml#ussecs.

[40] TreasuryDirect, "Debt to the Penny" for July 31, August 3, and August 4, 2009, available at http://www.treasurydirect.gov/NP/BPDLogin?application=np

[41] U.S. Department of the Treasury, Financial Management Service, *Treasury Bulletin*, June 2009, Table OFS-2, available at http://fms.treas.gov/bulletin/index.html. For more information about foreign ownership of Treasury securities, see CRS Report RS2233 1, *Foreign Holdings of Federal Debt*, by Justin Murray and Marc Labonte.

[42] Dupont, Dominique and Brian Sack, *The Treasury Securities Market: Overview and Recent Developments*, Federal Reserve Board, Federal Reserve Bulletin, December 1999, pp. 792-793, available at http://www.federalreserve.gov/ pubs/bulletin/1999/1299lead.pdf.

[43] Federal Reserve Bank of San Francisco, *What is a yield curve, and how do you read them? How has the yield curve moved over the past 25 years?*, July 2004, available at http://www.frbsf.org/education/activities/drecon/answerxml.cfm?selectedurl=/2004/0407.html.

[44] For more information, see CRS Report RS22371, *The Pattern of Interest Rates: Does It Signal an Impending Recession?*, by Marc Labonte and Gail E. Makinen.

[45] For information on the methodology used to calculate the constant maturity yields, see http://www.treas.gov/offices/ domestic-finance/debt-management/interest-rate/yield.shtml.

[46] Dupont, Dominique and Brian Sack, *The Treasury Securities Market: Overview and Recent Developments*, Federal Reserve Board, Federal Reserve Bulletin, December 1999, pp. 793-794, available at http://www.federalreserve.gov/ pubs/bulletin/1999/1299lead.pdf.

[47] U.S. Congress, House Committee on the Budget, *Challenges Facing the Economy: The View of the Federal Reserve*, 111th Cong., 1st sess., June 3, 2009., testimony available at http://budget.house.gov/hearings/2009/06. 03 .2009_Bernanke_Testimony.pdf.

[48] Report to the Secretary of the Treasury from the Treasury Borrowing Advisory Committee of the Securities Industry and Financial Markets Association, April 29, 2009, available at http://www.treas.gov/press /releases/tg111.htm

[49] U.S. Department of the Treasury, *February 2009 Quarterly Refunding Statement*, available at http://www.treas.gov/ press/releases/tg09.htm and *May 2009 Quarterly Refunding Statement*, available at http://www.treas.gov/press/releases/ tg1 10.htm.

[50] U.S. Department of the Treasury, Report to the Secretary of the Treasury from the Treasury Borrowing Advisory Committee of the Securities Industry and Financial Markets Association, February 4, 2009, available at http://www.treas.gov/offices/domestic-finance/debt-management

[51] For more information, see CRS Report RL34427, *Financial Turmoil: Federal Reserve Policy Responses*, by Marc Labonte.

[52] U.S. Congress, House Committee on the Budget, *Challenges Facing the Economy: The View of the Federal Reserve*, 111th Cong., 1st sess., June 3, 2009, testimony available at http://budget.house.gov/hearings/2009/06. 03 .2009_Bernanke_Testimony.pdf.

[53] For more information, see CRS Report RL31967, *The Debt Limit: History and Recent Increases*, by D. Andrew Austin and Mindy R. Levit.

[54] For more information, see CRS Report RL30346, *Federal Credit Reform: Implementation of the Changed Budgetary Treatment of Direct Loans and Loan Guarantees*, by James M. Bickley.

[55] For more information, see CRS Report RS22354, *Interest Payments on the Federal Debt: A Primer*, by Thomas L. Hungerford.

In: The U.S. National Debt: Background, Issues, Significance ISBN: 978-1-61761-767-6
Editor: Charlotte G. Wilson and Emily O. Brown

Chapter 10

EBBS AND FLOWS OF FEDERAL DEBT

Mindy R. Levit

SUMMARY

Financing the obligations of the United States has always been a central concern of Congress and the President. Levels of government spending and revenue collection are a focus of congressional debate in every fiscal year. Policy decisions and economic growth also play a large role in influencing federal debt levels over time. Historical trends can help illustrate the reasons behind large movements in debt levels. Understanding ebbs and flows of federal debt levels can be useful in synthesizing how budget policy affects the debt outlook.

Federal debt can be defined and reported in a number of ways. In the President's budget submission to Congress, information is presented on the federal surplus or deficit, gross (total) federal debt, debt held by federal government accounts (intragovernmental), and debt held by the public. In most years, debt held by the public has increased on a nominal basis. However, in order to compare the size of debt to the size of the economy over time, debt held by the public will be measured in this chapter as a percentage of gross domestic product (GDP) to control for effects such as inflation and economic growth.

A variety of factors, including spending levels (outlays), revenue collections (receipts), and economic growth, affect movements in the levels of federal debt. These factors are used in this chapter to identify changes in debt levels. Movements in debt cannot always be anticipated. Policy decisions that have led to major ebbs and flows in debt as a percentage of GDP have largely occurred around wars. Future changes in debt levels are likely to occur as a result of entitlement spending. Most recently, debate over the Emergency Economic Stabilization Act of 2008 (P.L. 110- 343) included concerns about increasing debt levels. Business cycles and economic growth also play a significant role in debt movements.

World War II resulted in unprecedented levels of debt as a percentage of GDP as a result of rapidly increasing outlays which outpaced GDP growth. After the war ended, debt as a percentage of GDP fell in nearly every year over the next three decades as a result of strong economic growth. Rapid increases in defense spending along with tax cuts in the 1980s began a decade-long trend of rising debt as a percentage of GDP. The early 1990s were characterized by tax increases, a recession, and rising debt as a percentage of GDP. This was followed by several years of budget surpluses and a strong economy, which led to declines in debt as a percentage of GDP by the end of the decade. Currently, tax cuts, increases in spending, and a weak economy reversed the downward trend, resulting in rising debt levels.

Though debt levels today are not at their highest point in history, future levels of debt appear to be a great concern to many. Funding the promises of the entitlement programs and recently passed federal financial assistance could result in pursuit of a large cut in other types of spending or an increase in tax revenues as a percentage of GDP to attempt to fulfill these commitments.

Financing the obligations of the United States has always been a central concern of Congress and the President. Levels of government spending and revenue collection are a source of congressional debate in every fiscal year. Policy decisions and economic growth also play a large role in influencing federal debt levels over time. Most recently, debate over the Emergency Economic Stabilization Act of 2008 (P.L. 110-343) included concerns about increasing debt levels and raised some questions about the future fiscal health of the country. Observations of historical trends can illustrate the reasons behind large changes in debt levels. Ultimately, there are many implications to consider when setting policy initiatives and agendas with regard to federal debt. Understanding ebbs and flows of federal debt levels can be useful in synthesizing how budget policy affects the debt outlook.

This chapter will define the measures of debt, discuss the mechanisms of how debt levels change, and use historical examples to illustrate the factors causing debt movements over the last seven decades. In addition, some policies which may affect the future budgetary outlook and the debt will be discussed.

FEDERAL DEBT

Federal debt can be defined and reported in a number of ways. In the budget submission to Congress, the President is required by statute to report essential information about government debt.[1] These budget documents contain data on the federal surplus or deficit, gross (total) federal debt, debt held by federal government accounts (intragovernmental), and debt held by the public.[2] Changes in debt held by the public closely correspond to each fiscal year's unified surplus or deficit.[3]

Gross federal debt is composed of debt held by the public and intragovernmental debt. Intragovernmental debt is the amount owed by the federal government to other federal agencies, to be paid by the Department of the Treasury. This amount largely consists of money contained in trust funds, such as Social Security, that has been invested in federal securities as required by law.[4] Debt held by the public is the total amount the federal government has borrowed from the public and remains outstanding. This measure is generally considered to be the most relevant in macroeconomic terms because it is the amount of debt sold in credit markets. Debt held by the public will be the debt measure used to describe the ebbs and flows of debt in this chapter.

In most years, debt held by the public has increased on a nominal basis. Nominal measures of debt, however, do not control for inflation. Therefore, debt held by the public will be measured as a percentage of gross domestic product (GDP) in this chapter because it adjusts for inflation and relates the size of the debt to the size of the economy. As long as an economy grows faster than the debt, it may become better equipped to handle increasing amounts of debt because interest payments on the debt are less burdensome to the economy as a whole.

In nearly every year since the establishment of the country, the government has accumulated debt.[5] World War II (WWII), however, represented a new era in debt levels and the role of the United States in the global economy. Because of this, an examination of debt levels since 1940 is used in this chapter to show ebbs and flows of debt levels and how they have changed over the last seven decades. Selected historical examples will illustrate the sources of federal debt movements over this period.

Figure 1 depicts GDP growth and the changes in gross debt and debt held by the public as a percentage of GDP between 1940 and 2007.[6] The gap between the line depicting gross federal debt and debt held by the public represents intragovernmental debt. Gross debt as a percentage of GDP in the 1940s reached unprecedented levels, not seen before or since in the United States (due to WWII). As a percentage of GDP, gross debt reached its peak in 1946 (121.7%). The minimum level was reached in 1981 (32.6%). Gross debt as a percentage of GDP was lower in FY2007 (65.5%) than during the decade immediately following the WWII period and in the mid-1990s. In terms of debt held by the public, the FY2007 debt-to-GDP ratio (3 6.8%) was lower than those seen between 1940 and 1965, 1986 to 1999, and 2004 to 2006. Intragovernment debt holdings as a percentage of GDP have increased steadily since 1984 as evidenced by the widening gap between the lines depicting gross debt and debt held by the public. This indicates that the amount of money held in the trust funds and other government accounts is increasing. The future implications of this will be discussed towards the end of this chapter.

Causes of Changes in Federal Debt Levels

A variety of factors influence debt levels including spending levels (outlays), revenue collections (receipts), and economic growth. Debt levels increase or decrease due to changes in outlays and receipts, which are influenced by economic conditions, demographic trends, workload changes, and legislative action. Though movements in debt can be defined in a number of ways, these factors will be used in this chapter to identify changes in debt levels. In order to make an appropriate comparison over time, outlays, receipts, and debt will be measured as a percentage of GDP in order to control for economic effects. For example, if there is a high rate of inflation in a single year compared to the previous year, it may appear that outlays or receipts increased significantly although they actually have not.

Spending

Spending levels are determined by mandatory and discretionary programs. Mandatory spending levels (i.e., funding obligated by laws other than annual appropriations, e.g., Social Security) concern some budget analysts due to increasing health costs and the retirement of the Baby Boom generation. When first implemented, the portion of the federal budget necessary to pay for these mandatory programs was much lower than it is today.[7] Discretionary spending is provided through annual appropriations acts. Over time, the share of discretionary spending as a percentage of total federal spending has declined. Projections of large future increases in mandatory spending are expected to place further strain on the budget.[8] In the absence of other economic or policy changes, increases in spending levels result in larger deficits or smaller surpluses. Deficits will increase debt held by the public and will generally lead to increases in gross debt as a percentage of GDP. On the other hand, decreases in spending with all else equal will lead to larger surpluses or smaller deficits, generally resulting in decreases in both gross debt and debt held by the public as a percentage of GDP.

Receipts

Economic performance heavily influences receipt levels. During periods of sustained growth, revenue collections through income, corporate, and capital gains taxes will generally be stronger and result in larger collections by the Department of the Treasury in the absence of changes in law. Conversely, economic weakness generally decreases receipts. Individuals may see a decline in their incomes and corporations might experience a decline in profits. In the aggregate, this can cause a decrease in receipts collected. Changes in receipt levels also have an impact on the debt. With no other changes to policy or the economy, increases in receipts will result in larger surpluses or smaller deficits which can decrease debt held by the public as a percentage of GDP and will generally lead to decreases in gross debt as a percentage of GDP in the absence of other policy changes. The opposite will occur with declines in receipt levels.

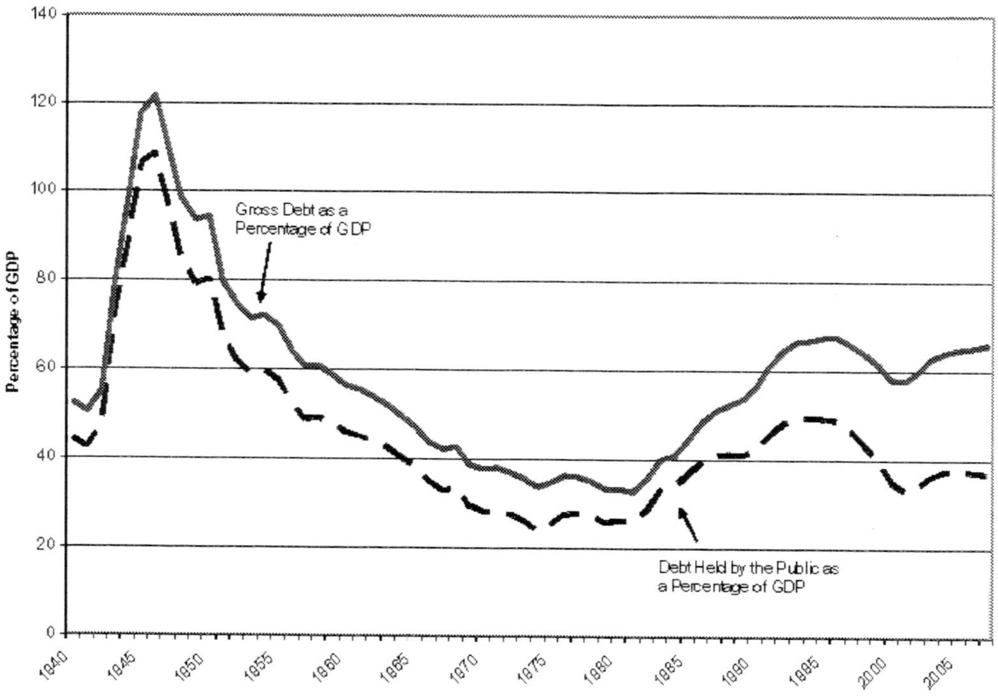

Source: Office of Management and Budget, *FY2009 Historical Tables*.
Note: The **Appendix** includes individual fiscal year data corresponding to **Figure 1**.

Figure 1. Ebbs and Flows of Debt as a Percentage of GDP, 1940-2007

GDP

Overall economic health is often measured by the growth rate of real GDP. Economic indicators, such as debt, are often evaluated using GDP as a base because it facilitates comparisons over time. Economic growth may allow an economy to absorb higher levels of debt. Even though interest payments increase as debt levels rise, they can be offset by a higher potential tax base thereby reducing the burden on the economy.[9] GDP growth will generally result in a decrease in the ratios of both the gross debt and debt held by the public as a percentage of GDP in the absence of changes in spending and receipts. During the period analyzed in this chapter (FY1 940 to FY2007), GDP growth did not necessarily result in the expected movements in debt as a percentage of GDP, showing that other factors influenced changes in debt levels.

Macro-economic Interaction

Movements in spending, receipts, or GDP (described above) can occur simultaneously or as a result of each other. Economic fluctuations tend to automatically cause short-run changes in the annual deficits because spending and revenue levels are affected as growth stimulates employment and individual income or recession reduces consumption and increases reliance on government programs.[10] For example, in a strong economy, new jobs are often created. In response, if the unemployed become employed and earn higher incomes, additional tax revenue will be generated. In contrast, in a weak economy, people may lose their jobs, which could lower tax revenue and increase government expenditures on programs such as unemployment insurance and food stamps (i.e., automatic stabilizers).

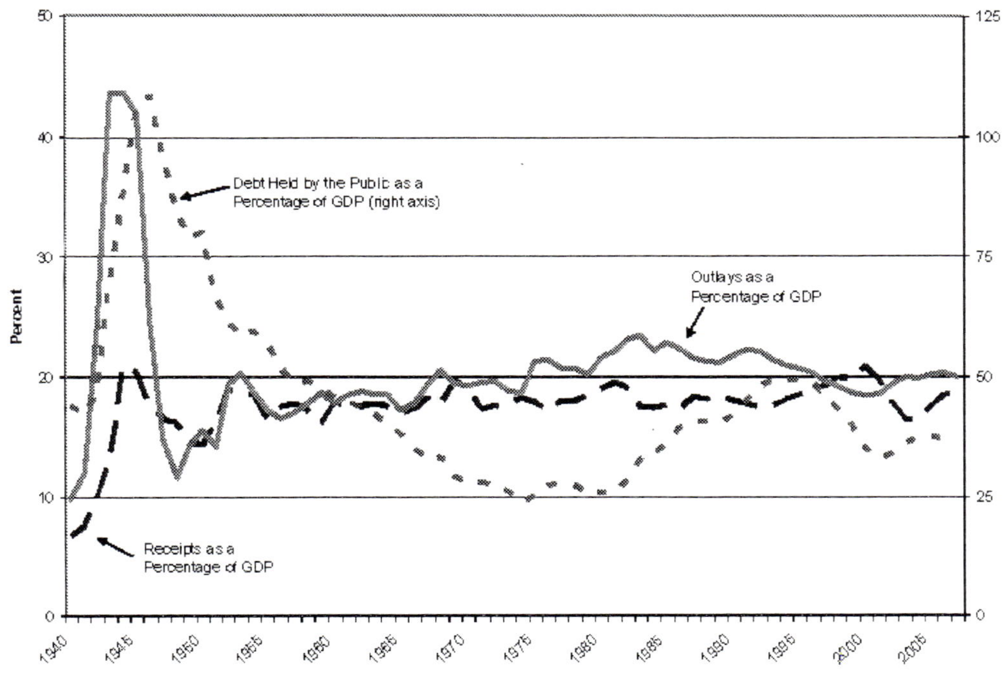

Source: Office of Management and Budget, *FY2009 Historical Tables*.
Note: The Appendix includes individual fiscal year data corresponding to Figure 1.

Figure 2. Receipts and Outlays as a Percentage of GDP, 1940-2007

If the growth in debt levels exceeds growth in the economy over the long term, an inherently unstable situation will result.[11] Debt levels, influenced by these changes, are also affected by policy decisions made by the President and Congress. Some policy analysts assert that the fiscal situation in the United States is unsustainable and represents a threat to economic stability necessitating significant changes in fiscal policy.[12]

As is shown in Figure 2, outlays greatly exceeded receipts during WWII. As the war ended and spending fell, receipts and outlays remained relatively equal as a percentage of GDP for the next several decades. Though small deficits existed in most years, growth in GDP exceeded the growth in borrowing causing the debt as a percentage of GDP to fall. Starting in the 1 980s and continuing to today, outlays have significantly exceeded receipts in most years. With the exception of the surpluses of the late 1990s, debt held by the public increased as a percentage of GDP. Between 1998 and 2001, revenues exceeded outlays as a result of strong economic growth, creating a short period of declining debt as a percentage of GDP.

Standardized Budget Data

The Congressional Budget Office (CBO) calculates standardized budget figures to assess the impact of economic cycles and policy changes on the debt. This data series estimates the level of receipts and outlays if the economy fully employed its resources, and is useful in determining the impact of recessions or tax cuts on the level of revenues and outlays.[13] The change in standardized data over a specific period provides a rough estimate of the effects of policy changes on receipts, outlays, and the deficit because economic and temporary factors have been stripped out. These CBO data will be used during discussions of certain historical periods in which the economy and policy decisions appeared to have significantly changed debt trends.

TRENDS IN DEBT: SELECT HISTORICALEXAMPLES

Changes in debt cannot always be anticipated. Policy decisions leading to major ebbs and flows in debt as a percentage of GDP have largely occurred around wars. Entitlement spending will also likely result in future changes in debt levels. Most recently, debate over the Emergency Economic Stabilization Act of 2008 (P.L. 110- 343) included concerns about increasing debt levels. In most cases, these events led to or are expected to lead to upward movements in debt due to immediate or out-year spending requirements. In addition, the economy, through its effects on revenues and outlays, has also played a significant role in debt movements. Over time, however, the effects of strong or weak GDP growth have not always resulted in predictable debt movements. In some instances, strong GDP growth was outweighed by increases in spending or decreases in tax revenues, causing debt as a percentage of GDP to increase instead of decrease. At other times, a strong economic performance led to declines in debt as a percentage of GDP.

Data on revenue collection, spending, and economic growth can illustrate how debt has moved over time. The historical examples below will be used to illustrate how some of the major changes in debt over the last seven decades have been affected by outlays, receipts, GDP growth, and economic interactions during specific periods.

World War II and the Effects on Debt

In December 1941, the U.S. entered WWII. War-time spending priorities had a greater impact on the debt than anything else in the six decades since. WWII resulted in unprecedented levels of debt as a percentage of GDP. Outlays, as a percentage of GDP, doubled between 1941 and 1942 and nearly doubled again between 1942 and 1943. Between 1940 and 1943, outlays rose from 9.8% to 43.6% of GDP. These increases were almost entirely a result of increases in defense-related spending, which rose from 1.7% of GDP in 1940 to 37.5% of GDP in 1945.[14] Total spending remained at the 1943 rate for the next two years and fell quickly in 1946 as the war ended. By 1947, outlays had essentially returned to their 1941 levels, hovering around 15% of GDP for the next several years. The six years of spending increases and their lasting effects resulted in a doubling of debt held by the public as a percentage of GDP rising from 44.2% in 1940 to 108.6% in 1946. The debt nearly equaled or surpassed GDP between 1944 and 1950.

Enormous changes in the economy resulted from the policy choices made during this period. GDP growth, while strong during most of this period, rising nearly 50% between 1940 and 1950, was not enough to compensate for the effects of the huge increases in spending. Despite strong economic growth, spending levels as a result of the war caused massive increases in debt as a percentage of GDP.

Entitlements and War Spending

After WWII ended, debt as a percentage of GDP fell in nearly every year over the next three decades. Several events highlighted the 1960s, including the Vietnam War and the expansion of entitlement programs related to healthcare. At the same time however, debt held by the public as a percentage of GDP was on a downward trend largely due to strong economic performance: GDP grew at an average annual rate of 4.6% during the decade.[15]

In 1965, President Johnson signed into law the Social Security Act Amendments of 1965 (P.L. 89-97), which expanded and created new programs providing health benefits for elderly and poor Americans.[16] These programs, modeled after New Deal era entitlement programs, granted specific monies to people who met certain conditions related to age, income status, or economic circumstance. At the time, these programs did not constitute a large portion of government spending. During the first fiscal year that Medicare and Medicaid were in effect (FY1 967) they consumed slightly over 9% of total federal mandatory spending. At that time, Social Security (i.e., old age and survivor's benefits and disability benefits under Title 2 of the Social Security Act) consumed more than half of the total amount that the government spent on mandatory programs. Spending on mandatory programs in FY1967 was 26% of total outlays and 5% of GDP.[17] Though not a large portion of total outlays at the onset, entitlements will alter the debate on the federal debt as more and more people begin drawing on the promised benefits, thereby consuming greater proportions of total outlays.[18]

In addition to these programs that created new government obligations, the country was also engaged in war in Vietnam. However, this conflict did not generate the same levels of increased wartime spending similar to WWII. Defense spending in 1960 equaled 9.3% of GDP, fell to 7.4% of GDP in 1965, before rising again to 8.7% of GDP by 1969. This was largely because the Vietnam conflict was significantly smaller in scale compared to WWII and defense spending had already increased in response to the Cold War.[19]

Outlays were higher than receipts during much of the 1 960s. However, the strength of the economy allowed receipts as a percentage of GDP to remain relatively constant during this decade. Tax increases also occurred in 1968 and 1969. In 1960 and 1969, there was a small budget surplus. Debt held by the public as a percentage of GDP stood at 45.7% in 1960 and fell to 29.3% in 1969. Outlays averaged 18.7% of GDP with revenues at 17.9%. Unlike the previous experience with war, GDP growth and economic expansion overwhelmed spending increases and allowed debt held by the public as a percentage of GDP to fall.

Defense Buildup

After declining for more than three decades from the peak of 108.6% of GDP in 1946 to 23.9% in 1974, debt held by the public as a percentage of GDP rose continuously during the 1980s and into the 1990s.[20] Rapid increases in defense spending combined with significant tax cuts enacted in response to recession led to unprecedented increases in the debt during peacetime. Defense spending rose from 4.9% of GDP in 1979 to peak at 6.2% in 1986. Between 1982 to 1989, annual defense spending remained around 6% of GDP. Over the same period, receipts fell from 19.0% of GDP in 1980 to 18.4% of GDP in 1989. Receipts hit their lowest level in 1986 at 17.4% of GDP. As the country continued to borrow more money, net interest payments rose from 1.9% of GDP in 1980 to 3.1% of GDP in 1989.

During the late 1970s and early 1980s, inflation played a major role in revenue collection. Because of inflation, households moved into higher tax brackets even though their real dollar income had not increased, a phenomenon known as bracket creep. In 1981, Congress passed the Economic Recovery Tax Act (P.L. 97-34), which systematically eliminated this long-term problem for parts of the tax system.[21] During times of high inflation before the 1981 act, bracket creep played a significant role in deficit reduction by increasing receipts solely as a result of the structure of the tax code.

As inflation began to fall in the early 1980s, the country also experienced two recessions, a relatively mild one in 1980 and a more severe one between 1981 and 1982, the deepest and longest in the post-WWII period to that point. High interest rates were largely seen as the cause of the economic downturn. In addition, government spending increased during this period to stimulate the economy in an attempt to create growth and incite a recovery.[22]

As a result of spending increases, inflation, and recessions, the deficit in 1983 reached its highest level as a percentage of GDP since 1946. CBO standardized data can be used to assess the contribution of these policy changes and economic conditions on the increases in the deficit. Table 1 shows the impact of these effects on receipts, outlays, and the budget deficit between FY1980 and 1983. The majority of the effect on both outlays and the overall deficit can be attributed to policy changes, rather than economic conditions despite the adverse conditions of the recessions. Outlays due to policy changes increased more than twice as much, as a percentage of potential GDP, during this period than actual outlays did. Actual outlays increased by less because of falling inflation. Overall, nearly 90% of the increase in the deficit can be attributed to policy changes.

Table 1. Standardized Budget Totals, 1980-1983 (Percentage of potential GDP)

	Total Budget		Standardized		FY1980 to FY1983 Percentage Point Change		
	FY 1980	FY 1983	FY 1980	FY 1983	Actual	Due to Policy Changes	Due to Economic Conditions
Revenue	18.6%	16.3%	18.6%	17.6%	-2.3%	-1.0%	-1.3%
Outlays	21.3%	22.0%	19.2%	20.8%	0.7%	1.6%	-0.9%
Surplus/Deficit	-2.7%	-5.7%	-0.6%	-3.2%	-3.0%	-2.6%	-0.4%

Source: CRS calculations based on Congressional Budget Office data.

Note: Numbers may not add due to rounding. Economic indicators include the effects of the business cycle and inflation on the budget. CBO calculates these measures using potential GDP, the level of output that corresponds to high levels of labor and capital use, because it excludes effects of the business cycle.

Congress and the President enacted several deficit reduction measures in an attempt to control increasing deficit levels in the 1 980s. One of the most well known was the Balanced Budget and Emergency Deficit Control Act of 1985 (also known as the Balanced Budget Act or Gramm-Rudman-Hollings, Title II of P.L. 99-177). The law attempted to eliminate the deficit by the early 1 990s through a process of sequestration, or automatic spending cuts if Congress and the President failed to enact legislation achieving this result. Under sequestration, spending would be automatically cut or cancelled if the estimated deficit exceeded the amount allowed under the act.[23] However, the primary goal of the Balanced Budget Act, to eliminate the deficit by 1990, was unsuccessful. Debt held by the public continued to rise for most of the next decade.

A Decade of Economic Fluctuations

The decade of the 1 990s was marked by two distinct periods. Tax increases and a recession characterized the first half while significant budget surpluses and a strong economy distinguished the later years. Due to the rapid increase in debt during the previous decade, additional deficit reduction measures were undertaken in the early part of the 1990s.[24] A strong economy, low unemployment, and other factors also helped to reduce deficits. Beginning in 1998, there were four consecutive years of surpluses, the first period of back-to-back surpluses in four decades. Strong economic performance developed steadily following the end of the recession in the early part of the 1 990s, which was marked by tax increases. Debt held by the public as a percentage of GDP declined for four successive years for the first time in almost two decades.[25]

Debt held by the public as a percentage of GDP increased in each year between 1990 and 1993, from 42.0% to 49.4%. However, between 1994 and 1999, debt held by the public as a percentage of GDP fell more than 16 percentage points from 49.3% to 33.0%.[26] Debt as a percentage of GDP fell during this period due to decreases in spending, increases in receipts, strong GDP growth, and the resulting economic interactions.

Spending in certain categories also fell, which contributed to the budget surpluses and lower debt as a percentage of GDP seen at the end of the decade. Following the disarmament agreement signed by Ronald Reagan and Mikhail Gorbachev in late 1987 and the fall of the Berlin Wall in 1989, defense spending declined. In 1990, the United States spent 5.2% of GDP on defense. By 1999, that number fell to 3.0%.

As defense spending began falling during the 1990s, tax increases were enacted as Congress and the President renewed efforts aimed at deficit reduction. The Budget Enforcement Act of 1990 (BEA, P.L. 101-508) replaced the existing sequestration process under Gramm-Rudman-Hollings with a new process involving deficit targets, discretionary spending limits, and "pay-as-you-go" requirements.[27]

However, meeting deficit reduction targets would have required massive cuts to key mandatory and discretionary programs.[28] The budget resolution for FY1991 (H.Con.Res. 310) agreed to by Congress set deficit reduction at 47% of the BEA target with one-third of the savings coming from revenue increases. Despite this, receipts fell from 18.0% of GDP in 1990 to 17.6% in 1993 largely as a result of the economic slowdown.

Beginning in 1992, GDP growth ranged from 3% to 5% annually through the end of the decade. Due to the strong growth and in combination with various tax increases in the Omnibus Budget and Reconciliation Act of 1993 (P.L. 103-66), receipts increased from 17.6% of GDP in 1993 to 20.0% in 1999. Low rates of unemployment also helped boost the level of receipts as more people had jobs and income, which generated tax revenue. Reliance on income security programs fell as a result from 2.7% of GDP in 1993 to 2.2% in 1999.

The budget surpluses that occurred during this decade surprised many budget analysts. As late as September 1997, CBO projected budget deficits into FY1 998 and beyond. The President's budget proposal for FY1998 also predicted a deficit. However, strong economic conditions led to a surprising and unexpected rise in revenues. Combined with a decrease in spending relative to GDP due to legislatively enforced spending cuts and strong economic growth, the annual budget deficits expected from FY1998 through FY2001 became surpluses. The budget surpluses not only helped shrink the size of the national debt as revenues exceeded outlays but also reduced interest payments as a result of decreased levels of borrowing. In 1999, interest spending fell to 2.5% of GDP, the lowest rate in fifteen years.

Economic Downturn and Entitlements

The years of budget surpluses and declining debt, which continued until 2001, have since been replaced by budget deficits and increasing debt. Tax cuts and increases in entitlement spending have been two of the largest contributors resulting in this turn-around. In 2000, debt held by the public as a percentage of GDP was 33.0%. Though it fell in 2001, it has been rising since that time. Debt held by the public as a percentage of GDP reached its peak for the decade in 2005 (37.5%) and declined slightly in 2006 (37.1%) and 2007 (36.8%). It is projected to resume rising through 2009.[29]

In 2001 and 2003, tax cuts were passed which caused receipts to fall as a percentage of GDP. In 2000, before the tax cuts were enacted, receipts totaled 20.9% of GDP. By 2004, receipts fell over 4 percentage points to 16.4% of GDP, their lowest level since 1959. Receipts have been rising since that time to reach 18.8% of GDP in 2007. At the same time, federal spending rose from 18.4% of GDP in 2000 to 20.0% in 2007, increasing in five out of seven years during this period. The economy also showed signs of weakness. Annual GDP growth averaged 2.6% between 2000 and 2007, down from 3.5% during the surplus years of 1998 to 2001.

Declining revenue and increased federal spending led the country from its peak surplus as a percentage of GDP in FY2000 to deficit. The FY2004 deficit was the largest of the FY2000 to FY2007 period. Using CBO's standardized budget data to separate out the effects of the economy and policy changes on the surpluses/deficits, **Table 2** shows that policy changes between FY2000 and FY2004 had a larger impact on the budget balance than the economy. Policy changes had nearly equal impact on revenues and outlays and were responsible for roughly 60% of the total changes in these measures as a percentage of potential GDP. The change in the deficit as a result of policy decisions was of similar magnitude.

Currently, discussion surrounding the debt has focused on expenditures on Iraq, Afghanistan, and anti-terrorism measures; recently enacted federal financial assistance legislation; and deteriorating economic conditions. Though defense spending has grown as a percentage of GDP since 2000, it remains lower than the average share of GDP devoted to this spending since 1962. It is generally assumed that expenditures related to these programs will continue at some rate into the foreseeable future leaving the level of related long-term spending and its impact on the federal debt somewhat uncertain.

Even more unclear are the effects of the legislation enacted to provide federal assistance to the credit and financial markets. To date, the government enacted the Housing and Economic Recovery Act of 2008 (P.L. 110-289) and specific provisions in the Emergency Economic Stabilization Act of 2008 (Division A of P.L. 110-343) devoted to providing financial stability to these industries. Along with financial intervention in Bear Stearns and AIG, the resulting outlays generated by these actions could be significant.[30] Combined with the recent rising unemployment and slow rates of economic growth, the new spending provided through this legislation could increase debt as a percentage of GDP, at least in the short-run. At the present time, the effect on the federal debt is hard to determine as the Treasury expects to recoup some of these outlays by selling the assets at a future date.

Table 2. Standardized Budget Totals, 2000-2004 (as a percentage of potential GDP)

	Total Budget		**Standardized**		**FY2000 to FY2004 Percentage Point Change**		
	FY2000	**FY2004**	**FY2000**	**FY2004**	**Actual**	**Due to Policy Changes**	**Due to Economic Conditions**
Revenue	21.5%	16.2%	19.1%	16.2%	-5.3%	-2.9%	-2.3%
Outlays	19.0%	19.8%	18.2%	18.7%	0.8%	0.5%	0.3%
Surplus/Deficit	2.5%	-3.6%	0.9%	-2.5%	-6.1%	-3.4%	-2.6%

Source: CRS calculations based on Congressional Budget Office data.

Note: Numbers may not add due to rounding. Economic indicators include the effects of the business cycle and inflation on the budget. CBO calculates these measures using potential GDP, the level of output that corresponds to high levels of labor and capital use, because it excludes effects of the business cycle.

In addition to this spending, the largest mandatory spending programs have grown significantly during the last decade. In 2000, spending on Medicare, Medicaid, and Social Security equaled 7.4% of GDP. In 2007, this number rose to 8.4% of GDP representing a one percentage point increase in just seven years.[31] The long-term consequences on future debt as a result of these mandatory programs may also be great cause for concern as the Baby Boomers approach retirement age.

How IntragovernmentalDebt Affects Gross Debt

Changes in the gross debt do not always track closely with budget surpluses or deficits because gross debt includes debt held by the public and intragovernmental debt. Intragovernmental debt is the amount owed by the federal government to other federal agencies, to be paid by the Department of the Treasury. Intragovernmental debt, required by law to be held in the form of Treasury securities, largely consists of money contained in trust funds such as Social Security. The amount contained in these trust funds is largely determined by payroll taxes collected less benefits paid.

Why is it important to examine this measure of debt? In 1982, intragovernmental debt as a percentage of GDP reached its lowest level. It has steadily risen since that time from 6.6% to 28.6% of GDP in 2007. This money has been used to finance other government spending while supplying Treasury I.O.U.s to the Trust Funds from which the borrowing has occurred. In 1983, major reforms to the Social Security program were recommended by the Greenspan Commission to stave off impending Trust Fund insolvency. These reforms led to increases in payroll tax collections, among other changes.[32] As a result of these changes in law, the level of surplus in the Social Security Trust Fund rose and the Treasury has been borrowing from it, thereby increasing intragovernmental debt.

Increases in gross debt as a percentage of GDP as a result of intragovernmental debt are a significant concern over the long run. In their 2008 report, the Social Security trustees projected that in 2017 the Trust Fund will begin to owe more benefits than what it collects in payroll taxes.[33] As the Trust Fund begins to redeem its Treasury securities in order to pay benefits to retirees, additional strains on the budget and debt levels will be created as large amounts of money from general revenues are needed to fund these Social Security benefits. In addition, the funds from the surplus currently being used by the government to fund other programs will no longer be available, putting strain on the funding for these programs.

Further, the liabilities to future generations of elderly from scheduled Social Security benefits do not show up in the debt. Funding the promises of the entitlement programs are difficult to fully measure. CBO calculates a fiscal gap measure which quantifies the reductions in spending and revenues necessary to generate fiscal stability over a given period. They project that a permanent and immediate combination of spending cuts and revenue increases amounting to 5.2% of GDP will be necessary in order to *maintain* the present level of debt (as a percentage of GDP) 50 years from now.[34] This amount is significant because outlays and revenues have each historically amounted to about 20% of GDP. Enacting this change amounts to a one-quarter cut in spending or a one-quarter increase in revenue collection or some combination of the two at a time when the country is facing a retiring Baby Boom generation. Standard economic analysis predicts that this could reduce domestic investment, worker productivity, and real wages further affecting the economy in the short run.[35]

CONSIDERATIONS FOR CONGRESS

Debt is affected by annual policy decisions on the levels of spending and revenue. Spending and revenues are also influenced by economic growth and GDP. As it has over the past decades, the United States will continue to face fiscal challenges. Though the accumulation of debt has always been a concern, some future challenges are already visible. As more people retire and become eligible for mandatory program benefits and if per capita healthcare costs continue to increase, these programs will consume greater portions of the budget unless policy changes are implemented. Potential changes could include benefit cuts, tax increases, or programmatic changes.

Effective fiscal discipline is necessary to balance the budget and rein in the debt. This would require less spending, increases in revenue collections, faster than average economic growth, or a combination of these things. Many economists agree that having some federal debt is a good thing because it builds credit which allows for more favorable borrowing terms. It encourages investment within the country because federal debt is seen as relatively low-risk and safe. However, debt is not free and the interest payments that accompany it can put further strains on budgets. Taking no action to reduce the projected growth in the debt potentially might lead to insolvency at some time in the future, implying that the government would have to default on its obligations.

APPENDIX. FISCAL SITUATION, 1940-2007

Fiscal Year	Gross Debt as a Percent of GDP	Debt Held by the Public as a Percent of GDP	Intragovernmental Holdings as a Percent of GDP	Outlays as a Percent of GDP	Receipts as a Percent of GDP	GDP Growth (%)
1940	52.4	44.2	8.2	9.8	6.8	4.1
1941	50.4	42.3	8.2	12.0	7.6	13.7
1942	54.9	47.0	7.9	24.3	10.1	17.8
1943	79.1	70.9	8.3	44	13.3	17.0
1944	97.6	88.3	9.2	43.6	20.9	11.6
1945	117.5	106.2	11.3	41.9	20.4	3.3
1946	121.7	108.6	13.1	24.8	17.6	-6.2
1947	110.3	96.2	14.1	14.8	16.5	-5.1
1948	98.4	84.5	14.0	11.6	16.2	0.2
1949	93.2	79.1	14.1	14.3	14.5	2.5
1950	94.1	80.2	13.9	15.6	14.4	2.2
1951	79.6	66.9	12.8	14.2	16.1	11.4

(Continued)

Fiscal Year	Gross Debt as a Percent of GDP	Debt Held by the Public as a Percent of GDP	Intragovernmental Holdings as a Percent of GDP	Outlays as a Percent of GDP	Receipts as a Percent of GDP	GDP Growth (%)
1952	74.3	61.6	12.7	19.4	19.0	4.6
1953	71.3	58.6	12.8	20.4	18.7	5.0
1954	71.8	59.5	12.3	18.8	18.5	0.0
1955	69.5	57.4	12.1	17.3	16.6	3.7
1956	63.8	52.0	11.8	16.5	17.5	5.5
1957	60.5	48.7	11.8	17.0	17.8	1.6
1958	60.7	49.2	11.6	17.9	17.3	-0.7
1959	58.5	47.8	10.7	18.7	16.1	5.1
1960	56.1	45.7	10.4	17.8	17.9	4.1
1961	55.1	44.9	10.2	18.4	17.8	1.1
1962	53.4	43.7	9.7	18.8	17.6	5.7
1963	51.8	42.4	9.4	18.6	17.8	4.2
1964	49.4	40.1	9.2	18.5	17.6	5.7
1965	46.9	38.0	9.0	17.2	17.0	5.5
1966	43.6	35.0	8.6	17.9	17.4	7.3
1967	41.9	32.8	9.1	19.4	18.3	4.5
1968	42.5	33.4	9.1	20.6	17.7	3.1
1969	38.6	29.3	9.2	19.4	19.7	4.7
1970	37.6	28.0	9.7	19.3	19.0	1.2
1971	37.8	28.1	9.7	19.5	17.3	1.6
1972	37.0	27.4	9.6	19.6	17.6	4.2
1973	35.7	26.1	9.6	18.8	17.7	6.3
1974	33.6	23.9	9.7	18.7	18.3	2.7
1975	34.7	25.3	9.4	21.3	17.9	-1.8
1976	36.2	27.5	8.7	21.4	17.2	3.8
TQ	35.2	27.1	8.1	21.0	17.8	0.0
1977	35.8	27.8	8.0	20.7	18.0	5.8
1978	35.0	27.4	7.6	20.7	18.0	5.2
1979	33.2	25.6	7.6	20.2	18.5	4.4
1980	33.3	26.1	7.2	21.7	19.0	0.3
1981	32.6	25.8	6.7	22.2	19.6	2.0
1982	35.2	28.6	6.6	23.1	19.1	-1.1
1983	39.9	33.1	6.8	23.5	17.5	2.1
1984	40.7	34.0	6.7	22.2	17.4	7.6
1985	43.9	36.4	7.5	22.9	17.7	4.5
1986	48.1	39.4	8.6	22.4	17.4	4.1
1987	50.5	40.7	9.8	21.6	18.4	2.6
1988	51.9	41.0	11.0	21.3	18.2	4.5

(Continued)

Fiscal Year	Gross Debt as a Percent of GDP	Debt Held by the Public as a Percent of GDP	Intragovernmental Holdings as a Percent of GDP	Outlays as a Percent of GDP	Receipts as a Percent of GDP	GDP Growth (%)
1989	53.1	40.6	12.5	21.2	18.4	3.8
1990	55.9	42.0	13.9	21.8	18.0	2.4
1991	60.6	45.3	15.3	22.3	17.8	-0.3
1992	64.1	48.1	16.1	22.1	17.5	2.6
1993	66.2	49.4	16.8	21.4	17.6	3.0
1994	66.7	49.3	17.4	21.0	18.1	3.6
1995	67.2	49.2	18.0	20.7	18.5	3.1
1996	67.3	48.5	18.8	20.3	18.9	3.1
1997	65.6	46.1	19.5	19.6	19.3	4.5
1998	63.5	43.1	20.4	19.2	20.0	4.2
1999	61.4	39.8	21.6	18.7	20.0	4.4
2000	58.0	35.1	22.9	18.4	20.9	4.3
2001	57.4	33.0	24.4	18.5	19.8	1.2
2002	59.7	34.1	25.6	19.4	17.9	1.2
2003	62.5	36.2	26.3	20.0	16.5	2.1
2004	64.0	37.4	26.6	19.9	16.4	3.7
2005	64.6	37.5	27.1	20.2	17.6	3.1
2006	64.9	37.1	27.8	20.4	18.5	3.0
2007	65.5	36.8	28.6	20.0	18.8	2.3

Source: Office of Management and Budget, *FY2009 Historical Tables*.

End Notes

[1] 31 U.S.C. § 1105(a).

[2] The Department of the Treasury also provides daily and monthly reports on debt levels, available at [http://fms.treas.gov/]. For the purposes of this chapter, the fiscal year data reported by the Office of Management and Budget will be discussed unless otherwise noted.

[3] Budget surpluses and deficits are measured in three ways: on-budget, off-budget, and unified. The unified surplus or deficit is the sum of the on-budget and off-budget surpluses or deficits. On-budget surpluses and deficits compose the majority of gross federal debt. The two Social Security Trust Funds (OASI and DI) and the Postal Service are off-budget and are part of intragovernmental debt.

[4] U.S. Executive Office of the President, Office of Management and Budget, *Budget of the U.S. Government, Fiscal Year 2009, Analytical Perspectives*, Feb. 2008, p. 408.

[5] Despite nearly paying off gross debt in several fiscal years in the 1 830s and 1 840s, rapid increases in gross debt levels occurred for the first time in the early 1 860s as a result of the Civil War. In nominal terms, debt rose from $90.6 million in 1861 to nearly $2.7 billion by 1865 and marked a new era in government borrowing at that time as debt equaled more than one-half of national income. Paul Studenski and Herman E. Krooss, *Financial History of the United States: Fiscal, Monetary, Banking, Tariff, including Financial Administration and State and Local Finance*, 2nd ed. (New York: McGraw-Hill, 1963), pp. 100, 116, 125, 152.

[6] In this chapter, all references are to fiscal years unless otherwise specified.

[7] For a more detailed discussion, see CRS Report RL33074, *Mandatory Spending Since 1962*, by D. Andrew Austin.

[8] For a more detailed discussion, see CRS Report RL34424, *Trends in Discretionary Spending*, by D. Andrew Austin.

[9] CRS Report RL3 1590, *The Federal Government Debt: Its Size and Economic Significance*, by Brian W. Cashell.

[10] For a more detailed discussion, see CRS Report RL3 1235, *The Economics of the Federal Budget Deficit*, by Brian W. Cashell.

[11] Along with economic growth, interest owed on prior borrowings also plays a role in the growth of the debt. Even if the United States stopped accumulating debt today, the interest payments on the debt currently held will continue until the debt is repaid. For a more detailed discussion, see CRS Report RL3 1590, *The Federal Government Debt: Its Size and Economic Significance*, by Brian W. Cashell.

[12] For more information, see CRS Report RL32747, *The Economic Implications of the Long-Term Federal Budget Outlook*, by Marc Labonte.

[13] The Congressional Budget Office eliminates the effects of both business cycle adjustments and short-lived economic fluctuations in the standardized budget figures. Short- lived fluctuations could include changes in capital gains realizations, the effects of changes in inflation on interest payments on the federal debt, and timing changes in federal payments and receipts. These budget estimates are measured as a percentage of potential GDP which quantifies the level of output corresponding to a high level of capital and labor use and therefore do not precisely match the historical budget figures calculated by OMB. U.S. Congress, Congressional Budget Office, *The Cyclically Adjusted and Standardized Budget. Measures*, Oct. 2008, available at [http://www.cbo.gov/ftpdocs/97xx/doc9768/ 10-03-StandBudget.pdf], accessed on Oct. 6, 2008.

[14] Defense spending reached its peak in 1944 at 37.8% of GDP.

[15] Between 1941 and 2007, GDP grew at an average annual rate of 3.8%, so the growth rate experienced during the 1960s was noticeably faster than average.

[16] Since its implementation, Medicare has been expanded several times to include additional categories of people (e.g., disabled) and benefits (e.g., prescription drugs). The same law which established Medicare also created Medicaid, which combined several existing welfare programs into one benefit for the poor. For more information, see CRS Report RL337 12, *Medicare: A Primer*, by Jennifer O'Sullivan.

[17] These entitlements have had a greater impact on spending levels and the debt in recent times. In FY2007, Medicare and Medicaid consumed 39% of total mandatory spending and Social Security (OASDI) accounted for 40%. Overall, mandatory spending consumed 53% of total government outlays and 11% of GDP. This means that over the last 40 years, mandatory spending on Medicare and Medicaid has increased by 30 percentage points of GDP while Social Security's portion has fallen by 12 percentage points. At the same time, total federal spending on mandatory outlays as a percentage of GDP has more than doubled over the same period.

[18] U.S. Congress, Congressional Budget Office, *The Budget and Economic Outlook: An Update*, Sept. 2008, p. 1.

[19] CRS Report RL3 1176, *Financing Issues and Economic Effects of American Wars*, by Marc Labonte and Mindy Levit.

[20] Between 1976 and 1978, debt held by the public as a percentage of GDP remained relatively constant. Office of Management and Budget, *Historical Tables*, February 2008, p. 5. From 1950 to 1980, debt held by the public as a percentage of GDP rose in the following years: 1950, 1954, 1958, 1968, 1971, 1975, 1976, 1977, and 1980. In only two of these years was the increase greater than 1% (1.1% in 1975, 1.5% in 1976).

[21] The provisions of the act with regard to bracket creep became effective beginning in 1985. U.S. Department of the Treasury, Office of Tax Analysis, *Revenue Effects of Major Tax Bills*, OTA Working Paper 81, December 1981. However, real bracket creep still exists due to long-term trends of rising real income.

[22] U.S. Congress, Congressional Budget Office, *The Outlook for Economic Recovery: A Report to the Senate and House Committees on the Budget - Part I*, February 1983, p. 9.information, see CRS Report 98-721, *Introduction to the Federal Budget Process*, by Robert Keith and CRS Report RL3 1137, *Sequestrction Procedures Under the 1985 Balanced Budget Act*, by Robert Keith.

[24] For more information, see CRS Report RS22098, *Deficit Impact of Reconciliation Legislation Enacted in 1990, 1993, 1997, and 2006*, by Robert Keith.

[25] In the 1990s, debt held by the public as a percentage of GDP declined during deficit years because GDP grew faster than the debt itself thereby decreasing the ratio. Because of this, declines in the debt-to-GDP ratio are more common historically than budget surpluses.

[26] Debt as a percentage of GDP fell further in 2000 and 2001.

[27] For more information, see CRS Report RL34300, *Pay-As-You-Go Procedures for Budget Enforcement*, by Robert Keith.

[28] On August 20, 1990, CBO issued initial sequestration reports for FY1 991 which estimated the FY1 991 deficit at \$165.2 billion, \$101.2 billion over the deficit target issued in the BEA. Outlays for defense programs would have had to be cut by \$50.6 billion (entailing uniform reductions of 41.8%) and outlays for nondefense programs would also have had to be cut by \$50.6 billion (entailing \$2.1 billion in cuts for programs with automatic spending increases or programs covered by special rules, and \$48.5 billion in uniform reductions of 38.0%). The report from CBO was only advisory and the numbers differed slightly from those reported by OMB and ultimately transmitted to Congress.

[29] Office of Management and Budget, *FY2009 Mid-Session Review*, July 2008, Table S-13.

[30] For more information see CRS Report RS22956, *The Cost of Government Financial Interventions, Past and Present*, by Baird Webel, N. Eric Weiss, and Marc Labonte; and U.S. Congress, Congressional Budget Office, *CBO's Analysis of Dodd Substitute Amendment for H.R. 1424*, Oct. 1, 2008.

[31] Medicare Part D, created by P.L. 108-173 on January 1, 2006, has contributed to some of this increase. In calendar year (CY) 2007, Part D expenditures amounted to 0.37% of GDP. Total Medicare expenditures rose from 2.28% of GDP in CY2000 to 3.18% of GDP in CY2007. Therefore, between 2000 and 2007, total Medicare expenditures rose 0.90% of GDP, with the creation of Part D accounting for approximately one-third of this increase. Medicare contributed nearly all of the total increase in spending on Social Security, Medicare, and Medicaid between 2000 and 2007. For data on Medicare expenditures, see U.S. Centers for Medicare and Medicaid Services, *2008 Annual Report of the Boards of Trustees of the Federal Hospital Insurance and Federal Supplementary Medical Insurance Trust Funds*, available at [http://www.cms.hhs.gov /reportstrustfunds/downloads/tr2008.pdf], accessed on September 18, 2008.

[32] U.S. Social Security Administration, *Report of the National Commission on Social Security Reform*, available at [http://www.ssa.gov/history/reports/gspan.html], accessed on Oct. 7, 2008.

[33] U.S. Social Security Administration, *Status of the Social Security and Medicare Programs, A Summary of the 2008 Annual Reports*, available at [http://www.ssa.gov/ OACT/TRSUM/index.html#C], accessed on Aug. 27, 2008.

[34] U.S. Congress, Congressional Budget Office, *The Long-Term Budget Outlook*, December 2007, pp. 5-7.

[35] In the long run, the increase in national savings as a result of the reduction in outlays or increase in spending would either increase investment or reduce the trade deficit. For a more detailed discussion, see CRS Report RL3 1590, *The Federal Government Debt: Its Size and Economic Significance*, by Brian W. Cashell.

CHAPTER SOURCES

The following chapters have been previously published:

Chapter 1 – This is an edited, excerpted and augmented edition of a United StatesCongressional Research Service publication, Report Order Code RL31590, dated February 3, 2010.

Chapter 2 – This is an edited, excerpted and augmented edition of a United StatesCongressional Research Service publication, Report Order Code RL31967, dated February 16, 2010.

Chapter 3 – This is an edited, excerpted and augmented edition of a United StatesCongressional Research Service publication, Report Order Code RS21519, dated March 18, 2010.

Chapter 4 –This is an edited, excerpted and augmented edition of a United StatesCongressional Research Service publication, Report Order Code RL31913, dated March 18, 2010.

Chapter 5 – This is an edited, excerpted and augmented edition of a United StatesCongressional Research Service publication, Report Order Code RS22354, dated April 15, 2010.

Chapter 6 – This is an edited, excerpted and augmented edition of a United StatesCongressional Research Service publication, Report Order Code RS2231, dated March 24, 2010.

Chapter 7 – This is an edited, excerpted and augmented edition of a United StatesGovernment Accountability Office publication, Report Order Code GAO-10-498, dated May 2010.

Chapter 8 – This is an edited, excerpted and augmented edition of a United StatesCongressional Research Service publication, Report Order Code RL30520, dated March 12, 2010.

Chapter 9 – This is an edited, excerpted and augmented edition of a United StatesCongressional Research Service publication, Report Order Code R40767, dated August 18, 2009.

Chapter 10 – This is an edited, excerpted and augmented edition of a United StatesCongressional Research Service publication, Report Order Code RL34712, dated October 20, 2008.

INDEX

N

O

P

Q

R

S

T

U

V

W